Be Your Own Business!

The Definitive Guide to Entrepreneurial Success

Contributing Editor
LaVerne L. Ludden, Ed.D.

Park Avenue

Be Your Own Business!

The Definitive Guide to Entrepreneurial Success

© 1998 by JIST Works, Inc.

Published by Park Avenue Productions
An imprint of JIST Works, Inc.
720 N. Park Avenue
Indianapolis, IN 46202-3490
Phone: 317-264-3720
Fax: 317-264-3709
E-mail: jistworks@aol.com
World Wide Web Address: http://www.jist.com

Copy edited by Carol Light

> **See the back of this book for additional JIST titles and ordering information.**
> **Quantity discounts are available.**

Printed in the United States of America
1 2 3 4 5 6 7 8 9   03 02 01 00 99 98
Library of Congress Cataloging-in-Publication Data

We have been careful to provide accurate information throughout this book, but it is possible that errors and omissions have been introduced. Please consider this in making any career plans or other important decisions. Trust your own judgment above all else and in all things.

ISBN 1-57112-082-3

CONTENTS

3   Buying a Business or Franchise 147

4 Becoming a Consulant or an Independent Contractor 241

Conclusion

Why Businesses Fail 291

Resources

Index 319

About
This Book

The world of work has changed dramatically, and career aspirations and expectations continue to evolve to reflect those changes. The turbulence resulting from waves of restructurings and downsizings has voided the old corporate contract that implied a guarantee of lifetime employment to loyal workers. Because of the insecurity of corporate employment, many employees considering leaving their current positions now prefer to try a new career direction—entrepreneurship. They want to be their own business.

Traditionally, most work has been organized into jobs that are permanent and full time in nature. Experts suggest, however, that work is now undergoing a significant change. Today the trend is toward a less permanent but more flexible workforce. Many businesses now hire staff for temporary jobs organized for specific projects or time periods. Others subcontract work to consultants or small businesses. These changes in the workplace, called *outsourcing*, are opening up many opportunities for people to start their own businesses.

The perceived risks associated with starting a business have actually decreased in proportion to the rising risks associated with depending on a full-time corporate job for financial security and emotional well-being. Many workers

1

have rejected the belief that they can easily replace a job with a more fulfilling position. Their experiences looking for new employment over an extended period of time have revealed this belief to be a myth. The corporate trend of outsourcing has reduced the number of full-time jobs available within large corporations, even as the number of people competing for those remaining jobs has increased.

Consequently, many people who would prefer traditional full-time corporate employment now have become acknowledged entrepreneurs, choosing to describe themselves as independent contractors earning interim income through foot-in-the-door assignments. Often these assignments are with potentially attractive employers who may not have full-time openings, but who still have work that needs to be done. Independent contractors have an opportunity to prove their skills before trying to secure traditional employment, should an opening arise or be created. Thus, some people have found that wearing an entrepreneurial hat can be an effective job search strategy.

Another development is the rise of the situational entrepreneur. Some departing employees are now using the windfall of an attractive severance package to buy a business, not because they are committed to entrepreneurship but because they want to buy a job. For various reasons, perhaps because of their age or economic status, they believe that their chance to earn a solid income is better served by entrepreneurship than by seeking another full-time job in the corporate world.

Many women who encounter a "glass ceiling" in the workplace are choosing to start their own businesses. Consequently, a high percentage of new entrepreneurs are women. Highly effective female managers find they can often achieve more success, both financially and personally, when their skills are applied to managing their own businesses.

A growing number of retirees are finding that they can begin a new career by starting a business. As corporate restructuring continues to force more employees into early retirement, the trend toward a higher percentage of retirees becoming entrepreneurs will likely continue. For small business owners, retirement is a choice rather than a mandated change on reaching a designated retirement age. In fact, many people in their seventies and eighties are continuing to run small businesses.

Whatever your reasons for reading this book, you should find it of practical value in helping you make a thoughtful career decision. Chapter 1, "Are You an Entrepreuenur?" helps you assess whether you have what it takes to be an entrepreneur, and the remaining chapters give you an understanding of the nuances of different entrepreneurial options.

Chapter 2, "Starting a Business," is a must-read chapter, regardless of which entrepreneurial option is of interest to you. It's the heart of this book, and it gives you an overview of fundamentals essential to running any business successfully. Chapters 3 and 4, "Buying a Business or Franchise" and "Becoming a Consultant or an Independent Contractor," each explore the issues pertaining to the specific options named in their titles. These two chapters are organized so that you can select and read the sections that most interest you. For example, you may be interested only in buying a franchise, so you need to read "Buying a Business or Franchise." However, we recommend that you read the entire book. You will find information in each chapter valuable in achieving success in your desired situation.

Even if you ultimately decide to stay in the corporate workforce, the entrepreneurial mind-set you will acquire by working through the exercises and absorbing the information in this book should serve you well in your career. Employees who can demonstrate the qualities of innovation, initiative, and sensitivity to the marketplace needs associated with entre-preneurs are becoming increasingly respected and valued by employers.

The best of luck on whichever path you choose.

Chapter 1

ARE YOU AN ENTREPRENEUR?

For many people, entrepreneurship has become an alluring fantasy—a possible solution to all of their career difficulties. However, because making the move to entrepreneurship is such a major life transition, it is essential to examine your motivations honestly. If you make any career change for impetuous or escapist reasons, your decision can easily come back to haunt you, especially when the going gets rough. Now is the time to assess whether you are moving positively and wisely toward a new career goal or merely moving away from the rigors of a demanding job.

Whatever the challenges in your career to date, you may discover that entrepreneurship does not offer an easy way out. In fact, you may find yourself coping with some of the same negative issues that caused you to reexamine your career goals in the first place. For example, in your corporate life, you may have disliked having a boss; however, as an entrepreneur, your clients and customers will be your new bosses. Or, as an employee, you may resent having to market yourself to obtain job interviews; however, as an entrepreneur, your skill at sales and marketing will be one of the most critical factors in your success.

Because there can be a greater risk in making a career shift to entrepreneurship than in remaining in the familiar corporate world, you need to question your motives carefully. You must also examine which of the various challenges of entrepreneurship are likely to be most difficult for you. The insights you gain from this personal assessment will place you in a stronger position to resolve any conflicts and dispel any naive assumptions before they can harm your business.

EXERCISE 1.1

Key Motivators

Check all of the motivators below that apply to you.

_____　1. I want to be my own boss.

_____　2. I'm resistant to a job search effort.

_____　3. I have identified a new business idea or opportunity.

_____　4. I have a specific idea, hobby, or interest that I believe could become a viable business.

_____　5. I feel I can achieve more in my life by becoming an entrepreneur.

_____　6. I want to take advantage of an unexpected opportunity that has come my way.

_____　7. I want to take advantage of a financial windfall.

_____　8. I am discouraged or angry at corporate life.

_____　9. I believe my job opportunities may be limited because of my age or skill level.

_____　10. I am seeking a career change more compatible with retirement.

_____　11. I need an outlet for my creativity.

_____　12. I'd like to be famous.

_____　13. I want a career that aligns better with my personal values.

_____　14. I want to avoid a likely relocation if I seek a new job.

_____　15. I feel that my lifestyle and personal priorities are better met through entrepreneurship.

_____   16. I want to achieve great wealth from my own ideas.

_____   17. I am seeking a source of temporary revenue.

_____   18. This is my once-in-a-lifetime chance to take a risk.

Now select the three that are most important to you and rank them in descending order of importance.

1. _____

2. _____

3. _____

Consider which of these motivators is valid and strong enough to merit the time, effort, and money required to become a successful entrepreneur. As you continue through the exercises in this book, try to identify any motivators that may be based on misconceptions about what it's like to be an entrepreneur, rather than on reality.

Do You Have What It Takes?

Only you can answer this question. Success in any endeavor is largely a matter of motivation and commitment. Your attitude is vital to your success, and a need to achieve often creates its own success.

The following exercise will help to reveal your entrepreneurial profile. Are your natural business strengths on the creative side or on the management side? Be honest. Answer the questions as you think you really are, not as you wish you were or think you should be. When you finish, ask people who know you well to verify your answers. If you find a discrepancy between their perceptions and your own, proceed with extreme caution. You simply must know how to leverage your strengths and cover your liabilities in order to succeed as an entrepreneur.

EXERCISE 1.2

Interest/Competency Appraisal

On a scale of one to five (with five being the strongest level of agreement), rate yourself on the following:

_____ 1. I prefer to read fiction rather than nonfiction.

_____ 2. I'm an organized person. I approach tasks in an organized, methodical way.

_____ 3. I love variety and spontaneity and find routine boring.

_____ 4. I like to know the goal and the plan for reaching it before proceeding with an important task.

_____ 5. I'm street-smart. I understand how to look at a business unit to determine its effectiveness and efficiency.

_____ 6. Other people frequently tell me that I tend to see things that others don't.

_____ 7. I'm an excellent planner.

_____ 8. Opportunity is much more important to me than security.

_____ 9. I've had formal training and experience in business planning.

_____ 10. I'm profit-oriented rather than idea-oriented. I love to make money.

_____ 11. Throughout grade school and high school, I preferred art and literature to math and science.

_____ 12. My tendency is to be a nonconformist.

_____ 13. Throughout my working life, my jobs have generally been management-oriented rather than creativity-oriented.

_____ 14. I spend much of my free time thinking about and playing with new ideas.

_____ 15. I have a good understanding of finance as the language of business.

_____ 16. I've turned many ideas into tangible products or processes.

_____ 17. I'm good at detail. I'm comfortable with moving things step-by-step toward an objective.

_____ 18. I've had many more jobs throughout my life than my colleagues at work.

_____ 19. I have a high tolerance for uncertainty. I work effectively even when the outcome is unclear and the work is unstructured.

_____ 20. I work best in an environment where there's orderly progress toward predetermined goals.

High scores (fours and fives) on questions 1, 3, 6, 8, 11, 12, 14, 16, 18, and 19 indicate that your interests tend toward the creative side of running a small business. High scores on questions 2, 4. 5, 7, 9, 10, 13, 15, 17, and 20 indicate that you gravitate more toward the management side of running a business.

Generally, people tend to be more competent in those areas where they have a strong interest. Obviously there are exceptions, but careful reflection about your high and low scores should tell you a great deal about whether creative abilities or management abilities are your strong suit in starting a business of your own.

Most people are not good at both. Creative types may easily see new ideas to exploit but are often ineffective managers. Exceptional business managers often marvel that they were unable to see new business opportunities until they were pointed out to them.

Are you strongly oriented in one direction, or are you somewhere in the middle? To start a business and manage it successfully, you need both creative and managerial skills. If you are strong in one and weak in the other, you're a candidate for failure in your new venture.

The good news is that you can learn what is needed to shore up your weak side. This book will emphasize both sets of skills and will take you through the creation of your business idea to the development of your business plan. The bottom line is this: To be successful in your commitment to a business, you must have creative ideas married to solid small business management skills. The marketplace has zero tolerance for incompetence in either.

An Overview of Your Options

If you think you have what it takes to become an entrepreneur, you need to begin to narrow your options. Which is the best entrepreneurial option for you? Your personality, skills, and opportunities will make one of the following most appealing to you:

▷   Starting a business

▷   Buying a business or franchise

▷   Becoming a consultant or an independent contractor

Each of these options will be discussed more extensively later in this book. The following section offers a quick summary of some of the pros and cons of each of the three entrepreneurial options. As you review each one, add to the list any personal pros and cons that reflect your unique preferences and situation.

Starting a Business

Potential Pros

▷   Being your own boss

▷   Creative challenge of bringing an idea to fruition

▷   Potential for high rate of return

▷   Ability to shape the company from the beginning

▷   Opportunity to build something of enduring value with your name on it

▷   _____

▷   _____

▷   _____

Potential Cons

▷   Cash flow fluctuations

▷   Potential problems due to lack of business and marketing skills

▷   Lack of built-in support system and feedback

▷   Must bear complete responsibility

▷ Little to no leisure time

▷ Can't buy in volume

▷ _____

▷ _____

▷ _____

Buying a Business or a Franchise

Potential Pros

▷ No need to develop an original idea

▷ Proven product and track record

▷ Established customer base

▷ Established vendor/supplier relationships

▷ Employees, equipment, and facilities already in place

▷ Lenders have more confidence lending to an existing business

▷ Some sellers may provide buyer financing

▷ Immediate cash flow may permit a small salary

▷ Very little initial investment may be required

▷ Franchise may provide recognized name and appearance

▷ Franchise products and services are standardized

▷ Access to franchise training approach or system

▷ _____

▷ _____

▷ _____

Potential Cons

▷ Searching for the ideal business is time-consuming

▷ Determining the value of the business can be difficult

▷ Finding sources other than business brokers who represent sellers may present difficulties

▷ Substantial research may be required to determine where the product or service is in its life cycle

▷ Slower growth rate may occur because the business is neither new nor free of an existing reputation

▷ May be difficult to test the waters on a part-time basis

▷ Will be locked into the franchise's products, suppliers, procedures, and advertising budget

▷ Possible difficulties protecting franchise locations

▷ _____

▷ _____

▷ _____

Becoming a Consultant or an Independent Contractor

Potential Pros

▷ Offers the chance to be on your own

▷ Eliminates getting mired in company politics and red tape

▷ Start-up costs are minimal

▷ Allows you to control your time

▷ Provides opportunity for variety

▷ Carries no mandatory or customary retirement age

▷ Offers potential for high annual income

▷ Work is closely related to your proven expertise

▷ Time until break-even stage is relatively short

▷ Offers ability to explore possibility of full-time employment with a company

▷ Provides an opportunity to manage and direct your own career

▷ Potential tax benefits include many deductions

▷ More opportunity for work and life balance

▷ _____

▷ _____

▷ _____

Potential Cons

▷ Intense competition from other consultants

▷ No built-in support system or social network

▷ Lack of organizational authority to impose solutions

▷ No set schedule or routine

▷ Blurred line between work and leisure time

▷ Irregular cash flow

▷ Must do your own marketing or use third-party brokers

▷ Constant need to improve skills and expertise to remain marketable

▷ Lack of typical corporate benefits

▷ Lack of corporate status and authority

▷ Must do your own record keeping and pay estimated taxes

▷ _____

▷ _____

▷ _____

Review your personal pros and cons for each of the entrepreneurial options and consider the following questions:

▷ Are there some recurring themes?

▷ Are some pros particularly important to you?

▷ Do they outweigh other factors you have recorded as cons?

▷ Would some cons be so negative that they would place your entrepreneurial venture at great risk?

▷ Do one or two of your cons far outweigh other factors you have recorded as pros?

Every business option has advantages and disadvantages. If you had difficulty filling in the pros and cons for these options, you need to do more research before committing to one of them. You must be absolutely certain that you have eliminated other entrepreneurial options for good reasons before following your chosen path. You may find that it's wise to delay your final decision until you've completed this book.

EXERCISE 1.3

Where Are You Now?

Answer the following questions as candidly as you can. Refer back to your answers as you research your options.

1. Why are you interested in becoming an entrepreneur?

_____

_____

_____

2. Would you rather find a job that pays well or strike out on your own? Why?

_____

_____

_____

3. What are your greatest concerns about pursuing an entrepreneurial option?

_____

_____

_____

4. Do you have an idea for a business? If so, describe it below.

_____

_____

_____

_____

5. What need does your product or idea meet in the marketplace?

_____

_____

_____

_____

6. Which of your skills and experiences do you believe will help you become a successful entrepreneur?

_____

_____

_____

_____

7. Which entrepreneurial skills and experiences do you feel you may lack at this time?

_____

_____

_____

_____

8. How long can you go without income?

_____

_____

Change and Transition

To successfully make the transition from employee to entrepreneur, you may find an understanding of the difference between change and transition helpful. Change is an event. For example, the following life experiences are all changes:

▷ Going to college

▷ Getting married

▷ Becoming a parent

▷ Buying a first home

▷ Relocating

▷ Starting a new job

▷ Becoming an entrepreneur

Transition is the gradual process that you go through to accept a changed situation. This process of acceptance is so complex that people usually go through distinct phases before the change feels comfortable. Transition involves letting go of the old, allowing yourself to feel confusion and fear, and then committing to a new beginning.

EXERCISE 1.4

Transition Word Association

This exercise will give you insight on your feelings about your possible career transition. Circle the words that best describe how you feel.

Self-pity	Betrayal	Fear
Self-doubt	Paralysis	Enthusiasm
Optimism	Confusion	Overwhelmed
Anger	Disbelief	Uncertainty
Anxiety	Stress	Motivation
Energy	Stimulation	Excitement
Determination	Curiosity	
Denial	Shock	

You may find that some of the words you chose were contradictory: some were positive, and some were negative. Mixed feelings are common when an individual goes through a transition. You will find that you'll move through three stages, which are listed below with their associated emotions:

ENDINGS	CHAOS	COMMITMENT
anger	fear	enthusiasm
shock	confusion	optimism
disbelief	self-doubt	perseverance

It's helpful to review your word choices as you move toward becoming an entrepreneur. As you become more committed to the change, you'll find that you'll choose more positive words to describe your feelings.

Making a Successful Transition

The following two case studies will help you understand how feelings and emotions can lead you into trouble, hindering your efforts to build a successful business.

Entrepreneurial Case Study 1

Tom was a 46-year-old executive who had recently separated from an accounting firm. At his preceding firm, he had noticed that his employer hired programmers and junior accounting staff on an interim basis to handle the demands of peak periods and special requests and that the need for these temporary employees seemed to be increasing. This trend appeared to be a new way of doing business for his firm as it continued to downsize the permanent, full-time professional staff.

Tom decided to open his own executive search business, specializing in interim assignments. In his preceding job, he had developed strong client relationships. He also had an excellent knowledge of fiscal affairs. He believed that these attributes, along with his interpersonal skills, would serve him well in the executive search business. Moreover, because the start-up costs were minimal, Tom believed he could gain a quick understanding of whether the interim search business was right for him, without a large investment of his savings.

Tom's first steps were to secure inexpensive office space; hire a secretarial assistant who was an independent contractor; and lease basic office equipment, including a computer. Then he called all of his old contacts and told them of his new business venture. He also placed an advertisement in selected newspapers to announce that he was specializing in interim programming and accounting positions. Tom understood very well how to reach his market.

However, what happened next was very disconcerting to Tom. He was so swamped with orders for interim personnel that he soon became frantic and overwhelmed. When Tom realized that he needed to quickly build an inventory of qualified applicants, he called corporate friends in various human resources positions to request any available resumes of good people who had not been hired for accounting or programming positions. He obtained very few resumes.

Tom was dumbfounded. He spoke with an entrepreneurial consultant about his business problem. The consultant encouraged Tom to call his potential business clients back and tell them that he wasn't quite ready to begin. However, Tom was so upset by the loss of personal credibility such an action would create that he decided to pull the plug on the business instead. Within a couple of months, he was out of business. Although he had only lost about $5,000, he was so burned by this experience that he needed several months to recover his emotional equilibrium.

He regrouped and decided to enter the same business again, this time as a much wiser man. Tom selected a former colleague from his accounting firm as a partner in the hope that the two of them together would manage to overcome almost any business problem. However, Tom failed to check on the man's personal status. Later he found out that his new partner was in the middle of a messy divorce, which was causing him financial difficulties.

Tom ended up loaning his partner money from his own pocket. Soon afterward, this business venture also failed. Tom eventually returned to corporate life as an employee for another accounting firm and gave up thoughts of other entrepreneurial pursuits.

Discussion Questions

What were Tom's major motivators and emotions in starting his first business?

_____

_____

_____

Overall, how well did Tom handle the transition from being an employee to becoming an entrepreneur?

_____

_____

_____

What can you learn from his approach?

_____

_____

_____

Entrepreneurial Case Study 2

Merry was a 28-year-old woman from a major telecommunications corporation, where she was a mid-level administrator with a college degree. After leaving her company, Merry attended an entrepreneurial workshop to explore further her desire to operate her own dry-cleaning business.

During the time she held a full-time corporate job, she had worked on weekends at a local dry cleaner so that she could learn how to run a dry-cleaning business daily. One of her strategies while working at the dry cleaner's was to talk at length with the customers to learn more about their needs. She discovered that the current owner could easily have increased his sales volume had he invested in more modern equipment, offered extended hours, and aggressively expanded his market.

To learn more about the owner's competitors, Merry took some of her own clothing to other dry-cleaners. While visiting each of these dry-cleaning establishments, she made a special point to observe the quality of their customer service, their equipment, the range of cleaning services available, and the standard business procedures they used.

Merry then attended a seminar to learn sales and marketing approaches most suitable for her business community. She liked the ideas of distributing flyers in local clothing and shoe stores and placing advertisements in inexpensive community papers.

Merry sensed that the owner of the business where she worked was restless and tired of his business. She offered to buy him out shortly after he mentioned to her his desire to retire. Because of the timing of her offer, she was able to buy the business at an excellent price. Soon Merry was running a thriving dry-cleaning business, and within five years, she had added two new stores.

Discussion Questions

What were Merry's major motivators and emotions in starting her business?

_____

_____

_____

Overall, how did Merry deal with the transition from being an employee to becoming an entrepreneur?

_____

_____

_____

What can you learn from her approach?

_____

_____

_____

How Will Your Life Change?

Now you need to examine your own unique transition issues. If there is one overriding question you need to consider at this stage in exploring your entrepreneurial options, it is how your life will change—and how you will feel about those changes.

EXERCISE 1.5

Lifestyle Issues

Note your feelings and concerns regarding how each of the following factors will change as you continue on your path to entrepreneurship:

Status: _____

_____

Identity: _____

_____

Social Network: _____

_____

Support: _____

_____

continued

Feedback: _____
_____

Time: _____
_____

Balance: _____
_____

Stress: _____
_____

Accountability: _____
_____

Family: _____
_____

Lifestyle: _____
_____

Health: _____
_____

Risk: _____
_____

Security: _____
_____

Finances: _____
_____

Which of these factors do you think will be your greatest challenge as you proceed through your career transition? What can you do to make your transition easier and faster? You may want to discuss your reactions to these factors with your family, friends, and colleagues.

Family Issues

If you commit to starting a business, you're not the only one making a sacrifice: your entire family will be affected. To create the highest level of support possible for your new venture, you should allow family members to have input. Select the questions below that are appropriate to your situation and ask family members for their answers. You will find their input will help you clarify existing issues and make decisions.

Questions

▷ What are the top three reasons for you to start a business?

▷ What are the top three reasons for you to not start a business?

▷ Where do you want to be in five years? How will you get there?

▷ What's the price for each of your family members? How will running this business affect your relationship with your spouse or partner? What will change?

▷ If children are involved, what are their concerns? How will their lives change?

▷ Which leisure activities will be affected? How?

▷ How will you balance your personal life with your business life? Will your partner or any children be involved in the business? What will their roles be?

▷ Will belt tightening be necessary? Where? For how long?

▷ If the business should fail, what are the consequences? Are they acceptable?

Time to Work

Because work and lifestyle are so inextricably tied together, you must look not only at how much time you'll spend at work, but also at the inevitable changes that will occur in your lifestyle. Most successful business owners spend much more than forty hours a week at work. Running a small business requires stamina, long hours, and sacrifices of leisure time and activities. Are you willing to accept these terms?

The balance—or the lack of it—between work and personal life depends on how you spend your time. As you evaluate any business, one of your primary concerns should be to obtain an accurate assessment of the time required to run the business. Will it enable you to lead the life you want? Here are some questions to consider as you analyze the time requirements for running a business:

1. How much time per week do you want to devote to the business?

2. How much time is the current owner devoting? What's the industry average?

3. What is being done that adds no value to the business? How much time does it require?

4. Are there key employees who could take on additional responsibilities?

5. Are there activities that can be outsourced to save time?

6. Is it possible to save time by improving efficiency? How?

7. Is it possible to combine leisure activities with business activities?

8. What would happen if you worked one day less per week?

Usually there is a correlation between the time you spend running your small business and the revenue and profit generated. Your ability to service debt, your monthly cash flow, and your operating expenses will all be affected by how much time you spend on the job. It's up to you to weigh the costs and benefits of your new business.

Stress Analysis

A little stress seems to contribute to both motivation and accomplishment, but excessive stress can be very bad news. You would be wise to assess the extent to which the business you are contemplating is likely to contribute to your stress index. You may then be able to make the required adjustments to ensure that you avoid your heavy-duty stress triggers. But first you need to know what they are.

EXERCISE 1.6

Stressor List

What are your stressors? Perhaps you feel very stressed when you're confronted with an overwhelming number of tasks coupled with tight deadlines. Or perhaps you find working in an unstructured environment that requires rapid-fire decisions with little margin for error more than you can take. Review your work and personal experiences and think about specific situations when you were aware of a high degree of stress. List the specifics of such stressful situations on the following lines:

1. _____

   _____

2. _____

   _____

3. _____

   _____

4. _____

   _____

5. _____

   _____

continued

6. _____

_____

7. _____

_____

8. _____

_____

9. _____

_____

10. _____

_____

Compare your list with the following list of situations that many small business owners have found to cause high levels of stress. If these same circumstances raise your blood pressure, proceed with caution. Ask yourself which stressors you can live with and which ones will be a problem for you.

  ▷ Obtaining enough money to cover monthly operating expenses
  ▷ Rapidly growing the business
  ▷ Problems with employees
  ▷ Problems with vendors
  ▷ Dealing with questionable business practices
  ▷ Lawsuits or the threat of lawsuits
  ▷ Problems with accounts receivable
  ▷ Perceived or real incompetence
  ▷ Being spread too thin
  ▷ Brutally competitive environment
  ▷ Insurance problems

▷ Feelings of life being out of balance

▷ Uncertainty and risk of failure

▷ Lack of family support

Financial Considerations

Finding the money to launch and maintain your business venture—be it large or small—is critical to your success. Many otherwise able and realistic entrepreneurs spend far too much time planning a business only to find that they were not realistic about the amount of money required or its likely source.

Many would-be entrepreneurs believe that funding for their entrepreneurial venture will come from one or more of the following sources:

Banks. Bank loans to you for your business will differ from home real estate loans. You must secure the loan by using your personal assets as collateral, such as a house or an investment account. If the business fails, the bank could seize these assets.

Venture Capitalists. Venture capitalists are generally interested in new businesses only when they can realize very aggressive profits.

Investors. Money for your venture sometimes will come from other investors, but only in certain circumstances. For example, you may receive contributions from family and friends who believe in you and will provide gifts of cash, loans, and investment capital in exchange for a percentage stake or shares in the business. If you are buying an existing business, sometimes the seller will assist you by giving you a note secured by the assets of the business.

The Small Business Administration. You do not deal directly with the SBA; your bank does. You may be eligible for an SBA loan, but only when you have been turned down twice by a bank. Your business must come under the definition of a small business, according to your industry. Your SBA loan must also be secured by assets, such as real estate and inventory, and the loan generally will be limited to 7 to 10 years. In addition, most banks require that your investment or equity in the business be substantial.

The reality is that in the vast majority of entrepreneurial situations, the money for the venture will have to come from you. Do not expect banks, venture capitalists, or business investors to have the same level of confidence as you do in your idea. Are you willing to furnish the capital necessary to become a successful entrepreneur? If so, what assets do you have that can be tapped to fund your enterprise? Some typical sources for investment capital include the following:

▷ Your savings account or other liquid capital

▷ Your personal borrowing power, such as withdrawals on credit cards or loans against 401(k) funds, investment funds, or insurance policies.

▷ Your business borrowing power, such as a home equity loan.

▷ Your ability to raise cash from liquidation of assets, personal property, or possessions

▷ A severance payment

Because you will probably have to provide most or all of the funding for your business, you must have a clear picture of all aspects of your personal financial situation. The following exercise will help you accomplish this task.

EXERCISE 1.7

Your Personal Financial Profile

The following profile lists standard assets, liabilities, income sources, and expenses. Fill in the spaces for those items that pertain to your current financial situation. When you reach the end of the exercise, your calculation of your total available capital will give you an accurate picture of where you stand as a potential financial resource for your business.

I. Your Personal Assets   **Fair Market Value**

A. Cash and Cash Equivalents

    1. Checking/Savings Accounts   _____

    2. Money Market Funds   _____

    3. Treasury Bills/CDs   _____

    4. Life Insurance (Cash Value)   _____

    5. Accounts Receivable   _____

    6. Other (specify) _____   _____

B. Securities

    1. Bonds   _____

    2. Stocks/Stock Options   _____

    3. Stock Mutual Funds   _____

    4. Other (specify) _____   _____

C. Tax-Deferred Annuities

    1. (Specify) _____   _____

    2. (Specify) _____   _____

    3. (Specify) _____   _____

D. Nonliquid Assets

    1. Investment Real Estate   _____

    2. Limited Partnerships   _____

    3. Business Interests   _____

    4. Other (specify) _____   _____

E. Retirement Plans

    1. Individual Retirement Accounts   _____

    2. Savings Plan/401(k)   _____

    3. Profit-Sharing Plan   _____

    4. Other (specify) _____   _____

F. Personal Assets

    1. Primary Residence   _____

    2. Secondary Residence   _____

    3. Furnishings/Antiques   _____

    4. Jewelry/Furs/Art   _____

    5. Automobiles   _____

    6. Other (specify) _____   _____

    Total Assets: _____

continued

II. Your Personal Liabilities		**Outstanding Balance**

A. Investment Liabilities

    1. Brokerage Account Margin/Loans   _____

    2. Investment Real Estate Mortgages   _____

    3. Investment Partnership Notes Payable _____

    4. Other (specify) _____   _____

B. Personal Liabilities

    1. Home Mortgage   _____

    2. Second Home Mortgage   _____

    3. Auto Loans   _____

    4. Other Bank Loans (specify)   _____

    5. Credit Cards   _____

    6. Income Taxes (Federal, State, and Local) _____

    7. Other (specify) _____   _____

    Total Liabilities: _____

III. Net Worth Summary	**Balance**

A. Total Assets   _____

B. Total Liabilities   _____

    Net Worth (Total Assets – Total Liabilities): _____

IV. Current Income Sources	**Gross Monthly Income**

A. Your Salary/Severance   _____

B. Your Spouse's/Partner's Salary/Severance _____

C. Social Security Benefits   _____

D. Pension Benefits   _____

E. Investment Income   _____

F. Other (specify) _____   _____

    Total Monthly Income: _____

	Monthly Total
V. Living Expenses	
A. Monthly Fixed Expenses	_____
1. Mortgage/Rent Payments	_____
2. Investment Real Estate Mortgage	_____
3. Investment Partnership Notes Payable	_____
4. Other Loan Payments	_____
5. Constant Premium Life Insurance	_____
6. Alimony/Child Support	_____
7. Other (specify)	_____
Subtotal 1:	_____
B. Monthly Variable Expenses	
1. Household Maintenance/Supplies	_____
2. Property Taxes	_____
3. Heat	_____
4. Electricity	_____
5. Telephone	_____
6. Food	_____
7. Clothing	_____
8. Medical	_____
9. Personal Care/Hygiene	_____
10. Variable Premium Life Insurance	_____
11. Health Insurance	_____
12. Homeowner's Insurance	_____
13. Automobile Insurance	_____
14. Transportation	_____
15. Automobile Maintenance/Repairs	_____
16. Automobile Gas/Oil	_____
17. Newspapers/Subscriptions/Books	_____
18. Dry Cleaning/Laundry	_____
19. Estimated Taxes (if applicable)	_____
20. Other (specify)	_____
Subtotal 2:	_____

continued

C. Monthly Discretionary Expenses

    1. Dining Out   _____
    2. Entertainment/Movies/Shows   _____
    3. Vacations/Travel   _____
    4. Gifts   _____
    5. Charitable Gifts   _____
    6. Other (specify) _____   _____

    Subtotal 3:   _____

D. Limited Duration Expenses

    1. Education   _____
    2. Home Improvements   _____
    3. Automobile Loan/Lease Payments   _____
    4. Other Bank Loan Payments   _____
    5. Other (specify) _____   _____

    Subtotal 4:   _____

    Total Monthly Living Expenses
    (Add Subtotals 1 through 4):   _____

VI. **Your Cash Flow Summary**   **Monthly Totals**

A. Total Monthly Income: _____
B. Total Monthly Living Expenses   _____

    Your Monthly Cash Flow
    (Monthly Income – Monthly Living Expenses): _____

Now that you have completed your Personal Financial Profile, you can estimate the amount of capital available to you to finance your venture:

Amount of liquid assets available
in savings and checking accounts: _____

Amount of borrowing power on your
home through home equity: _____

Amount, if any, of severance: _____

Possessions (such as car, home, jewelry, etc.)
you would be able to liquidate: _____

Investment assets: _____

Insurance policies with loan
provisions, if applicable: _____

Bank line of credit on your
personal account/credit cards: _____

Retirement assets (review for
penalties for access):   _____

Other (such as loans from family
or friends):   _____

Total Available Capital: _____

Keep your total available capital calculation in mind as you explore your
entrepreneurial options. Also, consider how much of your own capital you are
willing to put at risk. This decision is an individual and subjective one that only
you can make.

Drawing Conclusions

This chapter has given you an overview—and a reality check—of an
important career change issue in your life. At this time, you may not be
ready to make a final decision. Nevertheless, you need to begin drawing
some conclusions about your suitability for a career as an entrepreneur in
order to successfully move forward from this point.

EXERCISE 1.8

Clarifying Questions

Answer the following questions spontaneously and candidly:

1. Which would be the best direction to take now in my career?

   _____

   _____

   _____

2. What career options seem most appropriate for me now?

   _____

   _____

   _____

3. What are the pros and cons of each option?

   _____

   _____

   _____

Option 1:

   _____

   _____

Option 2:

   _____

   _____

Option 3:

   _____

   _____

4. What is my biggest need or issue right now about proceeding with an entrepreneurial option?

    _____

    _____

5. Will an entrepreneurial option provide more personal or professional satisfaction to me than a corporate position? In what ways do I expect more satisfaction?

    _____

    _____

If you decide to pursue entrepreneurship further, you will need to complete some key steps explored in this chapter:

1. Clarifying your motivations and expectations

2. Discussing the relevant issues with your family and key other people

3. Planning the time for your entrepreneurial effort

You must also honestly assess what essential business skills and knowledge you lack—and make the efforts necessary to bridge those gaps.

EXERCISE 1.9

Experience Gap Analysis

This exercise will help you pinpoint your strengths and weaknesses as an entrepreneur. Each of the skills listed is an essential component of starting a successful business. While you don't need to be expert in each of them now, you do need the reality check of a candid self-assessment. Your particular venture may require additional skills and knowledge as well.

For each of the skill areas listed below, rate your knowledge on a scale of 1 to 10, with 10 as the highest score. Then, on the lines provided, list the experience you have in that area and any actions you need to take to acquire any necessary additional experience.

continued

I. MARKET RESEARCH AND ANALYSIS   Rating

1. Sizing a market   _____
    Experience: _____
    Action: _____

2. Sizing a market future   _____
    Experience: _____
    Action: _____

3. Determining potential market share   _____
    Experience: _____
    Action: _____

4. Assessing physical factors influencing a market
    (such as location, weather)   _____
    Experience: _____
    Action: _____

5. Assessing economic and social factors
    influencing a market   _____
    Experience: _____
    Action: _____

6. Tracking marketing trends   _____
    Experience: _____
    Action: _____

7. Assessing your competition   _____
    Experience: _____
    Action: _____

8. Calculating/projecting sales volume   _____

   Experience: _____

   Action: _____

9. Familiarity with financial practices and
   guidelines for your industry   _____

   Experience: _____

   Action: _____

10. Ability to recognize a good business opportunity _____

    Experience: _____

    Action: _____

II. MARKET PLANNING   **Rating**

1. Forecasting sales   _____

   Experience: _____

   Action: _____

2. Determining product mix   _____

   Experience: _____

   Action: _____

3. Pricing products or services   _____

   Experience: _____

   Action: _____

4. Distributing products or services   _____

   Experience: _____

   Action: _____

continued

5. Selling products or services   _____

    Experience: _____

    Action: _____

6. Advertising products or services   _____

    Experience: _____

    Action: _____

7. Maintaining customer relations   _____

    Experience: _____

    Action: _____

8. Maintaining a warranty   _____

    Experience: _____

    Action: _____

9. Developing new products   _____

    Experience: _____

    Action: _____

10. Creating a marketing strategy   _____

    Experience: _____

    Action: _____

III. OPERATIONS   Rating
General

1. Maintaining supplier relations   _____

    Experience: _____

    Action: _____

2. Networking with industry contacts   _____

   Experience: _____

   Action: _____

3. Purchasing goods and services   _____

   Experience: _____

   Action: _____

4. Controlling and maintaining inventory   _____

   Experience: _____

   Action: _____

5. Selecting a site   _____

   Experience: _____

   Action: _____

6. Designing layout and work flow   _____

   Experience: _____

   Action: _____

7. Designing a building security system   _____

   Experience: _____

   Action: _____

Retailing

1. Merchandising   _____

   Experience: _____

   Action: _____

continued

2. Providing customer services
   (such as refunds, repairs)   _____

   Experience: _____

   Action: _____

3. Creating displays (such as fixtures, lighting, signs) _____

   Experience: _____

   Action: _____

Manufacturing

1. Selecting machinery and equipment   _____

   Experience: _____

   Action: _____

2. Negotiating maintenance contracts   _____

   Experience: _____

   Action: _____

3. Tooling   _____

   Experience: _____

   Action: _____

4. Maintaining facilities and equipment   _____

   Experience: _____

   Action: _____

5. Costing   _____

   Experience: _____

   Action: _____

6. Scheduling production _____

   Experience: _____

   Action: _____

7. Designing production methods _____

   Experience: _____

   Action: _____

8. Implementing quality control _____

   Experience: _____

   Action: _____

9. Packaging _____

   Experience: _____

   Action: _____

10. Shipping _____

   Experience: _____

   Action: _____

11. Implementing safe work practices _____

   Experience: _____

   Action: _____

V. FINANCIAL PLANNING   **Rating**

1. Assessing total start-up capital needs _____

   Experience: _____

   Action: _____

continued

2. Assessing long-term capital needs   _____

   Experience: _____

   Action: _____

3. Creating personal sources of capital   _____

   Experience: _____

   Action: _____

4. Developing outside sources of cash   _____

   Experience: _____

   Action: _____

5. Nurturing local private investors   _____

   Experience: _____

   Action: _____

6. Leasing   _____

   Experience: _____

   Action: _____

7. Assessing cash flow requirements   _____

   Experience: _____

   Action: _____

8. Making profit/loss projections   _____

   Experience: _____

   Action: _____

9. Developing a balance sheet   _____

   Experience: _____

   Action: _____

10. Analyzing financial statements and projections _____

    Experience: _____

    Action: _____

V. ORGANIZATION PLANNING   Rating

Legal

1. Knowledge of legal forms   _____

    Experience: _____

    Action: _____

2. Knowledge of formation requirements   _____

    Experience: _____

    Action: _____

3. Understanding of liability exposure   _____

    Experience: _____

    Action: _____

4. Negotiating contracts and leases   _____

    Experience: _____

    Action: _____

5. Understanding tax implications   _____

    Experience: _____

    Action: _____

6. Obtaining licenses   _____

    Experience: _____

    Action: _____

continued

7. Understanding of local, state. and federal laws _____

   Experience: _____

   Action: _____

Insurance

1. Understanding of risk management _____

   Experience: _____

   Action: _____

2. Knowledge of fire insurance _____

   Experience: _____

   Action: _____

3. Knowledge of auto insurance _____

   Experience: _____

   Action: _____

4. Knowledge of crime risk management _____

   Experience: _____

   Action: _____

5. Understanding of fidelity bonds _____

   Experience: _____

   Action: _____

6. Knowledge of liability insurance _____

   Experience: _____

   Action: _____

7. Knowledge of health and disability insurance   _____

   Experience: _____

   Action: _____

8. Knowledge of life insurance   _____

   Experience: _____

   Action: _____

9. Knowledge of Workers' Compensation   _____

   Experience: _____

   Action: _____

VI. STAFFING   **Rating**

1. Developing job descriptions   _____

   Experience: _____

   Action: _____

2. Recruiting employee prospects   _____

   Experience: _____

   Action: _____

3. Hiring (selecting, interviewing, evaluating)
   competent staff   _____

   Experience: _____

   Action: _____

continued

4. Developing personnel policies   _____

   Experience: _____

   Action: _____

5. Setting wages/salaries   _____

   Experience: _____

   Action: _____

6. Developing a menu of employee benefits   _____

   Experience: _____

   Action: _____

7. Training employees for future growth   _____

   Experience: _____

   Action: _____

Summarize on the following lines the action steps you have listed above for each of the Experience Gap Analysis categories. Use your summary as a guide through the rest of this book. The next chapter, *Starting a Business*, provides you with an overview of many of the basic skills you may find missing from your profile now.

I. Market Research and Analysis

_____

_____

_____

_____

_____

II. Market Planning

_____

_____

_____

_____

_____

III. Operations

_____

_____

_____

_____

_____

IV. Financial Planning

_____

_____

_____

_____

_____

V. Organization Planning

_____

_____

_____

_____

_____

Chapter 2

STARTING A BUSINESS

From identifying a market to developing an idea to designing a company, an entrepreneur must have both creative abilities and management skills. Many excellent managers have failed starting a business because their idea was flawed. Many others with an innovative idea have bombed because they had little knowledge of the fundamentals of running a business.

Certain basics apply to all businesses. In this chapter, you are introduced to the nuts and bolts required to launch a successful entrepreneurial venture. One of the major reasons that new ventures fail is the lack of a business plan. In this chapter, you learn how to develop the essential elements of a workable business plan: the idea, the marketing plan, the organizational plan, and the financial plan. The conclusion of this chapter describes the basic structure of a business plan. It explains how to write a business plan by using the individual elements introduced throughout the chapter.

Beginning at the Beginning

Every business starts with an idea. Many highly successful companies were started because the founder thought about the business in a new way. What were the business ideas that drove the success of Federal Express, Apple Computer, and H & R Block?

In the case of Federal Express, the founder saw a business need that was not being met: rapid, reliable delivery of small business packages. He targeted potential business prospects who had to have delivery overnight to avoid lost business or expensive downtime.

Apple Computer built a company around the incredible idea that a computer should be accessible to ordinary people who have no interest in investing large amounts of time learning complex instructions. Even though Microsoft Windows software has closed the gap, the Apple Macintosh is still considered the most user-friendly system available.

H & R Block is a classic example of targeting a narrow market niche. Prior to Block's start-up, tax returns were prepared by accountants or by the taxpayer. Block saw a real need and defined his idea as follows: we do only income tax returns. We do them for the common person. We do our work quickly. We do it at low cost.

The single most critical element that will determine your success or failure is your business idea. It is the very guts of your business.

Where Do Business Ideas Come From?

Most successful companies are started by individuals who are experienced in the industry or in a closely related one. Take a hard look at your industry. Wherever there is rapid change, there is opportunity. Wherever the needs of customers are changing, there is opportunity. Wherever there is an emerging trend, there is opportunity. Think of the businesses spawned by the move to digital technology: voice mail, cellular phones, automobile diagnostic equipment, and literally hundreds of computer-related businesses.

EXERCISE 2.1

Finding a Business Idea

This exercise is designed to help you develop an idea for your business. Often entrepreneurs' best ideas come from personal hobbies or interests, from a belief that they themselves can do a better job at something already on the market, from a response to a sudden opportunity, or from a perception of a market need. Answer the following questions to identify your business ideas. List all of your ideas without judging them.

For the items you list below, identify the sources of their appeal for you.

Hobbies, interests: _____

_____

Leisure time priorities: _____

_____

Skills you are motivated to use: _____

_____

Magazines you read: _____

_____

Trends that interest you: _____

_____

If you won a three-million-dollar lottery prize, how would you spend the money? How would you spend your time?

_____

_____

_____

continued

Do you know of an existing product or service in the marketplace that you could improve?

_____

_____

Do you know of a need that you could meet?

_____

_____

Do you know of a valuable product or service that is not currently offered in your geographical area?

_____

_____

Is there someone among your family or friends with a successful business who might be interested in expanding it?

_____

_____

What are the trends in your industry?

_____

_____

What business opportunities do they present?

_____

_____

Without the support of a workable idea, all of your efforts and resources will be misdirected—and wasted. The essential part is to make sure that your idea is market driven, which means that it must be connected to the needs and interests of your potential customers. Moreover, even assuming that your idea is a good business proposition, there is the question of what you bring to it. How well do your own experiences and skills mesh with the venture? Will your background help you make this effort a practical business success?

Becoming an Orange in a World of Apples

Failure rates for most new businesses are very high. How many stores, shops, and other small businesses have you seen fail within a few months of opening? If the owners of those businesses had asked themselves some fundamental questions about the purpose of their business and had defined how it would be unique, the new business might not only have survived, but thrived.

If you are to be a survivor and a thriver, you must build your business around a solid idea that creates a competitive advantage by its uniqueness. If your plumbing supply distributorship, lingerie boutique, or computer training company is nothing more than a copy of a competitor's business, you're inviting disaster. No matter how excited you are about your new business, customers will not desert current suppliers and come to you unless they have a compelling reason to do so.

"Ah, but I'll offer a lower price," you say. With few exceptions, small businesses that hinge their strategic advantage on price fail for two reasons. First, most customers buy on a combination of price and perceived value. Second, competitors almost always can meet or beat your price, and they may do so simply to put you out of business. Even when the numbers work—and they won't unless you can generate huge volume—competing on price is the worst possible strategy for most small companies.

Venture capitalists and other professionals who invest in new businesses look for four things:

1. Unique business ideas

2. Hard-to-copy competitive advantages

3. Large markets

4. Competent management teams

If these professionals consider the quality of the business idea the number one criterion, can you afford to risk your life savings on anything less?

EXERCISE 2.2

Clarifying Your Idea

In fifty words or less, state your business vision by writing a brief statement that summarizes your business concept and its purpose. Write the vision as though you were describing your new business to a potential investor.

My Business Vision: _____

_____

_____

_____

_____

_____

_____

The following questions will help you clarify your idea. Fully answering them may very well be the hardest work you do in putting your business together—and the most important. Don't move ahead with your new business until you have developed a satisfactory answer for each question.

1. What is the general industry or service area (such as retail, distributor, manufacturer, wholesaler) of your business?

   _____

   _____

2. What is the specific product or service (such as children's shoes, home remodeling, financial planning, publisher for the legal profession)?

   _____

   _____

3. Who is currently serving your intended customers?

   _____

   _____

4. How successful are they in terms of years in business, growth rate, and profitability?

_____

_____

5. What is their success based on? Few competitors? Exceptional quality? Innovative products or solutions? Speed? Reliability?

_____

_____

6. What is the essence of your business idea that will create a strategic advantage over your competitors?

_____

_____

7. What are the specific features of your business idea?

_____

_____

8. What are the specific benefits that your business idea provides for customers?

_____

_____

9. Could your business idea be copied easily and cheaply?

_____

_____

10. Are there patents, licenses, specialized processes, or proprietary information that could cause difficulties for competitors attempting to duplicate your idea?

_____

_____

continued

11. Describe the strategic advantage that your business idea will create.

_____

_____

12. Describe how your business idea will create the foundation for your business, why it will fuel the growth of your business, and how it will affect both customers and competitors.

_____

_____

Business Leverage Factors

Savvy entrepreneurs develop their business idea by creating new ways of serving customers. Consider these leverage factors for developing your idea and making it unique:

Do it faster. In many industries, downtime is big money. Many maintenance and repair businesses, parts suppliers, and even insurance carriers create their competitive advantage with fast turnaround.

Customize it. Rather than sell a mass-produced generic product or service, produce exactly the combination of product and service that each customer wants. Larger firms will find it difficult to compete because their business is built on mass production, where large numbers create economies of scale. A very small company can build to order at a profit.

High end it. Target the small number of customers in your market who want the best quality possible and will pay the price. This market is often too small for competitors to serve profitably.

Wrap around. Wrap your customers with an all-inclusive line of products and services. The success of Super Clubs in Jamaica offering high-, mid-, and low-cost, all-inclusive vacations is an example. Customers like the convenience of one-stop, hassle-free shopping.

Do it cheaper. Be careful here. Large supermarket chains and other retailers can operate on margins of one percent because they move huge quantities of goods. It's a lot tougher for a convenience store. However, if you have a way of dropping operating costs dramatically (proprietary technology, for example), and if the industry is price sensitive and you can maintain adequate profit margins, you may have a competitive advantage.

Offer product updating. Most companies create a product with a predictable useful life and built-in obsolescence. Perhaps your company can offer customers the benefit of continual updating to keep their product state-of-the-art. More and more small companies are making their mark through modular design, allowing quick, inexpensive component exchange. There are no industry limits here. Only a change in mind-set is required. Product updating could be done with clothing, office equipment, or financial services.

Do it better. Obvious as it sounds, this is one of the best business ideas. Customers are tired of shoddy products and poor service. If you can find a way to deliver consistently high-quality products and services, you will have a substantial competitive advantage.

What are the business leverage factors that make your business idea unique? Constantly ask yourself this question: "How can I be an orange in a world of apples?" If you cannot answer with clarity and confidence, your business is at risk.

Getting Feedback

As a beginning entrepreneur, you need to find out quickly if you have developed a workable business idea that potential customers will believe truly meets their needs. If you haven't, you will not succeed. This step represents the beginning of the market research process.

Seek out several potential customers or experts already in the business who are geographically distant enough not to be threatened by your interest. Describe your idea and solicit their candid reactions. Encourage them to be completely honest. Record their feedback, using a copy of this form:

EXERCISE 2.3

Feedback Recording Form

Date: _____

Name: _____

Title: _____

Company: _____

Phone: _____

Area of Expertise: _____

_____

_____

What are the strengths of this business idea? _____

_____

_____

What are the weaknesses of this business idea? _____

_____

_____

Is the targeted market appropriate? _____

_____

_____

What would you suggest for the next steps in the development of this idea?

_____

_____

Additional Comments: _____

_____

_____

Post-Interview Analysis. Based on this feedback, what is your next step?

_____

_____

Protecting Your Ideas

Many entrepreneurs are concerned about someone stealing their business ideas. Relax. First, great ideas are a dime a dozen. Most people, even if they recognize your idea as a great one, will not have the skills or motivation to turn it into a thriving business. It takes money, know-how, planning, excellent execution, and long hours to accomplish that goal.

Furthermore, if someone decides to use your idea, it must be reasonably easy to copy, which means that you should expect it to be copied if your business becomes successful. Competitive intelligence is practiced by every leader in every industry. But the idea is only the beginning. To win in business, you must stay ahead of competitors by constantly moving forward and developing your idea.

Most companies and savvy business entrepreneurs know the legal consequences of copyright, trademark, and patent infringement. Although you can't legally protect an idea, proprietary knowledge and products can be protected through patents, copyrights, trademarks, and employee noncompete agreements. If protecting your idea is a concern for you, discuss this issue with your lawyer and follow the guidance you receive.

Turning Your Business Idea into a Small Business

Now that you have a solid idea for your business, how do you turn it into a successful company? Before you dig into the details of actually setting up a company, you need to do some reality testing. Think carefully about your answers to these two key questions:

1. Is this business idea right for me?

2. Is this business right for the market?

Is this business idea right for you? Here's what you must consider:

Do I know enough about this industry to be a player? Find out if you measure up. Start by reading industry trade journals cover-to-cover. Seek out a good librarian to help you locate the publications you need. Seek out people already in the industry (not competitors) and interview them until you are clear about what it takes to be successful in the industry.

Am I excited about this idea? Starting a business is tough work. Successful entrepreneurs love the business they are in. Their enthusiasm keeps them going through the challenges of the start-up and the formidable task of managing the ongoing health and growth of their business. Is your business idea exciting enough and important enough to sustain you through the required hard work? If it isn't, you will find it difficult to stick with your idea long enough to be successful.

Can I make enough money? You have probably done some thinking about your compensation requirements. Will your business provide enough money for you? Through interviews and library research, you should be able to estimate what level of compen-sation is realistic.

Is this business right for the market? This question will require careful research. If you find the idea of market research intimi-dating, relax. It's not all that difficult. Essentially, what you want to find out is this: is there a sufficient market for my products and services, and, if so, where is it, and who are the individuals or organizations that would buy? How much will they buy, how often, and at what price? You will also need to know your competitors and their strengths and weaknesses.

Through market research, you will collect data, and through market analysis, you will interpret that information to determine the business viability of your idea. Together, these two tasks will enable you to create your marketing plan, which is an essential component of your complete business plan.

You need a marketing plan for "moving the goods" because nothing happens in business until somebody sells something. And if you're looking for outside financial help, you must have a clear marketing plan, one that is persuasive to a cautious investor or banker. The marketing plan should contain a sales forecast and a marketing strategy that explains how that forecast will be attained.

Conducting Market Research

One of the most common reasons businesses fail is insufficient research identifying potential customers, what they need, how to reach them, and what the competition has to offer. Because most outside investors require evidence of substantial market research from would-be entrepreneurs, it makes sense for you to obtain similar data before risking your own capital. Market research increases your likelihood of success because you obtain valuable feedback from the marketplace before making important decisions. The feedback protects you from costly mistakes that could deplete your resources.

Can you have your market research done for you? Yes, but the costs associated with reputable companies may be prohibitive. Besides, no one cares more about your money and your welfare than you do. You will be able to more accurately predict future earnings and ultimately improve profitability by personally collecting the necessary information from the appropriate people and then analyzing your results objectively.

Perhaps the greatest benefit of conducting your own market research will be the relationships you establish. If the relationships are positive, you can turn to these people for advice when you develop your market strategy —and you can return to them again and again for support. They may even become customers of your new business.

EXERCISE 2.4

Reviewing a Personal Decision

Select a personal decision from the past that you feel did not work out well. Choose one that relates to a move, a job change, or an important purchase. What pitfalls did you encounter in the decision process that you want to avoid in future? Analyze the experience by answering the following questions.

continued

1. What was the decision about?

    _____

    _____

2. What was the evidence that it was not a successful decision on your part?

    _____

    _____

3. What role did research play in that decision?

    _____

    _____

4. In retrospect, how would you have done the research differently?

    _____

    _____

5. What implications does this experience have for your research efforts in your entrepreneurial venture?

    _____

    _____

Two Methods of Market Research

The two market research methods are those of secondary and primary research. It is usually best to begin with secondary research. Secondary research involves collecting data that has already been gathered by others in printed material or databases of articles, statistics, speeches, trends, demographics, and so on. Secondary research provides more precise information about your industry, business, and customers than you would find if you did your own research.

As an emerging entrepreneur, you will need to find out everything about your industry and market to determine prospects for growth, competition, and potential problems. The resource list in the back of this book provides a valuable starting point for your market research.

Primary research involves firsthand collection of data and information. You can conduct primary research either by talking to people yourself, using a survey, or observing, such as counting traffic and shoppers.

The more information you can obtain about your target business, the better you will understand those factors that will contribute to the success or failure of your business.

EXERCISE 2.5

Market Research Warm-Up

Pick an object that interests you in the room. Pretend that you are interested in starting a business manufacturing and selling this product. The business will require a general investment of $20,000. You believe the business could be very successful. List below all of the questions you would like to have answered.

1. _____

2. _____

3. _____

4. _____

5. _____

6. _____

7. _____

8. _____

9. _____

10. _____

continued

Where would you find the answers to your questions?

1. _____

2. _____

3. _____

4. _____

5. _____

6. _____

7. _____

8. _____

9. _____

10. _____

Planning Your Market Research

Start your research by finding an experienced business librarian. Business librarians can be found in most large libraries, as well as in college or university libraries where business courses are offered. The librarian can direct you to the appropriate directories and databases containing the most valuable data relevant to your needs. If you can't locate a business librarian, a good reference librarian can be helpful.

The Small Business Administration (SBA) is a government resource you can use to access additional information and data. The SBA has numerous publications available that can help guide your research. And don't forget about the data and statistics available from your local Chamber of Commerce. Many trade and professional associations are also rich sources of industry trend data and statistics. Some of the larger organizations are listed in the resource section at the end of this book.

In researching your market, you will be looking for the following information:

1. Total size of the market in dollars.

2. Number of companies serving the market.

3. List of competitors within the geographic area where you will be doing business.

4. Percent of market share for each competitor.

5. Average annual gross sales and owner benefit for companies that are the size of the one you will build over three years. (Owner benefit is considered to be your entire annual compensation, including salary, net profit, benefits, and other perks.)

6. Estimated time until break-even. (The break-even point is the moment when the business income and the expenses to run your business become equal. After that point you should be making money.)

7. Industry potential. Five-year outlook. (Is it growing, mature, or declining?)

8. Cost and ease of entry. (Does it require sophisticated knowledge or substantial capital or both to start a business in this industry?)

9. Average sales per customer. (How much revenue you generate for each transaction and annually per customer.)

10. Average cost per sale. (What it costs to secure and retain one customer. Include items such as advertising, promotional materials, travel, commissions, and after-sale servicing.)

The next step is your primary research. Primary research consists of gathering information and data firsthand and drawing conclusions based on the findings. Here are some helpful techniques:

1. **Purchase the product or service.** If the product or service is a consumer item or a business service that can be utilized, you should purchase it. Make purchases from multiple locations and take notes on the differences in product and service. Purchase the competitors' products or services also, if possible.

2. **Talk to vendors, suppliers, bankers, accountants, and attorneys.** The suppliers and vendors to a business or industry are invaluable sources of information. They are often in a position to see changes in trends before the actual business owners do. Sometimes, as in the cases of accountants and lawyers, you may have to pay for the individual's time to obtain information. However, a small amount of money up front could provide the information that saves a tremendous amount of money down the road.

3. **Conduct surveys.** Surveys should be short, focused, and to the point. They can be conducted in personal interviews, mailed, or left to be filled out and returned later. Be aware, however, that there is a very small rate of return for mailed surveys—only about 1 to 2 percent will be returned.

4. **Use focus groups.** Focus groups are a standard form of primary research. They consist of potential customers of your product or service. You can hire a market research company to conduct a focus group, but the cost may be prohibitive. You can also conduct your own. Convene the group in a convenient location and ask relevant questions about your proposed product or service. It's helpful to have a sample product available, if possible. You may want to tape the session so that you can analyze the results later. Focus groups should consist of no more than ten to twelve participants and last no longer than one hour. In addition, participants should receive some compensation for their time—either money, a product or service, or lunch.

5. **Hang out.** This type of research can mean sitting in parking lots and counting cars on different days of the week and in different weather. It can consist of spending several weeks in the geographic area where a business operates or is to be located and watching behavior and recording comments. It can also mean immersing yourself in a particular business. And don't rule out the value of the information you can obtain by attending trade shows for the business or industry of your choice.

The Mind of the Customer

Although this market data is critical, markets don't buy products; individual customers do. If you're out of touch with your customers, you're out of business. So an important part of turning a great business idea into a great company is linking up closely with your potential customers so that you understand exactly what will get them to become your customers and stay your customers.

Customers will not abandon the companies that they currently patronize unless they have compelling reasons to do so. These reasons should be embedded as leverage factors in your business idea. But don't rely on your judgment: the only opinion that matters is that of your customers.

Where are your potential customers, and how do you reach them? If you don't know where they are, go back and do more market research. To reach them, contact business owners in a noncompeting territory and say something similar to the following:

> "I'm doing research on the (blank) industry, and I want to know exactly what customers want and don't want from their suppliers. I'm wondering if you could give me the names of a few customers I could interview as part of my research. I'd be happy to share what I learn with you."

You'll find that gaining access to customers is easy if you explain that you are doing research and are not trying to sell anything. Most customers are never asked for their input, and they will be flattered, even grateful, for the opportunity to express their views. After you have compiled your data, be sure to share it with your sources as you said you would.

When you survey customers, ask the following questions:

1. How long have you been a customer of this company?

2. Why do you do business with the company?

3. What was your best experience with the company?

4. What was your worst experience with the company?

5. How does the quality of the product or service compare with the quality of what is offered by the competition?

6. How well does the product or service meet your requirements?

7. What specific improvements are needed?

8. How much business will you do with the company this year?

9. What would convince you to give the company more business?

10. What must the company do to keep your business?

11. How should the product or service be priced?

12. What's important to you about the product? What's not important?

13. What would cause you to switch suppliers?

Scouting the Territory

If you are to gain your fair share of the market, you must know the strengths, weaknesses, and strategy of your competitors. Even if your idea is new, if it's a winner, you will soon have competitors trying to take your business away. Consequently, you must have a competitive strategy. And to develop a realistic competitive strategy, you need solid competitor information. Find out the answers to the following questions:

1. Who are the top performers in the industry and in your territory?

2. How would you describe their business ideas?

3. What are the key components of their strategies?

4. In what ways are the top performers alike? How are they different?

5. What are the core competencies of the top performers? (Core competencies are the critical skills and knowledge that drive the success of the business.)

6. What are the weaknesses of your competitors? (Examples might be poor distribution channels, poor location, high fixed costs, technology lags, inventory stockouts, poor customer response time,

zoning problems, lack of sales or marketing sophistication, poor after-sale service, poor understanding of customer needs, and illogical pricing.)

7. How have your competitors responded to new competition in the past?

8. How have your competitors increased market share?

9. What are the strategic advantages of your competitors? (Examples are low-cost provider, technology leader, first to market, best quality, fast turnaround, exceptional service, and exceptional reliability.)

10. What are the critical management strengths of the top performers?

One of the best ways to obtain this information is to talk to others in the business. Surprisingly, most people are willing to volunteer valuable information, so talk to as many sources as possible. The best strategy is to set up an appointment by phone and then visit in person. Clearly, if you want to be in the same business, the situation could be threatening to the person you are interviewing. Use your judgment. Sometimes the solution is a simple matter of traveling to a nearby area outside the limits of direct competition.

EXERCISE 2.6

Summary of Market Research

Use the following outline as a guide to summarize your findings. Wherever possible, cite two sources for greater accuracy.

A. Market/Customer Characteristics

Demographics. What are the demographic characteristics (total population, geographic location, gender, age, race, marital status, economic level, occupation) of your potential customers? _____

_____

_____

_____

continued

Lifestyle and Personality. What are the lifestyle (including social class) and personality characteristics of your potential customers? Which do you think are most important? What research supports this opinion?_____

_____

_____

_____

Attitude. What do your potential customers value most? Price? Quality? Style? Fashion? Originality? Uniqueness?_____

_____

_____

_____

B. Defining Your Target Market

Based on these characteristics, how do you define the specific target market for your business?_____

_____

_____

_____

C. Factors Influencing Market Trends

What factors significantly influence your target market? How can they be expected to influence your future market? Consider the following influences: the economy, location, season, technology, politics, laws and regulations, social and cultural influences, and any other factors. _____

_____

_____

_____

D. Competitive Analysis

Who are your biggest competitors? What percentage of the market do they collectively control? _____

_____

_____

_____

How many competitors are there in your market? Has the number of competitors changed in recent years? _____

_____

_____

_____

Has the market grown, remained the same, or become smaller in recent years? Is the market overloaded with competing firms? _____

_____

_____

_____

Analyzing Your Market Research

To create a solid strategic intent statement, you must avoid looking at your research results through tinted glasses. Giving up on your original idea when it proves not to be a good one (for example, because there is no market for it or because you will not earn a living from it for the foreseeable future) may represent the end of a dream, but your success as an entrepreneur is much more important. And that success needs to be built on the solid foundation of an idea that is a good business proposition.

Here are some typical responses to negative market data that you need to guard against:

The Denial Response. Aspiring entrepreneurs begin to uncover information indicating that their entrepreneurial efforts would not be successful. People often stop the research process at this point and continue to push ahead with their efforts, in spite of the negative data.

The Blinders Response. Aspiring entrepreneurs uncover conflicting data and analyze it only in a positive light. They may continue researching and interpreting the data in a more positive light than the information warrants. Or they may stop researching altogether and proceed on the basis of the misinterpreted data.

The Assumption Response. Aspiring entrepreneurs do no research. They base their business decisions on assumptions about entrepreneurial ventures or on gut feelings about the possibilities for success.

The more effective response to negative data is this:

The Objective Analyzer Response. Aspiring entrepreneurs compile data and bounce it off as many experts as they can find. Information is interpreted objectively, and each individual acts accordingly by (a) proceeding, (b) giving up the idea and pursuing other options, or (c) modifying the idea and resuming research.

From Concept to Reality

At this point, you should have a clear view of what your business would look like. You have defined your business idea, you know why it works, you know a market exists, you have listened to potential customers, and you have performed a competitive analysis. Your next step is to develop the foundation for your marketing strategy. You must address two basic issues: where to play and how to win.

A common reason for business failure is lack of focus—not deciding where to play and how. A targeted marketing approach generally results in lower risk and better results. Don't make the mistake of trying to be all things to all people. Make sure that you have the facts to back up your choices. Deciding to play in a market that is saturated or declining may not be such a hot idea, even if your idea is a great one. Jumping into a rising market without the required skills or capital is equally foolish.

How to win is simply to capitalize on the factors that will allow you to execute your business idea better than the competition. Here are some possibilities:

First to market. An ability to consistently get to market first with a new or improved product or service. This first-mover factor is a major competitive advantage.

Exceptional service quality. Many companies deliver mediocre or poor service. Many start-ups have knocked competitors out of the box by making exceptional service their top priority.

Marketing focus. Reebok, a world leader in sports shoes and clothing, doesn't manufacture anything. They are a world-class marketing company. All of their manufacturing is subcontracted, so they can concentrate their time and resources on marketing and sales. Because of the limited resources and time required to build the business, marketing focus is a high-leverage strategy for a start-up.

Other how-to-win elements are the leverage factors discussed earlier in this chapter. Some highly successful businesses combine several of these elements to create a competitive advantage that is difficult for competitors to emulate.

When drafting your strategic intent statement, you should keep the following in mind:

Brevity counts. It's much easier to write a thirty-page document than a one-pager that captures the core of your future success. Your strategic intent statement is a living document that drives every decision in your business. You must carry it around in your head every day. Your employees must do the same. Few people can carry thirty pages around in their heads.

Labels don't matter. The terms used up to this point aren't what matter; what matters is the process. The intent of this chapter is to provide you with a proven process to create your own unique success template. When you create your strategic intent statement, use whatever labels you want, as long as the final result is a clear blueprint for the success of your business.

Commit it to memory. If this statement is to be the guiding light for your business, it must become a part of you. Tape a copy to the bath-room mirror, tape another on the refrigerator, and carry one in your car. Read it until you breathe it.

Now summarize your direction in a strategic intent statement. This document will help guide the development of your marketing plan.

EXERCISE 2.7

Drafting a Strategic Intent Statement

Name of Your Business: _____

Business Idea: _____

_____

_____

_____

_____

_____

Strategic Differentiators: _____

_____

_____

_____

Where to Play: _____

_____

_____

_____

How to Win: _____

_____

_____

Formulating a Marketing Strategy

The ultimate reason for the failure of any new business is a lack of customers. No matter how wonderful your product or service is, it's highly unlikely that customers will simply show up. Prospective customers must be attracted and then convinced that buying is in their best interest. You can make many other mistakes and survive, but miscalculate your ability to find customers, and your business will be history.

Finding, winning, and retaining customers requires expertise in three areas:

1. **Marketing.** The means by which you define your customer base, determine their needs and wants, create appropriate products or services, and determine sales and distribution methods.

2. **Selling.** The process of finding prospects for your products and services and converting them to customers.

3. **Retention.** Your strategy to keep current customers buying.

To be successful, you must develop skills in all three of these areas. But first, you need to give more thought to narrowing your market niche to a customer group whom you can serve profitably, but one that is too small for larger competitors. The narrower your niche, the higher the conversion rate, which is the percentage of prospects who are converted into customers. The more narrowly you segment your market, the fewer competitors you will have. And narrow niching means lower customer sacrifice—the degree to which your customers have to compromise to get the exact product or solution they need.

Many entrepreneurs worry that if their niche is small, they may not have enough business. That's possible, but your market research should help you to identify the size of your market with great precision. A market with a total dollar volume of only a few million dollars, although too small for many companies in your industry, may be more than enough for you, even if your conversion rate is low.

Pricing Your Product or Service

After you've defined your market niche, you will need to determine the pricing of your product or service. While pricing is critical in order to cover costs and make a profit, deciding on a pricing strategy is not really a cost decision—it's a marketing decision. Your customer doesn't care about your costs. The perceived value of your product or service is the only factor that matters to the customer.

Cost-plus pricing, where a company calculates unit cost and then adds on the appropriate percentage of overhead costs plus a percentage for profit, is the most common—and the most ineffective—pricing strategy. It drives customers to competitors if your price is too high or leaves a great deal of money on the table that could have been yours if your price is too low. Cost-plus pricing totally disregards perceived value.

Value pricing, on the other hand, simply means understanding the perceived value of your product in the minds of customers and pricing accordingly. Consumers will pay plenty for better quality, faster delivery, ease of use, and exceptional service. Innovation, ability to customize, reliability, and many other factors can support a value pricing strategy. Here are some ways to use pricing to market your product or service:

1. **Loss leading.** Many retailers and some other businesses use a low price on a popular, high-volume product to draw customers in the door. Any losses are more than covered by the additional products that a predictable percentage of customers will buy.

2. **Volume discounts.** You should price high for the low-volume customer and then lower the unit price as volume per customer increases.

3. **Creaming.** This tactic involves singling out high-volume but non-price-sensitive customer segments within a market niche for special

attention. The product offering is usually changed by adding features and options or by modifying the product cosmetics to justify higher pricing.

4. **Bottom skimming.** This technique requires identification of a suitable number of price-sensitive customers who are happy with a generic product that can be identified and sold at very low cost.

5. **Option pricing.** Here a very basic product or service is offered with optional add-ons with high profit margins. The automobile industry has built its business around this pricing strategy.

6. **First-mover pricing.** If your product is first in the market, you have great sales leverage. While you're the only game in town, price high. As competitors copy you and begin to take your market share, lower the price.

7. **Top line.** If you're the best of the best and customers want what you have, you can charge high prices with large profit margins and be required to sell only a fraction of the volume of less well-positioned competitors. Small specialty retail boutiques in high-income areas use this tactic, as do many consulting companies and other professional service firms.

A business that adopts a market position as a high-volume, low-cost provider is asking for trouble. Small businesses simply do not have the economies of scale or enough market share to justify this kind of pricing. Don't make this fatal mistake.

Here's a general pricing rule: Low volume with high margins is always preferable to high volume with low margins. Pricing should be a critical plank in your overall strategy platform. Think through what value you're providing. Make sure it's aligned with what customers want. And then charge whatever the market will bear.

Cost Analysis

That said, it remains important to know and understand all of the cost factors that enter into producing your product or delivering your service. Basically, there are two broad categories of costs: the direct costs necessary to produce the goods or services for sale and the indirect or overhead costs associated with conducting your business.

Direct costs are costs for materials and labor used in the production of a particular item or the performance of a specific service. Materials are the parts and supplies that are used in the job, plus handling and shipping, if these costs can be allocated to a specific item or job.

The hourly wage multiplied by the number of hours spent on a job is the cost of labor. Sometimes this hourly wage is only the money paid directly to the worker, with the fringe benefits allocated to overhead. But, in many instances, the hourly wage is computed to include an allowance for such benefits as Social Security, unemployment insurance, and vacation time. As a rule of thumb, these benefits are calculated to be 20 to 30 percent of the hourly wage.

Thus, if your employee receives a base wage of $15 per hour, you would add $3.00 to $4.50 to the per-hour labor costs. If a job took two hours to complete and you used the expanded hourly wage, adding on the 30 percent for benefits, you would compute your labor costs at $39 per job.

To arrive at the total direct costs, you would add the costs of materials to the cost of labor. Continuing the preceding example, say you run an auto repair shop. The parts needed on a job cost a total of $60, which you would then add to your labor costs of $39. The total direct costs in the example add up to $99, which in turn is added to your overhead cost to arrive at the total cost of the repair job.

Indirect or overhead costs are among the more difficult costs to figure. Overhead is every cost that is indirectly connected with performing a service or producing an item. It includes such items as the rent on your property, supplies, postage, gas and electricity, phone, insurance, executive and secretarial salaries, and advertising. Usually, these costs are calculated on an annual basis. The problem is to convert these annual amounts to figures that can be used for a specific job—in other words, to arrive at an overhead dollar amount that can be used to calculate your unit costs.

The most common way in which an overhead dollar amount is calculated is to divide the annual or total overhead by the annual direct labor cost or the direct labor hours cost. When the salary is fixed, as in the example, you would use the annual direct labor hours cost. For a 40-hour week, this total would come to 2,080 hours, which in turn is multiplied by the hourly wage of $19.50. Thus, your annual direct labor hours cost is $40,560.

If we assume that your total overhead is $80,000 and divide into this figure the direct labor hours cost for the year, we arrive at a multiplier rate of 1.972, which in our example would yield $76.92 for the overhead cost for that original two-hour job. For most small businesses, it is estimated that the overhead rate is between 100 and 200 percent of the direct labor cost.

To determine the total cost of the job, you add the different costs together. Here is your calculation:

Direct material cost	$60.00
Direct labor cost	39.00
Overhead	76.92
Total cost of job:	$175.92

This is your price floor for the job. You cannot go below this figure without taking a loss. To arrive at your selling price, you add the profit you want to make and then compare it to what your competitors are charging.

Calculating Your Profit

To arrive at a reasonable profit, you have to know what your competitors charge for the same goods or services, and you must assume that their costs are very nearly the same as your own. If, for example, the auto repair shop down the block charges $211 for the same job that just cost you $175.92, then subtract the cost from the price charged, which leaves $35.08. If their costs are about the same as yours, you know they made a 17 percent profit. This level of profit percentage is common in many industries.

There are many ways to compute your profit. The way that was just described is a commonsense approach that more or less assures you of being in the right ballpark. Of course, this approach depends on your knowing accurately what your competitors are charging and what their costs are.

Another way to calculate your profit is to decide what your percentage of profit will be and add an appropriate markup to your total cost for the job. In our example, add 20 percent ($35.18) to the cost of $175.92 to arrive at a price of $211. Note that a 20 percent markup yields a 17 percent profit. After calculating the price by adding your markup to total costs, check it against your competitors to make sure that it's competitive.

There are other pricing mechanisms, but these are two of the most common. In any case, before making a firm decision on the price of your product or service, you should consult your accountant, as well as a marketing expert.

Sales and Distribution Channels

Your marketing strategy must also define how you plan to promote and distribute your product or service to customers at a profit. Every industry has its own proven methods of sales and distribution. Unless you have an excellent reason to buck traditional wisdom, stick with those methods. Using the proper channels of distribution can assure your business the greatest amount of profitable access to the customer.

Retail

Many consumer products and services are sold and distributed through storefronts. Here location, advertising, and name recognition are important. If yours is a retail business, do your homework. Know the answers to the following questions:

1. What is the demographic profile of the geographic area in which my business will be located?

2. Is the size of my market niche large enough to support my business in this area?

3. How many direct and indirect competitors do I have, and what percentage of the market do they own?

4. Will my location draw enough potential customers? How do I know?

Choosing a location will be discussed in more detail later in this chapter.

Direct Marketing

In direct marketing, various media are used to reach your customers—newspapers, magazines, catalogs, trade journals, radio, television, direct mail, and online computer services, to name a few. The advantages of direct marketing are substantial. It's easy to gauge the effectiveness of new marketing approaches by tracking customer response. Also, you have no sales force with its associated high costs. And a direct marketing campaign can be designed, developed, and launched in a few weeks.

Keep in mind, however, that effective direct marketing requires the skills of an expert. Your marketing piece must be so good that it moves your customers to buy, even if they have never heard of you. Your mailing list must be carefully selected to focus on your market niche. If you lack experience, seek professional help. Select an advertising agency or marketing consultant with a successful track record designing direct marketing campaigns for businesses similar to yours. Here are some questions to ask the experts:

1. Can my product be priced within the direct market price window? (The higher the selling price, the more difficult it is to sell through direct marketing.)

2. Are products similar to mine successfully sold through direct marketing? (A complicated or customized product requiring lots of explanation is difficult to sell this way. Also, very few people have successfully sold services through direct marketing.)

3. What are the best media options for my product?

4. If I'm using direct mail, do I know what I'll have to spend to get an adequate return? (A 2 percent response rate is about average.)

If your direct marketing strategy includes a direct mail campaign, remember the 60-30-10 Law: 60 percent of success is due to the quality of the list used, 30 percent relates to the right offer, and only 10 percent relates to the quality of the creative package.

Distributors

Distributors are resellers who distribute your product to other resellers or to the end user. A grocery or building supply chain is an example. Some distributors, like bookstores, may take the product on consignment from a national distributor. In the example of bookstores, the national distributor gets the product (books) from the publisher, who gets it from the author. A plumbing distributor may buy your faucets and then resell them to both wholesalers and retailers. A value-added reseller (VAR) may take your product and place it as a component of another product or repackage it.

If you can persuade a regional or national distributor to take on your product, you have developed a permanent sales pipeline with huge market potential. You would have to spend a great deal of money and time to develop even a fraction of the market that distributors may open for you.

The not-so-rosy side of this channel is the cost and the nature of the agreement. Distributors take a hefty percentage. Their price may require you to settle for smaller profit margins. Many distributors insist on the exclusive rights to market your product. If they should decide to dump you at the end of your contract, you could be caught with no customers. Here are some questions to consider:

1. Who are the distributors in my industry?

2. Are they the most cost-effective channel for my new business?

3. Can my business reliably meet my distributor's volume demands?

4. Will I be guaranteed a predictable volume of orders for an acceptable period of time?

You also need to determine whether to use one single channel or multiple channels. For example, you must decide whether to deal directly with one large distributor that maintains a sizable sales force, or opt instead to sell directly to a number of large retail outlets in the area. Small companies will often start with a single distribution channel and expand to a greater number as more financial resources build up.

Determining the type of intermediary to use also becomes an important issue. For example, some wholesalers perform many functions: buying, selling, storing, distributing, extending credit, and providing sales information. Other wholesalers are more limited and may not store merchandise or extend credit. A wholesaler may be desirable when greater distribution is required. If this is not the case, retailers may be preferred.

A small company with limited resources may also choose to work with a manufacturer's representatives or agents. This strategy can save the owner from the costs and effort associated with recruiting, training, and maintaining a sales force. In addition, established manufacturers' representatives may have better contacts that will enable them to sell the product. The fact that the profit margin on each item is far lower when sold through intermediaries may be outweighed by the fact that they can reach more customers.

It is essential in selecting an intermediary that the fit is right and that the intermediary understands your business strategy and image—and the roles that each of you are to play.

Rep Firms

Sales rep firms operate like real estate agents. For a percentage, independent sales reps will take on your product. The advantage is that you pay only for performance and avoid most of the sales overhead that you would incur if you had your own sales force. Because your business is driven by the sales order, in many cases you can build to order, keeping inventory at a minimum—a distinct advantage if inventory costs in your business tend to be high.

Keep in mind, however, that you have no control over the reps. If they are also representing a line of competing products, you may receive little attention. If they don't produce for you, you may be in deep trouble. You should never rely on just one rep firm. If you decide to go this route, hire several. Ask yourself the following questions:

1. What rep firms have been successful representing products similar to mine?

2. What assurances do I have that the firms I select will produce the required sales volume?

3. How can I monitor the activity of my reps?

4. What are my total sales costs if I adopt the rep option?

Company Sales Force

If your business requires any sophisticated selling, your best option is to employ your own sales force. Remember that no outsider is going to have the desire and commitment that you and your direct employees have. With your own sales staff, you have complete control. You can set sales targets; develop the most effective sales approach; try out new strategies; and, most importantly, stay very close to your customers.

Inside salespeople, either in a retail setting or in telemarketing, are easily monitored and relatively inexpensive. An outside sales force is another story. These salespeople spend much of their time on the road, unsupervised. And they're very expensive. The price of travel, hotels, meals, salaries, and benefits are only part of the price you must pay. The costs of recruiting, training, and managing add substantially to the total.

In a new business, an outside sales force is risky. Most people are simply not salespeople. The real producers are few in number and in great demand. Those with a track record gravitate toward large, established companies that can pay them well and have a reputation in the marketplace. That leaves the low producers and those with little or no experience. You simply don't know if a person will produce until you've spent a lot of money. Here are some questions to think about:

1. If your business requires salespeople, where will you find them—newspaper ads, employment agencies, personal referrals, recruits from the competition, or other?

2. What image is required—highly educated, professional, young, hip, techy, classy, refined, traditional, or other?

3. What knowledge is required—industry, product, customer requirements, competition, technology, computer literacy, or other?

4. What sales skills are required—low-level retail, high-level sophisticated retail, cold call, presentation, proposal development, needs assessment, consultative, closing, or other?

5. How will sales training be provided—formally by you, informally by you, in-house training by vendor, outside seminar, books, tapes, or other?

6. When can you afford to hire a sales force? How much will it cost, and how long will it take to break even?

7. If you are to be the sales force, do you have the required skills and experience, such as prospecting, qualifying, proposing, and closing?

8. If you cannot afford to hire a salesperson, and you do not have the required credentials, what will you do—do it yourself and hope for the best, find a partner strong in sales, work as a salesperson to gain the necessary experience, or other?

Marketing Costs

Industry averages from trade journals and industry associations will give you reasonably accurate numbers for the marketing costs associated with producing a certain amount of revenue. Remember, however, that these numbers are usually for established companies, not new businesses. The cost of attracting new customers is much higher than selling to existing customers. It will take you longer and cost you more to produce fewer customers in a new business.

Estimating marketing costs consists of creating an inventory of marketing-related products, promotions, and sales plans and then itemizing the costs. What are those costs? Typically, they include the following:

▷ Brochures, samples, and other sales literature

▷ Public relations

▷ Promotional meetings and seminars

▷ Direct selling costs

▷ Packaging

▷ Trade shows

▷ Advertising

▷ Warranties or guarantees

The key question concerning marketing costs is whether what you're spending is reaping an acceptable return. Here are some suggestions for low-cost marketing strategies with excellent returns:

Do your own PR. Make *use* of news releases, articles, and appearances on local radio and television stations. Write and distribute your own newsletter. Your local news media are always looking for business news; position what you give them as news, and you'll get a great deal of free press.

Offer a seminar. The investment community, lawyers, home improvement firms, software companies, and many other businesses use meetings and seminars successfully to promote their wares. Buy a how-to book or attend a seminar that tells you step-by-step how to use this strategy.

Take part in trade shows. Many companies realize a substantial percentage of their revenue through trade shows. Analyze this option thoroughly, however, because trade shows can be very expensive. Booth space, booth design and building, shipping, hotels, air fare, advance promotion, customer invitations, hospitality suites, and other costs can really inflate your overhead.

New business owners waste an incredible amount of money on advertising. Make it a priority to attend a seminar on the basics of advertising for the small business. In the meantime, here are a few suggestions to keep in mind as you develop your advertising plan:

Buy wholesale. Just as experienced business travelers never pay the standard hotel rack rates, experienced business owners never pay retail for advertising.

Place small ads many times. These small ads generate better results than splashy ads that run only once or infrequently. Watch a major network's nightly news program, and you'll see the same ads at the same time every evening. Repetition sells.

Know when and where to advertise. If your business is seasonal, plan advertising accordingly. Run ads on days your business is open and select media your customers use. Don't make the mistake of advertising industrial products or upscale consumer products in a local discount paper.

Make it easy and profitable to respond. Use coupons, discounts if bought by a certain date, and multiple ways to order. Be clear about what you are offering, and tell the customer how to order it right now.

Use multiple media and multiple ideas. Try newsletters, sponsorships, contests, frequent buyer programs, calendars, referral reward programs, endorsements, complimentary passes, discounts, and gift certificates. Think creatively.

Select help carefully. If you decide to use an agency, make sure that it has experience in your particular type of business. Ask to see examples. Ask where the ads ran, and check to see how long they ran. A long run means an ad worked; a short run means it didn't.

Selling Successfully

Until you find prospective customers and convince them to do business with you, you do not have a business. If you're in any business other than retail, you must be able to identify prospective customers by name, address, and phone number. Directories are the most common source for this information. Remember, you can never have too many prospects. Successful companies expend a great deal of energy to keep their prospect lists long and current.

If yours is a retail business, advertising and location are the two major factors influencing customer traffic flow. In most other businesses, however, an aggressive direct contact process is required. Even if you use direct mail or other promotional techniques, you'll still have to approach prospective customers by showing up on their doorsteps or by calling on the phone.

In most new businesses, cold calling is critical to success. Like it or not, how well you make cold calls will determine how quickly the cash begins to flow. Because the first step in persuading prospects to hear your story is to get an appointment, you must convince them that it's worth their time to investigate what you have to offer. In most cases that's accomplished over the phone.

We've all had to endure our share of memorized sales scripts. When you call prospective customers and ask them to meet with you, your message doesn't have to sound canned. If you keep the following rules in mind, you'll find that cold calling can be interesting and effective:

Rule 1. The purpose of the call is to get the prospect to agree to an appointment, not to sell your product or service.

Rule 2. The call should qualify the prospect and determine if the prospect has any need for your product or service.

Rule 3. The call should promote the benefits the prospect can expect from your product or service.

Rule 4. The call should conclude with a request for an appointment.

Baseball players and salespeople know that the more at bats you have, the more hits you'll have. If you sell one prospect out of every four, your hit rate is 25 percent. In most businesses, that's not a bad average. If your hit rate for cold calls to get a sales meeting is also 25 percent, that statistic means that to schedule one sales call, you must make four cold calls. Do the arithmetic, and you'll see that every completed sale requires sixteen cold calls.

If your sales pipeline is not constantly replenished with new prospects, you will fail. If the pipeline is full, you will flourish. Your sales activity numbers are the vital signs that will predict the health of your business. Talk with experienced people in your business. They can tell you with great precision exactly what sales activity level spells success.

EXERCISE 2.8

Calculating Your Sales Calls and Revenue

Use the following exercise to figure how many cold calls and sales meetings are required to hit your required number of annual sales. This annual sales goal can be calculated by dividing your first-year revenue projection by the average revenue generated per customer.

Industry prospecting hit rate: _____ %

Industry sales hit rate: _____ %

Number of prospecting calls per month: _____
{number of calls = (1 ÷ prospecting hit rate) x (1 ÷ industry hit rate)}

Industry average revenue per customer: _____

First-year revenue projection: _____
{first-year revenue = number of prospecting calls x industry average x 12}

Number of sales per year: _____
{number of sales = revenue projection ÷ industry average revenue per customer}

Use these numbers to help develop your sales forecast. The sales forecast should show dollar volume for each product or service, broken down by months, projected three to five years ahead. Ideally, it should also show to whom the product will be sold. This same basic formula can be used to calculate sales revenue for retail or direct sales.

For businesses with industrial customers (such as other businesses), the sales forecast should name the prospective buyers and attribute volume and product type to each one as precisely as possible. For retail businesses, the forecast should describe the class of buyer and buyers' characteristics.

The Customer-Focused Approach

Customers want knowledgeable salespeople who can help them identify their needs and then offer them exactly what is required to satisfy those needs. To accomplish this goal, you must develop excellent listening and questioning skills. If your questions are the right ones, your prospects will tell you exactly what you need to do to convince them to buy your product or service.

Customers buy for one of two reasons: fear of loss or hope of gain. Put another way, customers do not buy your product or service; they buy what your product or service can do for them. They buy the benefits that your product or service can provide. They buy the solution to their problem. Amateurs sell products; professionals sell solutions.

EXERCISE 2.9

Features and Benefits

Consider what problems your product or service can solve for your potential customers. Translate every feature of your product or service into a customer benefit. On the following lines, list the key features of your product or service on the left. Next to each feature, note the corresponding benefit.

Feature	Benefit
_____	_____
_____	_____
_____	_____
_____	_____
_____	_____
_____	_____
_____	_____
_____	_____
_____	_____

Customer Retention

All of the effort and costs associated with finding customers and convincing them to buy is wasted if you can't keep them. Finding, attracting, and winning customers is expensive, but losing them can be even more so. Customer dissatisfaction is bad business for three reasons:

▷ Lost revenue from the immediate sale

▷ Lost opportunity for future sales

▷ Loss of business reputation

Research shows that if customers are satisfied, they may tell one or two prospective customers. If they are delighted, they will tell three or four. If they are dissatisfied, they will tell ten to fifteen! Multiply that figure by several unhappy customers, and the word spreads quickly.

Most customers change suppliers because of the indifference of an employee. Perhaps an established business with many customers can get away with a few disgruntled ones, at least for a while. In a new business, losing even one customer is a big deal. Although you will need to spend time and money on building your customer base, don't neglect the importance of developing a plan for retaining them.

How much is a retained customer worth? Take your local supermarket as an example. If the average customer spends $300 a month, that means $3,600 a year in revenue per customer. If your supermarket can retain you for five years, you've contributed $18,000 in revenue. That's why most markets replace or refund with no hassle. The cost of losing customers is too high. To determine the value of just one of your customers, ask yourself the following:

▷ How many dollars will the customer contribute to your business in a year?

▷ If you provide acceptable service, how long will you retain the customer?

▷ What is your gross profit margin?

Here are some ideas for building your customer retention rate:

Talk to customers often. Ask them what you can do to better serve them. Ask them to immediately report any bad product or poor service.

Develop a service recovery process. Every business will make a mistake now and then. The best companies have a strategy to recover quickly.

Reward customers for their loyalty. Use discounts, special sales for long-time customers, and special gifts on special occasions.

Partner with customers. Learn everything you can about your customer's business so you can find a way to become a strategic partner.

Offer an unconditional guarantee.

Customers create your cash flow, pay your bills, and allow you to make a living. Without them, your business is nothing. Your marketing plan and your sales plan must detail how you will find, win, and retain the most precious part of your business—your customers.

EXERCISE 2.10

Developing Your Marketing Plan

A. **Sales Forecast.** Calculate your preliminary sales forecast, using the estimates you worked out in an earlier exercise called *Calculating Your Sales Calls and Revenue*. Provide projections for the next five years that reflect any anticipated changes in your market.

_____

_____

_____

_____

_____

B. **Strategy.** Develop a preliminary marketing strategy for your proposed business, based on the results of your market research and analysis.

1. What strategy will you follow in relation to the leaders in your market? Will you challenge them? Follow them? Or carve out a niche?

   _____

   _____

   _____

   _____

2. How will the strategy be translated into each of the following:

   Pricing? _____

   _____

   _____

   Advertising and Promotion? _____

   _____

   _____

   Distributor Relationships? _____

   _____

   _____

   Sales Approach? _____

   _____

   _____

   Customer Service? _____

   _____

   _____

Now that you have developed a clear picture of your product or service and how you will market it, it's time to think about the practical decisions that turn an idea and a strategy into a company.

The Legal Structure of Your Business

One of the most important decisions you will have to make regarding the start-up of your business is which legal form of ownership to choose. There is no best structure for all businesses. Many small businesses take different forms as they evolve, starting with a sole proprietorship and then moving through partnership to eventually become a corporation.

No matter which form you choose, the complexities of negotiating leases and contracts, securing licenses, and setting up the legal form require the help of a lawyer and an accountant familiar with small businesses. If your business is structured inappropriately, you could lose more than your business. You could also be required to pay substantially more taxes than necessary, and your ability to borrow may be severely limited.

To understand the many issues involved in choosing a legal structure, and to help you decide which form of organization will best serve your goals and needs, ask yourself these questions:

▷   Are you going into business by yourself?

▷   If not, how many others will be with you?

▷   How active will the others be in your business?

▷   What is the magnitude of the initial financing requirements?

▷   What degree of control do you want to retain over your business?

▷   How much regulation are you willing to tolerate?

▷   How much risk are you and your family prepared to accept?

Your answers to these questions should provide you with clues about the most suitable form of business for your personality and circumstances. Remember that your decision is not fixed in stone. You can always change the form of your organization to accommodate the changing needs of your growing business.

Laws that govern business formation are regulated by the state in which the business is located. A business's operations can further come under the jurisdiction of municipal and federal governments for licensing, permits, and other regulations. Remember, it is important to consult with an attorney who is an expert in the laws and regulations where you want to establish your business. There are six options that you should review:

- ▷ Sole Proprietorship
- ▷ General Partnership
- ▷ Limited Partnership
- ▷ Limited Liability Company
- ▷ Corporation
- ▷ Subchapter S Corporation

Each form has different applications affecting personal liability, management, and taxation. Each of those factors deserves consideration before you make a decision. Refer to the following section for an overview of the advantages and disadvantages of these major types of legal forms.

Sole Proprietorship

A sole proprietorship is the simplest business form. Usually, it is capitalized by the one person who has sole responsibility and control. It is the oldest and most common type of business. Three out of every four entrepreneurs elect this form, at least initially.

Forming a sole proprietorship is a simple matter of contacting the local city hall or the county clerk's office to ask if a business license is required in their particular area. You probably will need to pay a small registration fee. If you want to operate the business under a name other than your own, you will have to fill out a "Doing Business As" (DBA) form. Keep in mind that rights to that company name are limited to a specific state and do not extend to the entire country.

If your business is engaged in interstate commerce or related in any way to handling government property, you may also need a federal permit or license. Such licenses are also required for investment advisory services and businesses engaged in meat processing and transportation, operation of common carriers, or production of drugs or biologicals, to name a few. Retail businesses may also need to conform to local regulations regarding zoning and permits.

Of all of the legal forms, the sole proprietorship gives the owner the strongest control in managing the business. There are no partners to consult with or to second-guess decisions. You live with your decisions, good or bad. You may have employees with varying degrees of accountability, but the ultimate responsibility rests with you.

There are many advantages to having this much control over the operation. You do not share profits, for example. But there are also some disadvantages. One of the most noteworthy is the limitation on raising capital to fund growth or working capital needs. You cannot sell stock to raise money—and banks much prefer to loan money to corporations. Why? Banks and other financial sources may find lending money to individual proprietors too risky because they have limited net worth and therefore limited collateral for loans. Also, there is an ever-present risk that something could happen to the owner, rendering him or her incapable of managing the business and repaying the loan.

In a sole proprietorship, the owner and the business are one and the same as a legal entity, which has implications for liability and tax treatment. The most serious drawback of this legal form, in fact, is the problem of unlimited personal liability. If the business incurs debts during the start-up years that cannot be paid, creditors can move in to liquidate the business assets, and, if needed, lay claim to the personal assets of the entrepreneur (the house, automobiles, bank accounts, and so on). In light of the high rate of failure among start-ups, liability considerations are of the utmost importance. Generally speaking, the more substantial your personal holdings, the more you should probably consider the corporate form to protect them. In any case, you will want to consider your business insurance options carefully.

In terms of taxation, the sole proprietor's business income is treated as personal income. You pay tax only on the income generated. Because the business is you, you pay no additional taxes as a corporation would. Many enterprising individuals see a sole proprietorship as a great opportunity for avoiding taxes by deducting inflated business expenses. The IRS, however, assumes that a legitimate business must make money. Therefore, unless you make money in three out of five business years, the IRS will disallow a good number of your business expenses.

As an employee, you completed an individual income tax return each year when you filed your federal and state tax returns. As a sole proprietor, you do the same, but you add Schedule C (Profit or Loss From Business or Profession) to account for the profit or loss of your business. You must also file a declaration of estimated tax and pay quarterly tax on income that has had no tax withheld from it. The IRS supplies you with four declaration vouchers that you complete before the fifteenth of April, June, September, and January. You send these vouchers along with your payment of a quarterly portion of your estimate of your complete tax due for that year.

General Partnership

If you read the business section of your newspaper, you've undoubtedly seen numerous ads seeking business partners. Usually the hope is that you'll be able to bring capital and, sometimes, expertise. Or perhaps you've talked with friends or business colleagues about the possibility of striking out on a business venture together.

The legal and tax considerations for a partnership are similar to those of a sole proprietorship, but there is one big difference. In a partnership, you're legally liable for all actions of your partners. If your partner should get sued for half a million dollars and he doesn't have the assets to cover the obligation, guess who's on the hook for the full amount? For this reason, this form of business structure deserves very careful consideration.

Many start-up partnerships don't work out because they're born out of emotion, with great expectations and little else. To have a good chance for success, a business partnership should be thought through very carefully. To start, you should ask why you're thinking about a partnership in the first place. Here are some common—but poor—reasons:

▷ We're friends and just love being together.

▷ I lack the self-confidence I need to make it on my own.

▷ There's too much work for just one person.

It's not that business partnerships can't work. Even where spouses are the principals, partnerships can thrive if the personalities meld and the roles and responsibilities are clearly delineated. The key is making sure that the partnership is formed for the right reasons and has well-designed ground rules. What are the right reasons? Consider the following:

▷ Pooling of capital allows the partnership to start or buy a business that would have been beyond the financial reach of either individual alone.

▷ Combining individuals whose skills are strategic to the growth of the business adds credibility to the enterprise.

▷ Pooling skills to share the workload and decision making eases the burden of starting and running the business.

Many excellent partnerships are formed to take advantage of complementary skills and experience. The best situation is one in which the potential partners have already worked together for some time. If you're good at research and development and at managing a manufacturing operation, you don't need a partner who is a carbon copy. Instead, sales and marketing talent or financial management experience will round out the company. Look for a partner who will provide a natural division of labor and create synergy. Here's a laundry list of things to do when considering a partnership:

1. **Discuss personal business objectives.** Many partners later discover that their personal reasons for being in business are very different. If Bruce is in business because he wants to coast along and you're gung ho to build an empire, lots of luck. If you're interested in retaining earnings to grow and Bruce wants the profit right now, there's going to be trouble. You need to talk and talk some more until you and your potential partners have a clear understanding of what each wants out of the business.

2. **Develop a three- to five-year business plan.** This plan should describe precisely where you're going and how you're going to get there. Among other things, the plan should highlight revenue and profit goals, as well as growth objectives. Will new partners be recruited? How many and when? What are the criteria for being considered? Will employees be considered for partnership? Under what conditions?

3. **Agree on a management philosophy.** Nothing demoralizes employees more than having to deal with partners who can't agree on how to manage them. Both authoritarian and participative management have proponents. You must decide what's right for your company.

4. **Define the division of labor.** Decide what needs to get done and who's responsible for getting it done. Over and over, partnerships fail because the partners didn't take the time to define and agree on key roles. After roles are defined, stay out of your partner's sandbox.

5. **Develop a decision-making process.** Inevitably conflicts and differences will arise. How will disputes be resolved? Yelling louder is not the answer. If you have an odd number of partners, decision making could be as simple as majority rule. If possible, however, strive for consensus. Or you may decide that the partner who has responsibility for a given function has the final word in that area. The point is, you have to agree on how to agree.

6. **Define performance expectations.** This area is often a cause of serious conflict. Partners who must carry someone unwilling or unable to pull his or her own weight become very resentful. Partners who are workaholics often expect other partners to be just as driven. A frank discussion of work hours, time off, and personal business goals for each partner are areas that need to be covered. Are certain results expected of partners? If so, what are they? What happens if these goals are not met? How will partner performance be evaluated? By whom?

7. **Detail the compensation plan.** Both salary and variable compensation are at issue here. When you own your own business, there are many ways to hand out financial rewards. You and your partners must agree on an objective set of criteria. How will stock be awarded? How will price be determined? Will partners be expected to loan money to the company? If so, how much and under what conditions? May partners borrow against their equity? If so, under what conditions? What will be the terms?

8. **Define an exit plan.** Cash-out provisions and buy-out formulas take on great importance when your equity is at stake. Under what conditions may partners lose their partnership status? What's the process for removing them?

Like the sole proprietorship, a general partnership is easy to form and also relatively free from the more burdensome regulatory requirements imposed on corporations. But partnership formation should go beyond verbal understandings and handshakes. You should draw up a partnership agreement with the help of your attorney. Such agreements become legal instruments that spell out the role of each partner in the business and provisions for changes in ownership.

If you want to operate under an assumed name, some states ask you to file a "Certificate of Conducting Business as Partners" with the county clerk or the state. In most states where there is no written agreement, the Uniform Partnership Act gives partners certain protection. However, a written agreement is preferable.

Although a partnership files a federal income tax return, it is not subject to income taxes as such. The return is just for information purposes. Income for the business is taxed as personal income to the partner. Each partner's share is reported on Schedule E of his or her individual tax return. The partnership itself is not a taxable entity. Finally, the death of a partner, unless provided for in the partnership agreement, automatically terminates the partnership.

Limited Partnership

In certain states, the law allows the formation of a special form of partnership known as the limited partnership. Because of the more complex formation and regulatory requirements, the limited partnership is more like a corporation than it is like a general partnership. The most common reason business owners consider this legal form is to raise capital.

Limited partnerships typically have one or more general partners who manage the day-to-day operations of the business. Limited partners then invest capital or tangible property and, in return, share in the profits (or losses), but they are only personally liable up to the extent of their investment. These limited partners, although they share in the ownership, do not exercise control over the general operations of the enterprise.

A legal agreement must be drawn up for a limited partnership. It is significantly more complex than the optional general partnership agreements and requires active involvement by an attorney. The agreement, along with a Certificate of Limited Partnership, is filed with the state. Again, if you are using a fictitious name for your business, you are required to file the applicable form with your county clerk or state. The tax filing requirements for limited partnerships are the same as for general partnerships.

Limited Liability Company

A limited liability company (LLC) can be more desirable than other legal structures for a variety of reasons:

Tax purposes. LLCs are taxed as partnerships, rather than as corporations. This means, among other things, a single level of federal income tax and much greater tax flexibility.

Limited liability. Members of LLCs are not liable for the organization's debts, obligations, or liabilities; they are generally liable only to the extent of their capital contribution to the LLC.

Management flexibility. Unlike S corporations, there are no limitations on the number and type of owners, and unlike limited partnerships, all members may manage the company without losing liability protections.

Some types of companies that may find the LLC form advantageous are family businesses, service businesses, joint ventures, real estate businesses, and start-up businesses. However, businesses that expect their interests to be widely held or publicly traded may not find this option beneficial because the flow-through tax treatment will not be available.

An LLC resembles a partnership, but it is a legal entity distinct from its members. A business wanting to exist in the form of an LLC must meet the partnership requirements of the Internal Revenue Code. It must also file documents (such as Articles of Organization) with its respective state and meet the state's requirements for organization.

LLCs do have risks and disadvantages, such as the following:

> ▷ Some states may not recognize the limited liability feature of an LLC formed in another state, so members may still have personal liability.

> ▷ Not all states recognize the LLC form of organization, which may be troublesome for a multistate operation.

> ▷ Some LLC statutes can be rather restrictive—for example, regarding the ability to transfer one's interest.

If the IRS continues to rule favorably on the various state statutes, and as more states enact LLC legislation, the LLC may be expected to grow in popularity. Legal counsel is advised if you are considering this option.

Corporation

Sometimes called the "C" Corporation, or general corporation, this form is a separate legal entity apart from the owners or shareholders who manage and operate the business. In other words, the corporation has a life of its own. After it is formed, the corporation can buy and sell property, file lawsuits, merge or buy another company, and enter into contracts. Most importantly, it also pays taxes and is liable for its debts.

Corporations provide the maximum legal protection for their owners. Because a corporation is its own legal entity, it is separate from you—unlike a partnership or sole proprietorship. You are simply an employee of the corporation. Therefore, creditors, or those seeking reimbursement for alleged wrongs, are limited to suing for the assets of the corporation.

Individual investors, or the shareholders, are limited in the amount of their financial liability, up to their personal total investment. The corporation itself is potentially liable up to the value of the assets in the business. This limited liability feature is very attractive to individuals who want to protect their personal assets, should a legal action be initiated against the corporation or should the corporation become insolvent and its assets be insufficient to satisfy the debts incurred.

Another advantage of this legal form is the credibility it creates with banks and other lenders. These sources may be more apt to advance loans to an incorporated start-up venture with promise than to one that is not incorporated. However, lenders may insist on collateral and require the personal guarantee of the shareholders, as with any other legal form. You can count on the fact that your banker will require you to guarantee your loan with personal assets.

To maintain this corporate shield requires strict adherence to the many administrative requirements of corporate governance. State statutory laws permit the formation of corporations according to strict guidelines of registration, governance, and taxation. Each state's regulations vary in their complexity. Hire an attorney if you are seriously considering incorporating.

An attorney's fee for incorporating your business will usually run from several hundred dollars to a few thousand dollars. If you need a permit to issue stock or other securities, the fee will be higher. You can form your own corporation for a fraction of what an attorney will charge you, but laws to incorporate a business are complex. You need a professional who understands them and can save you hassles later.

To set up a corporation, one or more incorporators (depending on the state) file an application to the state office that grants corporate charters, usually the secretary of state. This Certificate of Incorporation, also known as Articles of Incorporation, lists the names and addresses of the shareholders and the corporation, the purpose and scope of the company's business, the amount of stock authorized, and other important information. The incorporators who apply need not be equal partners or major shareholders. For example, when sole proprietors incorporate, they often designate an attorney and an accountant as minor shareholders, if required by law. In most cases, the owner will be the sole shareholder at first.

The registration process includes a filing fee based on the value of the corporate stock, which is generally quite reasonable for a small business. In addition, you must pay an annual state franchise tax, which is based on the net income of the business. The initial tax varies from state to state. For start-up companies, the annual fee is usually a few hundred dollars, even if the corporation doesn't earn a profit.

After a corporation is formed, the officers or directors must adopt bylaws. These rules govern the operation of the business. Shareholder meetings must be held and minutes recorded in written form. In certain cases, you also may have preincorporation agreements among the officers, which your attorney also prepares.

If you select the corporation as your legal form, your tax reporting requirements are more complex compared to sole proprietorships and partnerships. If you draw a salary as an employee of the corporation, you report your total income (salary plus dividends) from the taxable year on a federal individual income tax return form. The corporation is required to withhold and pay federal and state income taxes on your salary, as well as Social Security and Medicare taxes.

Because it is a separate legal entity, the corporation files its own income tax return and pays taxes on its profits. This income tax form is filed either on a calendar or fiscal year basis (March 15 for the calendar year and by the fifteenth of the third month following the close of the fiscal year).

Double taxation is a real disadvantage of the corporate form when you are a shareholder paying tax on the dividends you receive after the corporation has already paid an initial tax based on its earnings. To avoid this double taxation feature, individuals may opt to form Subchapter S corporations.

Subchapter S Corporation

The preferred corporate status for most small start-ups is an "S" corporation. It was developed to serve the needs of the small business owner. In terms of corporate law and limited liability of shareholders, there is no difference between a general and an S corporation in the eyes of the states in which they are located. The S corporation retains many of the benefits of a C corporation but is taxed as if it were a partnership. The tax savings can be significant.

In an S corporation, shareholders (which may be only one person) are taxed on the total profit for the year at their individual rates, whether or not all of the income was distributed. In other words, profit and income are considered one and the same.

S corporations do have some restrictions. Only one class of common stock can be issued, and the company must be incorporated within the United States. The corporation is limited to thirty-five shareholders, who must be individuals, not corporations or partnerships. Some states place additional restrictions on S corporations, and the rules can change at any time, so it's important to seek help from your lawyer in deciding on the right structure for your situation.

The S corporation is a hybrid corporation that enables the business owner to enjoy the limited liability that a general corporation offers, but it is not taxed as a separate entity. This pass-through type of arrangement can be an ideal corporate structure for new or relatively low-revenue businesses. As in partnerships, the owners are allowed to account for the profits and losses (especially in early years) on their income tax returns in proportion to their ownership interests.

After you have elected to be treated as a Subchapter S corporation, you and other principal shareholders will report your appropriate shares of the corporation's taxable income or loss on your individual tax returns. This tax reporting situation is similar to how you report taxes for a partnership. The S corporation itself files an information return and pays no taxes other than normal state franchise fees.

While the S corporation has some significant tax advantages over the general corporation, including the elimination of double taxation, the administrative requirements of corporate governance remain the same. Consequently, you need to seek out tax advice from your attorney and your accountant.

Location

If your business is one where you deal directly with the public, the physical location of your business is a key determinant of its success. Restaurants, retail stores, copy and print shops, and many other businesses often rise or fall based on location. In fact, the core concept of the modern shopping mall is creating success for tenants based on a guarantee of a huge volume of potential customers. That's why the lease fees are so high.

Franchise companies, such as McDonald's and Jiffy Lube, have specialists who do nothing but site selection analysis. If these companies consider location so critical, so should you. That doesn't mean you have to be a specialist, but it does mean that you must carefully think through where to locate your business.

Suppose you wanted to open a convenience store on a busy six-lane commuter highway. If you decide to locate your business on the inbound side of the highway rather than on the outbound side, you would lose your shirt. Why? Because commuters don't buy bread, milk, beer, ice cream, and other incidentals on their way to work; they buy on the way home. Few people are going to battle traffic across six lanes to patronize your store.

Locating an upscale gift stop between a discount drugstore and a butcher's shop isn't likely to pull in the clientele you need. Selecting a retail location is more than counting heads to see if there's enough traffic —you need the right number and the right kind of customers. Check with your Chamber of Commerce or local business development association. They will often have detailed traffic studies available.

You can also research a location yourself. Stand outside the proposed site and count the passersby. It's a little more difficult to determine if they're the right people to buy your products, so you will have to look for clues. If you're selling mink coats and the potential customers dress in polyester, take the hint and move on.

Customer counts should also take into consideration the reason for the potential customer's trip. Locating a video store next to a community supermarket makes sense. So does locating a shoe repair shop next to a dry-cleaning establishment. Locating a clothing store adjacent to other clothing stores and restaurants next to other restaurants is done because the arrangement generates business for everyone.

Don't make the mistake of locating your retail establishment where you can negotiate a great deal on the space. Retail landlords know a valuable location from one that isn't, and the price will reflect the value of the site. An investment in "cheap" space could prove to be very costly in the long run.

EXERCISE 2.11

Retail Location Worksheet

Use this worksheet to record information for locating a retail operation.

The surrounding trading area: _____

_____

_____

Demographics of the population in the area: _____

_____

_____

Compatibility of neighboring stores: _____

_____

_____

Parking facilities: _____

_____

_____

Public transportation: _____

_____

_____

Volume of traffic (pedestrian and vehicular): _____

_____

_____

Type of building and store front: _____

_____

_____

If your business is not a retail business, location may be just as important but for different reasons. Manufacturing plants and wholesale enterprises should be more concerned about access to good transportation facilities for delivery of raw materials and for distribution of their products.

EXERCISE 2.12

Office/Production Location Worksheet

Use this worksheet to record information about the location for an office or production facility.

Costs of land, construction, materials, and leasing: _____

_____

_____

Cost of labor, transportation, and storage: _____

_____

_____

Utility rates for sewer, water, power, other: _____

_____

_____

Availability of trained employees: _____

_____

_____

State and local zoning: _____

_____

_____

Permitting processes and EPA requirements: _____

_____

_____

Local ordinances and regulations: _____

_____

_____

Tax structure: _____

_____

_____

Availability of space for growth and expansion: _____

_____

_____

Proximity to markets: _____

_____

_____

Quality of local services (police, fire protection): _____

_____

_____

Consider whether the location is on the way up or down; the cost of relocating can be fatal. Cost of living may severely limit the labor pool. What is the political climate? Is it likely to support your business interests? A business that depends on the local airport may be out of business if the local noise pollution lobby has enough muscle to close down the airport.

Equipment

Even if your business is a small service business, you need a phone system, some office furniture, and a computer. Many other businesses, particularly manufacturing, require a substantial equipment investment. As a fledgling entrepreneur, your impulse is likely to be to run out and buy brand-new equipment. Don't do it!

Because of the turnover rate in small business, nearly every industry has a sizable used equipment market. In most cases you will be able to equip your business at a fraction of the usual cost by purchasing used equipment. Take field trips to similar businesses and take careful inventory of the required equipment. Read the industry trade journals. You can uncover the sources for obtaining the specialized equipment you need with a little research.

Conserve your capital by buying only what you absolutely need. Don't buy equipment that will receive only occasional use. If you only make a few copies, do you really need a copy machine? If you simply must have it, consider leasing. Leasing often makes excellent sense and conserves your capital. It requires less up-front cash and your monthly lease payments allow you to conserve the cash needed to grow your fragile new enterprise. Check with your accountant to make sure that leasing is right for you.

Vendors and Suppliers

Establish a formal business relationship with suppliers before you open your doors. You can't complete a business plan unless you know your costs, so knowing what you'll have to pay for raw materials and inventory is essential. As you research sources of supply, pay attention to who the customers of your suppliers are. If they're all large companies, remember that a small potato like you is likely to be at the bottom of the priority list, particularly if demand outstrips supply. Instead, try to develop relationships with suppliers who service small companies.

Because your new business has no track record, don't expect credit. You probably will be required initially to pay cash on delivery. Would you let an unknown walk away with a hefty supply of your product based on a smile and a promise? Neither will your vendors. Remember the need for cash on delivery as you compute your starting inventory costs.

Creating a business relationship with a select few vendors may seem attractive, but be careful. If your supplier of critical widget parts goes belly up or is hit by a strike, you may be out of business. Although buffer stock is the answer for many firms, it's expensive. Whenever possible, try to have a backup supplier in the wings.

Companies that have a just-in-time (JIT) inventory system supported by their suppliers have a competitive cost advantage. This system can conserve capital and eliminate the cost of warehousing. Ask your supplier to help you set up a JIT system for your company.

Insurance

When starting a business, you must determine what insurance will be necessary to minimize your risks and protect your business. From a cost-of-doing-business perspective, insurance-related expenses are often the second highest expense incurred by entrepreneurs after those of payroll.

Obviously, if you have substantial business assets, you'll want them insured. Lenders will require it. Property and casualty insurance are as important for your business as they are for your home. Be certain that you understand what you're buying. Insurance premiums are less if your policy specifies asset value. That simply means that the current market value of the lost assets will determine what you will collect. In most cases, you will want a policy that guarantees asset replacement value. Used equipment and old buildings may serve your business needs well; however, if you suffer a loss, the cost of replacement may be many times the current market value.

Property coverage protects against all direct physical loss. It includes such specific areas as the following:

▷ Building, business, and personal property, including furniture, fixtures, and equipment

▷ Loss of income coverage (such as business interruption coverage) for loss of business income resulting from an insured property loss

▷ Theft (includes burglary and robbery) of business property

▷ Valuable papers and records coverage

Other important additional property coverage options to consider include the following:

▷ Actual cash value coverage (rather than replacement cost) for any building

▷ Exterior glass coverage

▷ Spoilage coverage

▷ Employee dishonesty coverage

▷ Accounts receivable coverage

▷ Money and securities coverage (extends burglary and robbery coverage)

Inland marine coverage includes a contractor's portable equipment (such as equipment mounted on a trailer or truck), tools, and most types of portable equipment.

In today's business world, liability insurance has become a standard operating expense. Nearly everyone knows a small business owner who has been sued. The odds are very good that you may be sued at some point. There's no such thing as a low-risk business these days.

If your business manufactures a product, product liability insurance should be seriously considered, particularly if there's any chance that the product may cause injury. Jury awards in recent years have been astronomical. Many companies have been put out of business because of extremely high and often unwarranted damage awards. Don't be naive enough to believe that justice will prevail. Even if it does, you may still end up broke.

Liability coverage protects you from paying the amount for which you are otherwise legally liable if there is an occurrence arising out of the ownership, maintenance, or use of your premises. This coverage would encompass your liability for products, as well as the following:

▷ Personal injury (due to false arrest, imprisonment, libel, slander, and other causes)

▷ Advertising injury

▷ Professional liability (relevant for some occupations, such as druggist, veterinarian, mortician, and optician)

If you are working out of your home, your homeowner's policy undoubtedly will require you to obtain a separate rider to cover property damage, injuries, or losses suffered by a client visiting you.

Another major form of coverage to consider is business vehicle coverage. Also known as commercial automobile coverage, this type of insurance is identical to coverage an individual would carry on a personal auto. The only difference, of course, is that the coverage relates solely to your business vehicle.

Workers' compensation insurance provides an income, as well as payment for medical and rehabilitation costs, to workers who are injured on the job. This coverage is mandated by state law and can vary among the states. You may also be required to pay for unemployment insurance. The state mandate applies to employees only, so if you have employees, you will need to cover them. You may want to consider this coverage for yourself, even if you have no employees, especially as you will no longer be covered by an employer. How much you pay depends on your location and the size and nature of your business. However, providing this coverage will add substantially to your operating costs.

Many business owners try to get around these employee-related insurance costs by hiring only contractors. The IRS takes a dim view of this practice, and the federal tax laws are being changed to reflect this attitude. Even though you think you have hired a contractor rather than an employee, you may discover that the IRS sees the classification terminology differently. To avoid a surprise, ask the advice of your accountant.

Health insurance is a concern not only for you, the owner, but also for your employees. You should have health insurance to cover expenses due to sickness or accidents and disability insurance to cover loss of income due to sickness or disability. An additional employee benefit might be group life insurance. Providing this benefit for employees can be a substantial expense; therefore, it is not uncommon for small business owners to ask employees to pay part or all of these costs.

Key person insurance protects the company against financial loss caused by the death of a valuable employee, partner, or owner. This type of coverage is usually a requirement for bank financing. In those situations where an attorney draws up a "buy-sell agreement" for such enterprises as partnerships, you will have two different options to consider that are funded by life insurance. The first is a "cross-purchase" plan, where each owner is the purchaser of life insurance. The second is the "entity" plan, where the corporation purchases the policy.

If you're overwhelmed by all of these insurance options, take heart. A qualified broker specializing in small business insurance can guide you through the complexities of finding the package that's right for you. Your agent can explain the various options and recommend the appropriate coverage. Your best bet is to consult an experienced commercial agent. Independent agents are usually more aggressive in finding low-cost coverage than employees of major insurance companies. However, before you consult any agent, you should have a protection plan in mind. Here are some steps you should take to formulate your plan:

1. **Write a statement.** What insurance will do for your company.

2. **Develop an insurance budget.** Be realistic about what you need— and be careful not to underinsure.

3. **Study insurance costs.** Investigate umbrella coverage. Find policies in which premiums are paid monthly and cancel automatically with no further liability if monthly payments are missed.

4. **Buy only what you need.** Insurance companies love to include lots of special coverages that add to the premium but are unlikely to be needed.

5. **Request high deductibles.** The idea is to protect yourself against catastrophic loss. Up the deductible and your premium will plummet.

6. **Review your insurance periodically.** Make sure that your coverage is adequate and your premiums are cost-effective.

Staffing

Now you need to decide the most efficient method for managing your operation. Start by developing an organizational chart to indicate the flow of communication and the delegation of responsibilities. In a small business, everyone is likely to be directly involved in producing and selling the product, particularly when a business is getting started.

The first step in evaluating the personnel requirements of your new business is to write out job descriptions and indicate the major responsibilities and tasks that have to be done. Determine the number of hours needed to accomplish each task each week. Determine the job specifications, listing the skills required to perform effectively. Both the *Dictionary of Occupational Titles* and the *Occupational Outlook Handbook* are good resources for developing job descriptions and requirements.

Decide whether to hire full-time, part-time, or temporary workers (such as independent contractors or agency personnel). Try to make do without full-time employees for as long as possible.

By writing out the job descriptions and job specifications, you are prepared for interviewing and should be more successful in hiring the right applicant. There are a variety of methods for finding potential applicants:

Referrals. Your network of friends, employees, acquaintances, suppliers, and customers often is the best source for locating candidates.

Personal recruitment. People doing similar jobs for someone else may be interested in working for a new business with a chance to grow.

Educational institutions. Area vocational high schools, trade schools, and colleges are excellent resources for part-time employees.

Employment agencies. These usually offer a wide range of pre-screened applicants. However, their fees can be expensive, ranging from 10 to 30 percent of the first year's salary.

Help wanted ads. These generate a large number of responses, but the ad needs to be clearly written with enough job specifications to discourage the unqualified from responding.

Walk-ins and write-ins. Unsolicited applications and resumes sometimes come along at just the right time.

Selecting Your Accountant

If there's one professional who will be indispensable to the long-term health of your company, it's your accountant. Selecting an accountant to help you manage your business will be one of the most critical decisions you will make. Companies thrive or die because of accounting practices. The *Yellow Pages* is not the way to find someone for work this critical to your enterprise. You need to find someone with a proven track record and enthusiastic endorsements from other business people.

In general, you can expect accountants to have the bulk of their experience in one of the following areas: retailing, manufacturing, service, or nonprofit organizations. Ask yourself, "What category do I fall into, and can this accountant serve my needs?" Check to see what percentage of your candidate's client base matches your category. Then ask for several references and check them in person. Find out what the accountant actually did for the client and the quality of the work performed. Explore questions such as the following:

▷   What are the accountant's strengths and weaknesses?

▷   Can the accountant help you save money or make money?

▷   How many clients has the accountant had in situations similar to yours?

Above all, check on timeliness. One of the biggest complaints business owners have about their accountants is a lack of timeliness. All the financial information in the world is worthless if it's not available when you need it to make business decisions.

Don't be shy about asking about fees. Will you be charged hourly or at a flat rate? Don't make a decision strictly on price; make it on value received for the price. An accountant who will be a strategic part of your business is worth more than someone who simply acts as a bookkeeper.

If your prospective accountant passes with flying colors, then decide if there's a philosophical match. If your accountant is ultraconservative and you're not, you may find yourself in conflict more often than you'd like. Be certain that the business views of your accountant align as closely as possible with your own.

Should you consider only certified public accountants? Not necessarily. Most small, closely held companies do not usually need a CPA. A public accountant can often do as well for your small business at less cost. Knowledge and experience are more important than credentials.

After you've found an accountant who fits the bill, how do you work with him or her to answer the critical financial questions and develop financial controls? Based on your plans for the company, your accountant should be able to tell you how much cash you will need going in to meet both the start-up costs and the operating expenses for the first year. He or she should be able to help you project when you will start making money—and how much. Your accountant should also be able to suggest some strategies for dealing with unforeseen contingencies and inaccurate forecasts.

Selecting Your Lawyer

As in the case of an accountant, securing the services of a lawyer is a requirement, not an option. If you don't already have a lawyer knowledgeable in the area of small business, you will have to locate one. The same rules used to select an appropriate accountant also apply here. Lawyers specialize. Don't use a divorce lawyer to assist you in starting a small business. Be certain that you select someone who has logged considerable time with new businesses.

You will want to have your lawyer involved in the early stages of starting your business. Don't wait until you're ready to launch your business. A seasoned veteran can help you craft an approach that ensures that you are uncovering problems early and accumulating critical information necessary to lay the groundwork for a business that is both legal and well protected.

Starting a business is fraught with areas where a misstep could prove disastrous. Your attorney will be able to make judgments about product liability and environmental conformance, two very serious issues. If the purchase of commercial real estate is part of the business you're planning, you need a lawyer who's knowledgeable in that arena. Potential buyers sometimes find that the existing use of the property is in violation of many local and state requirements. You could pay plenty to comply with zoning requirements, environmental restrictions, or structural codes regulating hazards such as radon, lead paint, asbestos, and waste water discharge.

Before you hire an attorney, sit down and talk specifics about the fee structure. Much of the trauma associated with sticker shock is due to not understanding exactly what is to be done and the fees to be charged. Make sure that you tell your attorney what you want and don't want. Agree on the scope of the work and an estimate of the dollar amount the attorney will charge. Never accept a bill "for services rendered."

Make it clear that you expect an itemized statement. Specific services might include forming a new corporation, obtaining permits, arranging environmental site evaluation, and real estate title search. The list can be much longer. If you communicate clearly that you want your attorney to be specific about the cost of each service, you'll avoid unpleasant surprises.

Your Banker and Other Free Professionals

Although your bank is probably not going to help you start your business unless the note is heavily collateralized by personal assets, your banker may be a wealth of information. A banker can examine your business plan with a practiced and dispassionate eye. And your banker's advice is free for the asking.

Many commercial loan officers have just the experience you need to help you evaluate your idea intelligently. Evaluating small businesses, after all, is what they do for a living. Before you approach them, however, get your act together. You need an accurate and detailed business plan, complete with financials.

It doesn't matter that you're not asking for a loan. If you're going to be in business, you're going to need a bank to serve your business. Bankers understand that you may need a line of credit, a loan against receivables, or maybe capital to grow the business down the road. Simply indicate that you'd like to have the bank serve your business needs after you're up and running. Then let your banker look at your plan and give you feedback.

There are other free sources of professional advice available as well. Many states have organizations that exist solely to help entrepreneurs. Check with your state's department of economic development or its equivalent. Also, contact federal agencies, such as the Small Business Administration (SBA). In addition, your state university's business school, as well as private business schools, are often looking for businesses such as yours for study purposes. You may make an excellent practical project—and generally the help you receive is quite good.

Your Financial Plan

One of the cornerstones of a business plan is the financial plan. This is the vehicle that translates all of your business assumptions, market research, and market analysis into a measurable format. The work involved in preparing your own financial plan is well worth the effort. You will learn what your business needs in order to operate, how to correct deviations that inevitably occur, and how to manage your business finances competently. Moreover, completing your own financial plan will enable you to justify your business needs to potential investors and lenders.

The language of business is money. The guts of any business plan, whether for a start-up or for an existing company, are the financials. About 85 percent of the people who start their own businesses do not understand how to use a balance sheet, income statement, or cash flow system to manage their company. It's no coincidence that the failure rate for small businesses is also about 85 percent.

An understanding of basic finance is essential if you want the odds on your side. Without this foundation, you can't develop a business plan or obtain a loan. You can't even answer the most basic questions, such as the following:

▷ Are my expenses in control?

▷ Is my pricing high or low?

▷ Can I afford to hire an employee?

▷ Can I afford new equipment?

▷ Do I have the necessary cash flow to run my business through a complete business cycle?

To put it bluntly, if you aren't competent in the basics of small business finance, you're not ready to start a business. If you're new to the world of finance, don't panic. Although this section is not exactly light reading, it's not rocket science either. Go through it slowly, making sure you grasp each concept. You will soon understand the language of business and be able to make intelligent financial decisions about your company. If you're already a pro in financial management, skim this section and move on.

First, what kind of financial records do you need to understand? The two primary ones are a statement of financial position, called a *balance sheet*, and an income statement, often called a *profit and loss statement*.

A Snapshot in Time

A balance sheet is very much like a snapshot. It's a picture taken at a particular point in time that profiles the company's assets, liabilities, and the owner's equity. It's expressed as of a particular date, usually the end of the fiscal year. Most small businesses use the calendar year as the fiscal year. However, choosing another date often makes accounting easier and less expensive. For example, if a company's shipments are highly seasonal, the low point in the inventory cycle would be a logical point to end the fiscal year because the time required to count inventory is minimal.

Essentially, the balance sheet illustrates a fundamental accounting equation:

Assets = Liabilities + Stockholders' Equity

The first half of the balance sheet records the company's assets. The second half lists the liabilities and the stockholders' equity. Notice the analogy to a child's seesaw, thus the term *balance sheet*.

Refer to the example of a balance sheet later in this chapter. Under assets, you'll notice several subgroups. The subgroup *current assets* refers to cash on hand and assets that can be converted to cash within one year.

There are also subgroups under liabilities. The first subgroup, balancing with current assets, is *current liabilities*. Current liabilities are short-term debts that must be paid within one year. Two common examples of current liabilities are accounts payable and bank lines of credit.

You can quickly see that the difference between current assets and current liabilities gives you a picture of the company's cash position or *liquidity*. Liquidity is the working capital that every company needs to manage cash flow effectively. It literally makes the difference between success and failure. A company without enough liquidity does not have enough cash to pay its bills and is in deep trouble.

Realize, however, that smart business owners keep actual cash on hand to an absolute minimum, putting the excess into short-term investments that will earn interest. Cash just sitting in the company checking account is not making money for the company.

After cash and short-term investments, the next most liquid asset is the *accounts receivable*. Accounts receivable are also considered current assets. When you look at your company's balance sheet, add the following: cash, short-term investments, and accounts receivable. That sum is what accountants call *quick assets*. Quick assets can be converted into cash relatively fast. They are another indicator of a company's financial health.

Often it's useful to express quick assets as a ratio called a *quick ratio*. By using a ratio, you can easily compare a company to an industry average. To calculate the quick ratio, divide the most liquid assets (that is, cash, short-term securities, and accounts receivable) by the current liabilities. The rule of thumb is that a ratio of one to one is the acceptable minimum. Aim for a ratio of two to one to give yourself a good cushion. Because business life is unpredictable, a company with the ability to raise cash in a hurry can more readily weather the inevitable storms that may hit any business from time to time.

Now divide the total of current assets by the total of current liabilities. The resulting number is called the *current ratio*. This ratio is a measure of the company's liquidity, or, in other words, its ability to meet short-term obligations. A ratio above two is considered strong. If the number is negative, watch out! There may be some exceptions to this rule of thumb, and your accountant can point them out. But generally, the current ratio will tell you a great deal about financial strength.

Keep in mind that all of this talk about liquidity is not a pointless, abstract exercise. Small companies simply can't afford to make big mistakes and just write them off. Failure to control liquidity can bring on bankruptcy in a flash.

The *long-term assets* are those holdings that would take more than one year to convert into cash. Like short-term assets, they are also broken down into subgroups. These long-term assets are *fixed assets,* such as furniture, fixtures, equipment, and real estate. Securities held as a long-term investment are also listed here. Occasionally, you may also find intangible assets (nonphysical property, such as a patent, a copyright, a trademark, or a crediting rating) listed on the balance sheet.

Long-term liabilities are the total company debt that is due more than one year from the date of the balance sheet. You may be surprised to find stockholders' equity listed as a liability. But it is listed that way because it reflects what an owner has invested in the company. In most privately held companies, the stockholders' equity is the retained earnings that were left in the company to help it grow, or, in some cases, to survive. It really can be viewed as a debt the company owes to the stockholders.

So, a balance sheet can tell you a great deal. It can tell you if the company has enough cash to run the business, what the assets are, and how the assets compare to the liabilities. After you have a basic understanding of what information is found here and why, you will be able to understand what your accountant is telling you about the health of your company. Study the sample balance sheet until you understand what each entry means on both the asset and the liability sides.

Where Money Comes From— and Where It Goes

The *income statement* compares the company's revenue to its costs. Revenue is simply the money received from customers, investments, and any other source that generates income. Costs or expenses are the price paid to do business. Unlike the balance sheet, which is a snapshot of the company's financial position at a particular point in time, the income statement gives a picture of what has happened over a period of time, such as a month, a quarter, or a year.

Like the balance sheet, the income statement tells quite a story. Look at the Sample Income Statement provided later in this chapter. The income statement begins by listing all sources of revenue or income. The next entry on the income statement is a breakdown of the cost of sales or materials required to do business. You will note that when the cost of sales (sometimes called *cost of goods sold*) is subtracted from the revenue, the result is listed as the *gross profit*.

Next is a line-item listing of what are called *operating expenses*. The operating expenses tell you what is happening to most of the cash generated by the business. How is the owner disbursing funds? What are the major costs of doing business?

The income statement can also help you spot problems. Scrutinize each line item to see if it makes sense. You must be able to read not only each line but also between the lines. Often the line items in the operating expenses don't mean exactly what they say. For example, if gross revenue seems lower than it should be and the expense listed for advertising is extremely low, there may be a cause-and-effect relationship. If freight costs seem high, it may be because the company can't seem to ship on time and must use expensive overnight delivery to deliver products to customers. Or, even worse, the freight costs may be unusually high because customers are refusing to accept shoddy merchandise.

There are still a few more items that should interest you about the income statement. First and foremost is the *net profit*. Net profit is what's left after the total of the operating expenses and the cost of goods is subtracted from the revenue. Net profit as a percentage of net sales is called the *profit margin*. The profit margin is an extremely important figure. The acceptable range for this margin will vary considerably from industry to industry. However, the median for all companies is roughly 5 percent.

If your company has a higher profit margin than others in the same business, you're in great shape. Excellent margins enable you to withstand business downturns—in addition to making you richer, of course. If the profit margin is very low, a couple of percentage points can make the difference between operating at a loss and operating profitably.

Interpreting the Financials

Study the sample financial records given here. The company balance sheet shows current liabilities exceeding current assets. Remember to watch out for this situation! It may well indicate that a company is in trouble. Yet, if you look at the income statement, you'll see that the company ended the year with a fine profit picture.

How can this be? The explanation is simple. The firm is a highly seasonal manufacturing business. All of the sales take place in the first quarter. All revenue comes in during the last quarter. Note the large interest expense of $150,000 on the income statement. That interest pays for a line of credit, which, in turn, pays operating expenses for nearly the entire year. So things are not always what they seem. That's just one example of why you need to work closely with your accountant to develop a financial strategy.

Sample Balance Sheet

Year Ending December 31, 19___

Assets

Current Assets

Cash	$ 2,000
Accounts Receivable	17,500
Inventory	312,000
Due from officers	200,500
Total Current Assets	532,000

Equipment

Leasehold Improvements	24,500
Auto	45,000
Equipment	250,000
Less: Accumulated Depreciation	(150,000)
Net Property & Equipment	169,500

Other Assets

Real Estate	375,000
Total Assets	$1,076,500

Liabilities and Stockholders' Equity

Current Liabilities

Notes Payable	$ 200,000
Long-Term Debt (Current Payments)	50,000
Accounts Payable	300,000
Accrued Taxes	110,000
Total Current Liabilities	660,000
Long-Term Debt (less Current Payments)	300,000
Total Liabilities	960,000

Stockholders' Equity

Common Stock, No Par Value, 250 Shares Authorized, Issued and Outstanding	30,000
Retained Earnings	86,500
Total Stockholders' Equity	116,500
Total Liabilities and Stockholders' Equity	$1,076,500

Sample Income Statement

Year Ending December 31, 19__

Sales	$2,000,000
Cost of Sales	1,200,000
Gross Profit	800,000
Operating Expenses	
Salaries	250,000
Consulting/contracting	25,000
Payroll Taxes	17,000
Lease Payments	35,000
Utilities	12,000
Telephone	6,000
Advertising	30,000
Repairs	2,000
Insurance	9,000
Travel & Entertainment	41,000
Depreciation	60,000
Auto Expense	20,000
Taxes	7,000
Office Supplies	14,000
Shipping	19,000
Legal & Accounting	3,000
Dues & Subscriptions	1,000
Miscellaneous	3,000
Total Operating Expenses	554,000
Other Expenses	
Interest	150,000
Income Before Taxes	$ 96,000

Remember that financial statements can be as misleading as they are enlightening. Many business people jokingly call the profit and loss statement the "pretend and lie" statement. To keep the stockholders happy, public corporations want to show as much profit as possible. Owners of privately held companies will try very hard to show as small a profit as possible. Every possible expense is paid through the company before the money is taxed, a practice far preferable to paying that same expense out-of-pocket with after-tax dollars.

The Lifeblood of the Business

The third financial instrument with which you must be familiar is the cash flow statement. In fact, the ability to manage the flow of cash in and out of your business is the leading indicator of whether you will make it in the world of small business. Cash flow is the lifeblood of business. It literally determines survival. Don't confuse it with profitability. Many a profitable company has gone bust because of its inability to manage the inflow and outflow of cash.

Here's an example. Suppose that your company, a small heating and air-conditioning firm, lands a contract to design and install a $250,000 system in a local office building. You're elated. It's your largest contract yet. The job will require all of your personnel for a month. The payroll per month is $25,000. You figure construction materials, subcontractors, and equipment will run you $125,000. That leaves you with a 40 percent gross margin of $100,000. Not a bad deal, right?

On the surface, it's a great deal. But, as is often the case, your customer turns out to be slow in paying his bills. You have no other business for the month, yet you have to meet a $25,000 payroll and pay your vendors and subcontractors another $125,000. You've just created $150,000 in overhead. Add that to your monthly fixed operating expenses, and you're looking at a prime reason for business failure.

Suppose also that you have several slow-paying customers, and one folds and doesn't pay you at all. On paper, your company looked great. Sales were higher than expected, and profit margins were better than ever. The problem is that your required disbursements were completely out of balance with the actual flow of revenue into the company checkbook. You're flat broke and can't pay your bills.

Cash flow planning is not easy. It requires looking into the future and making critical judgments about sales revenue, fixed and variable costs, and how quickly accounts receivable will turn into cash. It requires careful scheduling of inventory purchases and planning for capital investment.

When cash flow slows to a trickle, you'd better know the reason why. Is it a seasonal problem? Or a key customer with a large past-due receivable?

If the problem is temporary, adequate working capital or a line of credit may keep you afloat until you reach smooth sailing.

But what if the costs of doing business are actually exceeding revenues? A business owner who is confused about the company's financial status and who doesn't have reasonably accurate revenue projections and cost estimates has no control over the business. He's literally flying blind, without the critical data needed to make sound business decisions.

Why do so many business owners have such difficulty handling cash flow? They have no process for predicting cash requirements. Thus, they run out of money before they run out of month. Setting up a system to predict and manage cash flow is not nearly as difficult as you may think. Here's where you'll find your accountant's experience invaluable. Being familiar with the usual and customary expenses of running a business like yours, your accountant will be able to help you create a projected cash flow statement (often called a pro forma) from start-up to three years out.

Because cash flow management is the most critical skill needed to start and run a company, you will need more than an intellectual understanding of this skill. Ask your accountant to walk you through a cash flow analysis using the process outlined here. If your accountant suggests another system, make sure it's as simple as this one. The idea is not to make yourself into an accountant, but to give yourself a simple, effective system to manage cash flow. Here's how it works:

Step One

Create a Cash Flow Report Form like the following one shown. Customize the categories under *Cash Out* to fit your business.

Step Two

Use your projected figures for this exercise. Include every deposit and disbursement for a twelve-month period.

Step Three

1. Begin by recording $0 in the first month of the *Beginning Cash* row.

2. Record the figures for all other rows in the first month column.

3. Carry forward the number from *Change* (Cash Flow) into the next month's column. Record it as *Beginning Cash*.

4. Complete the figures for the rest of the year.

5. Look for the highest negative cash flow in any one month. That number gives you the dollar figure you'll need in cash reserve to break even.

Cash Flow Report

Month	1st	2nd	3rd	4th	5th	Other
Beginning Cash						
Cash Flow In						
Sales						
Receivables Paid						
Total Cash In						
Cash Flow Out						
Fixed Expenses						
Payroll						
Mortgage or Lease						
Other Fixed Overhead						
Variable Expenses						
Sales Expense						
Mfg./Service Delivery						
Other						
Total Cash Out						
Ending Balance						
Change (Cash Flow)						

Step Four

Complete a three-year cash flow analysis. Then create a simple line or bar graph to illustrate the ebb and flow of cash. Assuming that there have been no radical changes, you will be able to predict next year's cash flow requirements from month to month with great accuracy.

Start-ups typically have more cash flow problems than established companies. Here are some additional pointers to help you to free up cash:

Lease rather than buy. Check with your accountant to see which makes more sense for your situation.

Control growth. Growth uses lots of cash. Operating and capital costs escalate much faster than profit in most rapidly growing companies.

Get rid of excess inventory. Try to buy what you need as it's needed. Have your suppliers warehouse for you.

Don't tie up money in underutilized fixed assets. Contract out whenever possible.

Maintain tight credit policies. Bad debts can sink you like a stone.

Analyze accounts receivable agings monthly. Extending interest-free loans to customers is very expensive.

Pay sales commissions based on revenue received rather than sales written. You will find that salespeople become highly motivated to see that customers pay quickly if their commissions depend on collections.

Running a small business is economic Darwinism—survival of the fittest. Those who prosper have a roster of well-developed management skills. And cash flow management should be near the top of that list.

Financial Ratios

Just as a doctor can tell a great deal by monitoring your vital signs, financial ratios can tell you much about the health of your company. A ratio is simply a numeric way of showing the relationship between two factors—for example, between the total sales and the amount of profit.

Because there are generally accepted industry standards, you can use financial ratios to track how well your company is doing. *The Almanac of*

Business and Industrial Ratios, found in many business libraries, will give you an excellent feel for what is usual for your type of business. You can also ask your accountant to nail down what would be acceptable performance for your company.

There are some basic financial ratios that every business owner should monitor. A watchful eye on these numbers will give you financial control of your business. As you study the ratios below, it's helpful to have a balance sheet and an income statement in front of you. Or you can use the samples given earlier in this chapter.

Profit Ratio. Called the sales margin, this ratio is the fundamental indicator of business health. You compute it by dividing net income by gross sales. What's acceptable varies considerably from one industry to another. A 4 percent margin in discount retailing is above average, while the same margin for an ice cream producer or tool manufacturer would be poor. In the majority of small businesses, a profit margin of only a few percentage points is very risky.

Gross Profit Ratio. This ratio is computed by dividing the gross profit or margin by the gross sales. If this ratio is below the standard for your industry, it means your cost of sales is unacceptably high.

Operating Expense Ratio. This ratio is computed by dividing total operating expenses by gross sales. Again, each industry will have its own average. As your company grows, you'll be able to keep your expenses in line by monitoring this ratio. You can also compute a ratio for each line item in the operating expenses. Computer programs are now available to constantly monitor every line item of your operating expenses to ensure that they are within acceptable limits.

Current Ratio. Compute this ratio by dividing current assets (less inventory) by current liabilities. Remember that these figures are bills that must be paid during the next twelve months and assets that could be converted into cash within the same time frame. This is an important figure for you as a new business owner because it indicates your company's ability to meet its short-term financial obligations. A ratio of two is considered average for most industries, but here again, there are many exceptions. Be concerned if the current ratio is very low. It means that there's a question of whether your company will be able to pay its bills.

Inventory Turnover Ratio. This ratio is computed by dividing gross sales by total value of inventory. This ratio varies considerably by industry; however, there's cause to worry if the number is very low. This means the company has too much cash tied up in inventory in relation to sales. Carrying excess inventory is expensive.

Receivables Collection Ratio. Compute this ratio by dividing accounts receivable by sales per day. Find sales per day by dividing gross sales by 365. For example, if the accounts receivable are $20,000 and the average daily sales are $1,000, then the ratio is 20. In other words, receivables are collected in an average of 20 days. If the company bills 30-days net, this is an excellent ratio. On the other hand, if the same company has accounts receivable of $75,000, then the ratio is 75, or an average of 75 days to collect what is owed. This high ratio is unacceptable. Not only does this situation severely strain cash flow, but the probability of bad debt rises dramatically. Many small companies have been put out of business because this ratio was not controlled.

Don't underestimate the importance of understanding and using financial controls. You simply must master the fundamentals; otherwise, your business will be out of control.

Start-Up Costs

In order to develop your business plan, you will need to know how to develop revenue and cost estimates. Because your cash flow projections are predicated on assumptions about revenue, they should be as close to reality as possible. Guessing is not the answer. Because you probably have no track record, you must rely on the experience of others. Your local library will likely have some pertinent references. In addition, many industry associations have compiled extensive historical data concerning first-year revenue averages and start-up costs.

Don't rely only on secondary research. Select a number of firms outside the geographic area where you plan to do business and call them. Ask them what their personal experience was.

EXERCISE 2.13

Estimating Your Start-Up Costs

The following list will help you to estimate your start-up costs. You may find that some entries don't apply to you, and you may need to add other categories that are unique to your situation.

Decorating/Remodeling _____

Fixtures/Equipment _____

Install fixtures/Equipment _____

Beginning inventory _____

Licenses/Permits _____

Insurance _____

Opening advertising _____

Services/Cleaning, other _____

Stationery/Cards _____

Office and other supplies _____

Legal/Accounting _____

Other professional fees _____

Phone/Utility deposits _____

Signage _____

Books/Subscriptions _____

Lease deposit _____

Professional dues _____

Sales materials _____

Bank/Financial charges _____

continued

Other   _____

Total Start-Up Costs: _____

Now list all of your operating expenses for one month:

Rent   _____

Supplies   _____

Insurance   _____

Maintenance   _____

Advertising   _____

Utilities   _____

Taxes   _____

Employee comp/Benefits   _____

Delivery/Transportation   _____

Raw inventory   _____

Travel/Entertainment   _____

Postage/Shipping   _____

Other   _____

Total Operating Expenses: _____

Now multiply the operating expenses by three to determine your quarterly operating expenses. Add the start-up costs, and the total is what you will need to spend to open the doors and remain in operation for three months.

If you add your personal living expenses to this total, you'll know how much it will cost you to open your business and operate for three months while keeping your family out of the poorhouse.

Be careful about undue optimism. If you figure you will need three months to break even, make sure you have enough to survive six months at least. Most people underestimate what's required to ensure success.

Financing Your Business

Most entrepreneurs are overly optimistic about the expected performance of their business. One seasoned veteran put it this way: "Figure out how long it will take to lead the company to profitability and double it. Figure out how much money you'll need and triple it."

There is great truth in his message. No matter how well-prepared you think you are, there will be lots of things happening that weren't in your plan. Virtually every entrepreneur who has been through a start-up finds that the financing of the business wasn't given enough thought and attention.

This doesn't mean that the financial plan for your business should be overinflated. It does mean that you should plan in enough extra capital to take care of unforeseen contingencies. Start by asking yourself what could go wrong, and then make a long list. Here's a start:

1. I get sick, and I'm out of work for three months.

2. A water pipe bursts and floods my business.

3. A key employee accepts an offer I can't match three months after start-up.

4. My supplier raised her prices 25 percent across the board.

5. My star salesperson (me) isn't quite as hot as he thought he was.

6. Actual manufacturing time has turned out to be 50 percent more than expected.

7. My advertising isn't pulling in prospects, and I don't know why.

8. The delivery van blew an engine just after the warranty expired.

continued

9. A major technology breakthrough has made my key product line obsolete.

Add your own "what ifs" until you've exhausted every possibility. Now start attaching dollar figures to each contingency. Then rank them in order of how real the threat is. Forecasting revenue and normal operating expenses for a start-up is imprecise, and so is forecasting contingencies. But be sure to go in with your eyes wide open.

Many start-up models have the planner develop and justify a best case, a worst case, and a probable case plan. Experienced advisors encourage prospective entrepreneurs to bet the farm on a plan somewhat below the probable case scenario. Small business postmortems consistently find that a major reason for bankruptcy is inadequate start-up and operating capital.

Two Kinds of Money

Finding the money to do a start-up successfully is predicated on the assumption that you know how much money is required. For now, assume that you will require outside funding. There are essentially two kinds of financing: equity and debt. Equity means ownership. If you elect to seek equity financing, you will be giving part of the ownership of your company to whoever is putting in the cash. If your business is a partnership or a sole proprietorship, equity is defined as the owners' percentage of the total net worth of the company. Net worth is simply the value of the company remaining after all financial obligations have been met.

If, for example, you go into business with two partners and you each put in $50,000 and work full time in the business, each partner would usually have an equity interest of one-third. The profits are split three ways, and if the business is sold, the proceeds are split three ways. Obviously, it's also possible for partners to own any percentage of equity based on how much they ante up to start the business.

You may have heard of silent partnerships. In this situation, you and your silent partner invest different amounts and assume different equity stakes. A silent partner invests but does not assume an active role in the business. In some cases, the silent partner may be an advisor.

Here's an example. You invest $15,000. Your silent partner puts in $80,000. You work full time. Your partner does not work in the business. Equity is split 70-30: 70 percent for your partner and 30 percent for you. Any profits are also split 70-30. You might think this is unfair. After all, you're putting in money and developing a lot of "sweat equity" by working in the business full time. But remember, equity capital is risk capital, not a loan. If the business fails, your partner has lost $80,000 to your $15,000. Your partner is betting on little more than his or her faith in your ability to make the business successful.

If you elect to remain a sole proprietorship, you cannot sell equity in your company. By definition, you are the sole owner. If, however, you decide on a partnership or a corporation, you may sell equity to anyone for any amount, limited only by your corporate charter or partnership agreement. In a corporation, you'll be selling shares of stock.

While public stock offerings are tightly regulated by the Securities and Exchange Commission, private offerings within your state for 35 or fewer investors are not complicated and can be set up by your lawyer. That doesn't mean investors will flock to your doorstep. It simply means that the red tape and the cost to offer stock for sale are minimal.

The upside of equity financing is shared risk and additional capital with no payback. The downside is loss of ownership and profit. Many equity investors insist on more than 50 percent ownership. Even if you sell less than a controlling interest to several partners, together they may have the deciding vote. That means they can boot you out of the company at any time.

Debt financing is a loan. In a start-up, regardless of whether your company is a corporation, you are on the hook personally should your business fail. In most start-up situations, unless you're receiving a direct gift from Aunt Tillie, you will be expected to pay interest on the loan. If you're borrowing from a professional lender, such as a bank, you may be required to maintain certain financial ratios as discussed in the preceding section.

Unlike equity financing, debt financing requires payback. Usually the lender will require periodic payments of principal and interest within a few months of contracting for the loan. This requirement means that your new company is going to have to do more than pay its expenses and your compensation. It also must service its debt—a challenge, to say the least, for most start-ups. That's why banks, credit unions, and most other professional lenders take a dim view of financing newly formed companies. They know that undercapitalization and lack of management ability kill most new businesses.

What Lenders Want

All professional lenders are looking for the same information. First, why do you want the loan? If it's to avoid placing your own resources at risk, forget it. Virtually all lenders will require that you have a substantial amount of your own money on the line. They want to be sure you'll hang in there when times get tough.

Lenders will insist on a personal guarantee to repay the loan, backed by collateral. The collateral could be a bank account (or Uncle Harry's bank account if he's willing to cosign the note), stock, or your home. Don't even try to get money for a start-up without agreeing to collateralize the loan. Professional lenders will lend to an existing business because it has saleable assets, accounts receivable, cash flow, and a track record. As a new business, you have none of those assets.

If you make it to the next level, your creditor will want to know how much money you need and how you intend to use the funds. Simply saying, "I think forty to fifty thousand ought to do it" is not going to fly. If the money is to be used for supplies and equipment, specifically what are they? Why are they necessary? If you're asking for operating capital, exactly how will the borrowed funds be applied and over what period of time?

Of course, they'll want to see this information in writing—in detail. How much money do you have? How much do you need to start the business? How much will you need to stay in business? In short, they want a business plan with complete financials that will spell out realistic revenue projections for up to three years. Cash flow will be detailed month by month for the first year and then quarter by quarter for the remainder of the three years.

If providing all of this information seems like too much work for getting a loan, remember that lenders have a lot at stake. They insist that you demonstrate convincingly that you have the ability to repay the loan, with interest, on time. At the top of their list is their need to have some assurance that the cash flow will both pay the expenses of running the business and service the loan. Here's what you must do to prepare for seeking start-up capital from professional lenders:

1. **Prepare a complete business plan.** Use the information in this chapter to begin.

2. **Check your credit rating.** Your lender certainly will. A perfect credit record isn't necessary. Creditworthiness is.

3. **Show that you're committed to the business.** Invest a substantial amount of your own money.

4. **Learn everything you can about your industry.** Demonstrate that you have the management expertise to be successful.

5. **Be financially fluent.** Be ready to discuss balance sheets, income statements, depreciation, and other basics of finance.

6. **Document your track record.** Lenders believe that consistent success in a closely related field is a predictor of future success. Show how past experience has given you the skills you need.

7. **Demonstrate an ability to repay.** Conservative cash flow projections should show that cash will be there to meet your monthly loan commitments.

When you are rejected by a lender—and you inevitably will be, be sure to find out why. There are usually solid business reasons. The problem may be easy to correct. If several banks reject you for the same reason, you may want to rethink that aspect of your business plan.

Other Sources for Raising Capital

Savings and FAF (friends and family) are the most common methods of financing new businesses. Although some entrepreneurs have bootstrapped their enterprise with credit card lines of credit, most have reported that the stress was monumental.

If the funding is coming out of your pocket, you will have to think about personal expenses in addition to the start-up costs and expense of running your business. If you put your whole bundle into the business, what will you and your family live on until the business is producing the required income?

Be careful about tapping friends and relatives. How would you feel if you lost your parents' life savings? More than one family has been devastated by a failed business. If you do elect to accept funds from friends or relatives, put everything in writing.

Most people have heard of venture capitalists, but few understand what they really are. Venture capitalists are equity financiers. Unfortunately, most small start-ups are not candidates for their money. They're high-stakes gamblers who are looking for companies that can produce a 500 to 1,000 percent or higher return in just a few years.

Venture capitalists tend to fund projects that have national or international appeal, with huge revenue and profit potential. Although there are exceptions, most of their money goes into high-tech products with proprietary technology, and they expect the company to go public within five to seven years. They also demand a strong management team with heavy industry experience. If you fit this profile, you can find a directory of venture capitalists in your local business library.

There are also money brokers, often called *finders*, who find money for a fee. Don't ever pay a fee up front; pay only when you have the money in your bank account. The going rate for a finder is a hefty 5 percent. Find out first exactly what you're getting for your money. Is the broker going to give you a number to call or spiff up your business plan, introduce you to money people, participate in the negotiations, and sit on your board of directors? Contact those who have experience with money brokers in your local financial community to find likely candidates.

Angels are a little known but important source of equity financing. This group is made up of doctors, lawyers, CEOs, millionaires, investment groups, and others with money to invest. Unlike venture capitalists, they have varying performance criteria and play in virtually every industry.

The problem for most people is finding angels. Bankers, business school professors, and state and local business development organizations may be able to supply leads. In recent years, business schools with entrepreneurial MBA programs have become good sources for tracking down leads. Check the business schools in your area. Also check with your state's business development council.

Other private sources of capital are business incubators run by universities and local governments. They offer start-up counseling, attractive leases, vendor relationships, and sometimes loans. Some Chambers of Commerce operate venture capital clubs, which introduce small companies to interested investors.

The Small Business Administration is in the business of serving people who run a small business—or who want to run one. Part of that support is helping with funding. The SBA, however, does not lend money directly. It simply guarantees loans. This means that if your bank agrees to loan you money to start a business, the SBA will pay up to 90 percent of the note should you default. Obviously, your local lending institution is going to look on you more favorably. However, you will still have to invest a substantial amount of your own financial resources and guarantee repayment. You will also be required to present a compelling business case for funding.

The Small Business Administration also licenses small business investment companies (SBICs). SBICs are private sector organizations that are given access to federal money. They function as a hybrid of a bank and a venture capital company; they offer equity funding and long-term financing to the small business community. Minority enterprise small business investment companies (MESBICs) assist socially and economically disadvantaged entrepreneurs.

Two other government-sponsored organizations are the SBA's Small Business Institute (SBI) and business and industrial development corporations (BIDCOs). The SBI offers consulting and counseling assistance through a wide network of local universities. They also offer direct assistance to small firms. BIDCOs are organizations composed of financial institutions that spread out the risk of financing small businesses among their members.

Getting the money to do your deal isn't a one-time process. If your company is successful and grows, you will require additional funding. In fact, the more successful you are, the more money your company will need. After obtaining seed money to launch your business, you may need what is called *first-round financing* to take your company out of the start-up mode and move it to the next level.

Second-round financing will be required if you're on a significant growth curve because the working capital requirement will be more than what's available in retained earnings.

Third-round or mezzanine financing may fuel the next round of growth and stabilize your company. The point is, you will always be looking for money if your plan is to grow. You need to know not only what your money requirements are but also where to meet them.

Question your investors or lenders carefully. You will be involved with them for a long time. Will they be a valuable resource or a constant interference in the management of your business? Or will you be left to your own devices? What kind of reports will they require and how often? What strings are attached to the money? Will you be prohibited from seeking additional funding? Will you be required to maintain certain inventory levels? The list of questions you decide to ask may be long, but you need to ask them.

Finally, don't ever put more on the line than you're willing to risk. There are no guarantees in business. No matter how good you are, no matter how well you plan, you could lose everything. If your deal goes sour, are you prepared to live with the consequences?

Your Complete Business Plan

Someone once said, "Most people aim for nothing in life and hit it with amazing accuracy." When it comes to business, you can't afford not to plan. A business plan is a blueprint of your business. It defines your goals and details precisely how you will achieve them. With a plan, you will know what needs to be done and when—and what resources and skills will be required to do it.

Because a business plan details not only your goals but also how you will achieve them, the business planning process allows you to see the flaws in your thinking before you put your money on the line. Doesn't it make sense to make your serious mistakes on paper and not in the real world?

A business plan also gives you a way to monitor and control your business. Sophisticated business owners use monthly variance reports to review sales and expenses. A *variance report* is simply a monthly income statement that compares your business plan to what actually happened.

For example, suppose that your plan budgets $550 a month for postage. In checking your monthly variance report, you find that mailing costs were three times what was budgeted. On investigation, you find that an employee has been sending out all proposals by Federal Express. Variance reports quickly flag such financial deviations from your plan so that you can take action to fix the problem before it becomes serious.

A business plan combined with variance report monitoring will enable you to plan your second year in business with far greater precision. Start-up plans are less accurate because there's no track record on which to predict future performance. However, future planning decisions become much simpler and far more accurate if planned versus actual financials have been tracked for the preceding year.

In short, a well-conceived business plan can put you in control of your business. You'll ensure the safe launch of your start-up and have a powerful tool for monitoring performance. When it's time to plan for year two, you will know exactly what your cash needs are and be able to make growth decisions based on reliable data.

If this is your first attempt at constructing a business plan, don't despair. Take it one step at a time. First, decide on the purpose of your business plan. Plans that are built to attract investors or to secure debt financing are generally very detailed and focus on selling. An operational business plan is a tool used by management to control and monitor the business. It's short, focused on defining the business strategy and operational plan, and includes the financials.

Second, whether you're constructing a plan to operate your business or to seek financing, brevity counts. Since the advent of computer programs to automate the writing of business plans, along with the development of easy-to-use spreadsheet software, plans submitted to lenders now often contain reams of useless financial forecasts and meaningless data. Bankers and other professional lenders can spot a long-winded boilerplate a mile away.

Although your financier may need specific information to understand your proposal and why it's worthy of funding, the entire plan should be no more than twenty-five to thirty pages maximum. You may think that's impossible, but if you can't describe your deal clearly, simply, and quickly, you haven't thought it through enough.

The operating copy of your business plan should be even shorter—under five pages. If you need fifty pages to describe where you are going to play and how you're going to win, your purpose is foggy, and your strategy is muddy.

What's in the Plan?

Your business plan is the summation of what you've been working on throughout this chapter. Your business idea, your strategic intent statement, your marketing plan, your organization plan, and your financial plan—all are necessary elements of your complete business plan.

Make sure that you include a table of contents and a solid executive summary at the *beginning* of the document. An *executive summary* is a picture of your business plan in miniature. It should run no more than two pages and capture the essence of the entire plan. It should be conversational in tone, as if you were explaining your business to a stranger in three minutes or less. Professional lenders and investors read hundreds of business plans. You will have about one minute to grab their attention. A well-conceived and well-written executive summary may not guarantee financing, but a poor one will certainly guarantee rejection.

Here are some other common mistakes to avoid:

1. **Hyperbolic projections.** Nothing turns a prospective lender off faster than unrealistic revenue estimates and market share projections.

2. **Academic mumbo-jumbo.** An executive summary isn't a Ph.D. dissertation. Avoid jargon and replace long words with short ones wherever possible.

3. **Too much optimism.** Savvy lenders prefer to deal with entrepreneurs who go into new ventures with greater caution and solid backup plans.

4. **Unprofessional appearance.** Believe it or not, people submit handwritten, error-laden tomes that take months to prepare and seconds to reject.

5. **Not enough research.** This mistake is easily discerned and virtually guarantees rejection.

6. **Financials that lack detail.** Present your financial data in the usual and customary way. Be able to explain all financial assumptions.

7. **Inadequate information about yourself.** Summarize your background in enough detail that it documents well your ability to run the business.

8. **Product focus.** Lenders don't care about all the nifty features of your product. They care about the benefits provided to customers.

9. **Too much too soon.** High salaries and excessive perks turn off lenders. They want you to be willing to wait for your rewards,

Although writing a business plan is a great deal of work, make it your very best work. It's the best business success insurance you can have. After going through this exercise, many people have concluded that their business would probably not fly. Bad news? No, it was great news. The misery and money saved were worth every minute spent.

EXERCISE 2.14

Business Plan Outline

Use the following lines to begin your business plan.

I. Executive Summary

_____

_____

_____

II. Marketing Plan

_____

_____

_____

III. Organization Plan

_____

_____

_____

IV. Financial Plan

_____

_____

_____

V. Appendices

_____

_____

_____

Chapter 3

Buying a Business or Franchise

uying a business is the dream of many entrepreneurs. Business ownership can bring unparalleled personal fulfillment and financial reward. Those people most interested in buying a business often share the following characteristics:

> They are in a strong financial position.

> They have excellent contacts to develop a consortium of potential investors.

> They have reduced income needs and have no major financial obligations, such as mortgage or tuition.

> They are older and more experienced and believe themselves more likely to remain active in the labor force—and maintain their current income level—through entrepreneurship, rather than by corporate employment.

As you start out on your quest to find and buy a business, you should know that most aspiring business owners fail to find a profitable, secure business that fits their skills and interests. That's the bad news. The good news is that if you know what you're doing, the odds of finding the business that's right for you are quite good. This chapter, in conjunction with chapter 2, "Starting a Business," provides you with a complete blueprint for the successful acquisition of a small business that fits your needs as well as your wallet.

This chapter examines the purchase of an existing business or a franchise. An existing business can be purchased outright. You direct the business and can make all decisions about the product, service, structure, location, and other details of the business. A franchise is a business concept purchased from a franchisor. The franchisor chooses the goods or services that are sold. The location of your business must be approved by the franchisor. In return, you get a packaged business operation that has been successful in other locations. Both options are explained in this chapter.

Selecting a Business

Many people hope to buy a business without any idea of what's right for them. Even when their goal is clearly defined, most people have no idea where to look. Fewer still have any clue about how to evaluate a company's profit potential accurately, or how to place a selling price on a potential acquisition.

The decision about what type of business to buy should be based on what you know and what you enjoy. Why? Because you're going to be spending a lot of time running your business. Three useful ways to approach this selection process are listed below:

1. **Hobby or interest.** If you have a deep interest in a particular area, or a specific skill or expertise, you might want to look for a business that fits your interests and abilities.

2. **You can do it better.** Perhaps you have had an unpleasant or unsatisfactory experience as a customer of a certain business. You might want to transfer that knowledge or your conviction that you can do it better to a competitor business.

3. **Lack of product or service in a particular area.** Perhaps you were traveling and had the opportunity to be a customer of a business

that offered a product or service not yet offered in your region or city. You might want to look for a company that could easily expand its product mix into that area.

Financial Considerations

How much money is enough? You already took the time to sit down and determine your current financial position when you completed the Personal Financial Profile in chapter 1. That exercise will now help you to decide whether a prospective business is right for you from a financial perspective.

The first question is, What size business can I afford? There is a simple method to estimate what league you are in. It's called "The Rule of One-Third." The rule states that the down payment you make on a business will be roughly equal to one-third of the total purchase price. Therefore, if you add up all liquid assets that you are prepared to invest in a business and multiply that number by three, you will have the approximate dollar value of the company you can purchase.

Investable Assets x 3 = Business Purchase Price

For example, if you have $50,000 in savings, money market accounts, and certificates of deposit, and another $30,000 in stock, you have a total of $80,000 to invest in a company. By the Rule of One-Third, you can afford a company in the $240,000 range. This rule is subject to individual variation, but it serves as an excellent starting point.

The second money matter to discuss is the issue of salary. This calculation is simple, too, if you have completed your Personal Financial Profile. You know how much income you need for living expenses. Later in this chapter, you will learn how to determine how much money the current owner of a business is extracting from the company. These two figures must mesh, or you'll be in trouble. Simply compare your needs to the current owner's financial benefit, and you will find that making a decision will be easy.

Geographical Considerations

Some people would live on the far side of the moon just to have the opportunity to run a business. For others, however, no matter how attractive the business may be, there's just no way they would relocate. If you have roots in your community, do you really want to pull up stakes and move to where the business is?

If you're married and have children, the decision may be even more complex. You may be willing to live somewhere else, but do you want to send your kids to school there? Is it an environment where you want your kids to grow up? How does your spouse feel about it? Is he or she willing to give up a job, family and friends, a home, and a comfortable lifestyle to support your venture?

The possibility of relocating needs to be discussed before you begin investigating your opportunities. If you decide that you cannot relocate, your choices obviously will be restricted.

Location may or may not be critical to a business. If you're considering a company that serves a national or global customer base, you have many options. Service businesses that serve a wide region are also quite mobile—assuming that critical employees are willing to move. However, you may find that costs of labor, rent, heat, taxes, and other operating expenses will dictate where the business should be located.

In other businesses, such as retail, location is critical. It will make you or break you. If you are considering purchasing such a business, understand that it's not a wise idea to relocate a business that is thriving in its current location.

The point here is that the decision about where your company is located should be grounded in data that reflects what's good for the business. When considering moving a business, keep in mind that major cost-related changes could occur in any of the following areas:

Utility rates	EPA requirements
Taxes	Permit processes
Economic/Business climate	Expansion possibilities
Cost availability of labor	Proximity to vendors

Business regulations	Shipping
Cost of leasing	Zoning
Purchase of real estate	Local tax incentives
Cost of living	Local political climate

Why Traditional Search Methods Fail

The typical business buyer is not a professional buyer. The primary strategy will be quite predictable—reading the business opportunity ads in the newspaper and calling on business brokers. The result will be a long and frustrating experience because the vast majority of high-profit small businesses that are for sale are never advertised. Successful business owners don't want to upset key employees about their future with the company. In addition, news of a potential change in ownership may hurt the business. Business owners do not want to shake the confidence of customers and suppliers, nor do they want to give competitors an edge.

Business brokers generally represent sellers and concentrate on moving what they have in inventory. If you decide to work with a broker, select one who exclusively represents a business for sale and who also receives a retainer in addition to the contingency fee. This arrangement allows the broker to devote more time to researching the business and preparing a comprehensive offering package that includes vital background and financial information. Most brokers work on a contingency basis and are paid by the seller at the closing. The disadvantage of this arrangement to you is that brokers on contingency can't afford to invest a lot of time and effort in learning about a business that is for sale.

The expertise of these individuals and firms varies widely, from the relatively unskilled to the highly experienced and sophisticated. For the most part, business brokers are not regulated. Only fourteen states require that business brokers be licensed. Because of this lack of regulation, brokers should be screened carefully. Make sure you have answers to all of these questions:

▷ What deals has the broker completed?

▷ What is the broker's personal background? References?

▷ What is the broker's record of sales as a portion of total listings?

▷ How frequently does the broker's listing price correspond to the actual sales price?

A good broker can be instrumental in structuring the elements of a successful deal. Although many brokers are not expert appraisers, they can help you assess and qualify a business. They also can help mediate disputed points with the seller. Although brokers work for the seller, they have a strong interest in completing the sale. Some even facilitate locating sources of financing. If you can find a good broker and get on his or her priority buyer list, you have a slight chance of success. But the odds are not in your favor. Fewer than 20 percent of businesses are sold through business brokers.

Obviously, finding a profitable business with a willing seller is a tough job. You need a strategy for tapping into the market where the high-profit companies are—and the competing buyers aren't. Who knows about unadvertised businesses for sale? The following people may be able to help you:

▷ Bankers, lawyers, and accountants who deal with small companies

▷ Vendors and suppliers to small companies

▷ Business consultants who specialize in helping small firms

Make a list of individuals you know in these fields. As part of your initial research, call them and ask if they are aware of solid businesses that may be for sale. Also, ask for referrals to their colleagues who may be able to provide you with additional leads. After you obtain and research these leads, you will use a "go direct" campaign in which you directly approach the owners of the companies in which you're interested. This strategy meets with the most success.

The Start of the Search

Research is the backbone of your go-direct strategy to find and buy a high-profit business. First, it provides the information you need to identify companies that fit your geographic and interest requirements. Second, research provides the data that will enable you to make intelligent business decisions about markets and industries.

The research you conduct will be driven in part by your decision about geography. If you've made a decision to limit your search for a business to within an hour's drive of home, you can immediately see how that decision focuses your research. You will concentrate only on the prospective companies within your geographic range.

If you want to continue living in your area, limiting your search to only one industry is unrealistic. To some people, the industry is everything. To others, where they live is their top priority. This trade-off between geography and industry is often not an easy decision, but it must be made early in your search.

Let's assume you have resolved the issues of industry and geography. What's next? If you have decided to stay wide open geographically and open your search to several industries, you will want to start with industry research. If you are considering entering an industry that's new to you, you will need a great deal of information. Even if you are already in the field, you will find additional industry research to be very useful.

If geography is your top priority, save your industry research until you have identified companies that fit your general interests and are within the boundaries you've defined.

Industry Research

The resource list in the back of this book will help you to find much of the information you need. Another excellent source of specific industry information is trade journals. Trade journals are every bit as abundant as directories. At your library, you will find a directory of trade journals that will tell you what publications exist in your fields of interest.

Trade journals will make you an expert. If it's an industry issue, you'll find it covered. Study the journals carefully. Go back a couple of years. Notice the trends and changes. You will develop an excellent feel for the industry you are researching, to the point where you will find it easy to say either "I love it" or "I hate it."

EXERCISE 3.1

Industry Research Worksheet

Use this worksheet to record data about the industry you research. You can consider your industry research complete when you have the answers to all of the questions.

What are the key industry issues?

_____

_____

Is the industry growing or dying?

_____

_____

Who are the leaders and innovators? Why are they the leaders?

_____

_____

What has happened to the industry over the last five years?

_____

_____

How is technology affecting the business?

_____

_____

Is foreign competition having an impact?

_____

_____

What is the growth potential over the next five years?

_____

_____

What is the long-term growth potential for the industry?

_____

_____

What is the size of the industry?

_____

_____

What kinds of people are in the industry? What backgrounds do they have?

_____

_____

What kinds of skills and education are required?

_____

_____

How sophisticated is the industry in technology and marketing?

_____

_____

What is the mix between large and small companies?

_____

_____

continued

Who holds the greatest market share?

_____

_____

Can small firms compete effectively?

_____

_____

Who is making money and why?

_____

_____

How much, on average, can a small company do in annual revenue?

_____

_____

How much annual profit can a small firm produce?

_____

_____

How much capital investment is required to compete effectively?

_____

_____

What is the makeup of the employee population in a typical small company?

_____

_____

What are the industry problems? How are they being solved? At what cost?

_____

_____

What separates the real performers from the pack?

_____

_____

Do my interests and skills fit this industry closely?

_____

_____

Do my abilities and interests fit better in this industry than any other? Why or why not?

_____

_____

_____

_____

If this list seems intimidating at first, don't be alarmed. You will find that the problem will be too much information rather than not enough. Keep reminding yourself that the importance of making the right decision outweighs the time required to obtain accurate information.

Company Research

Now you need to move on to researching specific companies. Preliminary research needs to be done before you can approach the owner and sell yourself effectively. No matter what your information needs may be, there are many sources from which to choose.

Use directories to identify companies that are possibilities for you. Remember, if you're limiting your search to a specific geographic area, concentrate on the appropriate regional directories. If geography is secondary, focus on the appropriate industry directories.

EXERCISE 3.2

Company Research Worksheet

In a large notebook with alphabetical tabs, create a research worksheet like
the following sample:

Industry: _____

Company Name: _____

Owner: _____

Address: _____

Phone: _____

Products/Services: _____

_____

_____

_____

_____

Gross Sales: _____

Number of Employees: _____

Additional Data: _____

_____

_____

_____

_____

When you're ready to begin your go-direct campaign, you will have the names and addresses of the business owners you plan to contact.

After you have completed this first phase of your research, you will have a long list of good possibilities. All you will know at this point is that these companies look interesting and might be worthy of further consideration. You will have no idea if the company is profitable or if the owner has any interest in selling. You must narrow down the list so that you have a smaller set of companies where the owner is interested in the possibility of selling.

Contacting Prospective Companies

Now is the time to get in touch with the current owners to see if they are interested in selling. Your first contact with the prospective business seller should be through a letter. The message should be very straight-forward: "I'm interested in the possibility of buying your business. I'm financially and professionally qualified to do so. If you'd like to explore the issue, let's talk. I'll call you to get your answer." That's it.

When writing your letter, make sure that you do the following:

▷ Use high-quality stationery.

▷ Double-check all spelling, addresses, and names.

▷ Individualize: this is no place for a form letter.

▷ Type or print cleanly.

▷ Make the letter short and simple, yet powerful.

▷ Mark the envelope "Personal."

▷ Let your research show wherever appropriate.

▷ State that you will be calling and when.

Use the following example to help you construct your own letters:

Sample Approach Letter

Ms. Kathy Donohoe, President
Piper Employment Services
12 Charles Street
Portsmouth, NH 03801

March 12, 19__

Dear Ms. Donohoe:

Your impressive record in the personnel field proves your ability to get things done and bring innovation to an industry that sorely needs it. Three new offices in less than two years is a terrific track record.

I am in the market to buy a company like yours. I realize that selling may be a new idea for you, but if you'd like to explore the possibility, I'd like to meet with you and discuss what I have in mind. The meeting could be good for both of us.

I will call you Tuesday morning of next week.

Sincerely,

Michael Morrison

Making the Call

In your letter, you have indicated that you will call to follow up at a specified time. It's important that you do exactly what you said you would do, exactly when you said you would do it.

When the time comes to call prospective sellers, how well you handle the phone may determine whether you get the opportunity to buy the company. Be certain that you understand the purpose of that first phone call. You have sent an initial contact letter, and now you are following up, just as you said you would. Your call has only one purpose: to set an appointment to explore the possibility of buying the company. When the appointment has been set, end the conversation. Don't enter into a long discussion; the meeting is for *that* purpose.

Think through the concerns that the owner may bring up and plan your responses. The owner may flatly state, "I have no interest in selling, and that's final!" Obviously, then, it makes little sense to press for a meeting. In many cases, however, if the owner is convinced that selling the business is at least worth talking about, you will be able to arrange an exploratory meeting.

It's a good idea to role-play the initial phone contact with a friend until you feel completely comfortable with it. Above all, remember the goal of the phone call is to set an appointment. Be warm and friendly, but get the appointment set as quickly as you can, and then get off the phone.

If your experience is typical, you will have a success rate of 15 to 20 percent. Make twenty contacts and you will have four or five meetings lined up with potential sellers. Keep this ratio in mind, as it will help you to deal with the inevitable rejections. Remember that every time you hear a "no," you're one step closer to a "yes."

Not one in ten of your competitors will be using this strategy. It never occurs to most people to forget about going with the herd and instead go directly to the source. The direct route not only is easier, but also increases dramatically your odds of uncovering a highly profitable business for which there is virtually no competition!

Preparing to Meet the Owner

Although you will have a number of meetings with the seller before the final deal is done, the first face-to-face discussion with the owner of a prospective company is a very important one. You have several goals to accomplish at this meeting:

▷   To size up the company as a candidate for purchase

▷   To size up the owner so that you will have some idea of how best to deal with this individual

▷   To create the right impression in the mind of the owner

The owner must like you, respect you, and see you as competent; otherwise, you won't be taken seriously. Openness, friendliness, honesty, and professionalism are the operative words that should guide your strategy for these meetings.

Always try to arrange the first meeting at the business location. You can learn much simply by being observant. While visiting the site, check out the following clues to the business's health:

Look at the appearance of the facility. Is it clean, neat, and orderly? Appearances can tell you much about how the business is managed.

Observe the employees at work. Do they look happy and busy— or depressed and frightened? Morale problems are responsible for serious productivity problems.

Look carefully at raw inventory, work-in-progress, and finished goods. Later, as you examine the financial statements, you can see if what's claimed is roughly equal to what's really there.

Notice the fixed assets. Are they old and worn out? Old but well maintained? Does the business have the equipment it needs? Problems with equipment or other fixed assets could cost you plenty.

Notice how often the phone rings. Busy phones signify a busy business.

Get the owner to discuss customers. How many? What revenue per customer? What amount of repeat business? How is business generated? A steady flow of business from a solid customer base is the single most important dimension of a business.

Analyze the owner's personality and style. How does the owner make decisions? What's important to him or her? What are the owner's plans? This information will be critical when the time comes to construct a workable deal.

Using a Nondisclosure Agreement

Begin the meeting by addressing a primary concern of all business owners: confidentiality. You must be certain to allay the owner's fear of a breach of confidence. To do this, you will use a standard nondisclosure agreement.

In a nondisclosure agreement, you promise not to reveal any information about the business to anyone else without the express permission of the owner. The use of a nondisclosure agreement identifies you as a trustworthy business professional who understands and respects these concerns. Here's how to deal with this issue:

Step One. Use the sample nondisclosure agreement provided here. Prepare copies and have them available whenever you meet with a business owner.

Step Two. Early in your first meeting with the owner, emphasize your commitment to protecting the owner's privacy. Indicate that everything that the owner tells you, along with any written records you are given, will be treated with complete confidentiality. When it's necessary to share information with your advisors, promise that you will obtain the owner's prior approval.

Step Three. After you have explained your commitment to confidentiality, take out two copies of your nondisclosure agreement. Explain to the owner what they are, fill them out, and sign them. Ask the owner to sign them also. Keep one copy for your records and leave one copy with the owner. And then do what you promised: maintain the owner's confidentiality. Breach of contract could prove costly.

Sample Nondisclosure Agreement

Company Name: _____

Address: _____

_____

As a prospective buyer of the above-named business, I acknowledge receipt of personal and confidential information. I agree not to divulge such information to others, except to secure their advice and counsel, in which case I agree to obtain their commitment to the same confidentiality.

I further agree not to contact other owners, customers, suppliers, or employees regarding the business or business affairs of the above-named business without the knowledge and consent of the owner.

Date: _____

Your Signature: _____

Owner's Signature: _____

At this point, limit your discussion to broad issues that will not be threatening. Start by summarizing your background, and explain how you arrived at the decision to contact the owner. Then ask the owner how he or she came to be in this business. Ask the owner to share his or her background and to tell you what experience helped or hindered in managing the company. Before you leave this initial meeting, make sure that you both agree on what the next step in the deal should be and the timing for that step.

When you feel certain that the owner is interested in pursuing the sale, then you're ready to delve deeper into the confidential details of the business that will be necessary for you to analyze the company and begin negotiating a deal.

The information you collect will be the basis for discussion with your professional advisors. You will be providing them with a detailed picture of the business that will assist them in generating a list of additional questions that need answers. This valuable information from the owner will be the foundation for developing a full profile of the company.

What you are trying to do is benchmark this company. In a short time. you will have figured out what industry leaders are doing that makes them winners. You will be able to use that information as a yardstick to see how your target company measures up.

Use the following business profile worksheet to collect and organize information about the company you are considering. Use it as your interview guide with the business owner. Later, you will be able to compare what the owner has told you with your personal research.

EXERCISE 3.3

Business Profile Worksheet

Company Name: _____

Address: _____

_____

Owner: _____

Phone: _____

History from Start-up to Present: _____

_____

_____

_____

_____

continued

What products or services are offered? What's the mix? _____

_____

_____

_____

How is the location? What are the demographics? Are there any branch offices or other locations? _____

_____

_____

_____

How many years has the company been in business? Were there periods of expansion? When? _____

_____

_____

What are the owner's reasons for selling? _____

_____

_____

_____

Why did the owner originally buy or start the business? _____

_____

_____

_____

Is the industry embryonic, emerging, or mature? _____

_____

What was the revenue over the last five years? _____

_____

What was the profit for the last five years? _____

_____

Are there any hidden expenses? What are they? _____

_____

_____

_____

Are there any pending litigations, licensing difficulties, or patent problems?
What are they? _____

_____

_____

_____

Have there been any lawsuits in the last five years? What were they?
Who filed them and why?_____

_____

_____

_____

What was the disposition of each? _____

_____

_____

Are there any zoning problems? What are they?_____

_____

_____

_____

Are there zoning changes likely in the near future? What changes? _____

_____

_____

Are there parking problems? What are they? _____

_____

_____

continued

What are the regulations regarding signage? _____

_____

_____

What copyrights, patents, databases, customer lists, mailing lists, or other proprietary information does the business depend on? _____

_____

_____

_____

_____

What is the total dollar value of the inventory? _____

_____

How much is raw inventory, work-in-progress, finished goods? What is the value of each type of inventory? _____

_____

_____

_____

How often does this inventory turn over annually? _____

_____

What is the total amount of accounts receivable and accounts payable? ____

_____

_____

What portion of the accounts receivable is overdue 30 days? 60? 90? More than 90 days? _____

_____

_____

What is the bad debt history? _____

_____

What is the billing/pay cycle? _____

What is the fair market value for each of the following assets?

Furniture: _____

Fixtures: _____

Equipment: _____

Vehicles: _____

Leases: _____

Other assets: _____

_____

_____

If possible, get a list for each category.

What is the monthly rent? _____

Is the rent likely to change? _____

What is the duration of the lease? _____

Is it assignable? _____

What are the options and the restrictions? _____

_____

_____

Are there additional payments for taxes, insurance, or maintenance?
What payments? _____

_____

_____

If possible, get a copy of the real estate lease.

Is there any leased equipment? What equipment? _____

_____

_____

continued

What are the terms? _____

_____

_____

_____

Is the lease assignable? _____

Are there any items and equipment not included with the sale of the business? What items? _____

_____

_____

_____

Are there key customers? Who or what are these? _____

_____

_____

_____

How long have they been customers? _____

_____

_____

_____

What is the total number of customers? _____

What is the revenue per customer? _____

_____

_____

_____

What is the percentage of repeat business? _____

How is the advertising handled? _____

_____

_____

What is the budget? _____

Where is the advertising placed? _____

_____

_____

What is the frequency? _____

Are the results tracked? If so, how? _____

_____

_____

Get copies of any advertisements. _____

What is the sales and marketing strategy?_____

_____

_____

What are the sales projections for the next two years? _____

_____

How were they derived? _____

_____

What sales and marketing promotions are used? _____

_____

_____

Do you attend trade shows? What are the results? _____

_____

Get copies of any marketing materials.

Who is responsible for sales? _____

_____

What percentage of the total sales does the owner generate?_____

_____

continued

Who is the competition? _____

_____

_____

Do they operate differently? How? _____

_____

_____

_____

Do they have a competitive advantage? If so, what is it? _____

_____

_____

_____

Where are they? _____

_____

_____

What is their market share? _____

_____

What is the size of the total market? _____

How does your company position itself in the market? _____

_____

_____

What is your company's reputation in the marketplace? _____

_____

_____

What image does the company project? Why and how? _____

_____

_____

Is the company a low- or high-cost provider? _____

Is the company a technological leader? In what way(s)? _____

_____

_____

_____

Is the company a turnkey provider?_____

Is the product high or low quality? _____

Is the product noncompetitive? _____

What are the company's key business strengths? _____

_____

_____

_____

What are the key business weaknesses?_____

_____

_____

_____

Is there potential for add-on products and services? Which ones? _____

_____

_____

_____

Is there merger/acquisition potential? In what way? _____

_____

Are there outside factors that may influence the business positively or
negatively? What factors? _____

_____

_____

_____

continued

What is the company's current market niche? _____

_____

_____

Will it remain stable? _____

Are there untapped markets? Which markets? _____

_____

_____

Are there separate operations or divisions? What are they? _____

_____

_____

Are there distributors? Who are they? Where are they? _____

_____

_____

What is the business arrangement? _____

_____

_____

What percentage of sales are they responsible for?_____

How much time and money are spent servicing them?_____

_____

_____

What are the totals for rework and other avoidable costs? _____

_____

_____

How are they determined and tracked? _____

_____

_____

What is the figure for scrap? _____

Are there discounts and customer allowances? What are the amounts? _____

_____

_____

How do all these figures compare to industry norms? _____

_____

_____

What is the cost to enter the industry? _____

_____

What technical knowledge and experience are required? _____

_____

_____

How much time does it take to break in? _____

Is there a recent history of growth or change? Summarize. _____

How critical is the owner to the success of the business? _____

_____

_____

Competitor Interview Guide

As part of your investigative process, you must talk with industry competitors. Choose competitors from a noncompeting geographic area. Call them. You can take either of two approaches here. One approach is to say that you are thinking about buying a company in this field, so you would like to gather some information about the industry to help you make a decision. The best information would come from professionals experienced in the business, thus your call. The second approach is to say that you are doing research about this industry and that you would like to tap the individual's experience and get his or her opinion about the state of the industry.

EXERCISE 3.4

Competitor Interview Worksheet

Use this worksheet to record information collected from competitors.

Competitor Name: _____

Person Interviewed: _____

Position with Company: _____

Who are the major players in the industry? _____

_____

_____

Which are the best companies in the industry? Why? _____

_____

_____

_____

What is the market size? _____

_____

What are the untapped markets? _____

_____

What changes are occurring in the industry? How are these changes
impacting the business?_____

_____

_____

What do you have to do to make money in this business? _____

_____

_____

What are the industry problems? _____

_____

_____

What kind of background do you need to get into this business? _____

_____

_____

What will the industry be like five years from now? _____

_____

_____

What is the best way to increase market share? _____

_____

_____

How do you keep overhead down? _____

_____

_____

How much time and money should be devoted to research and development?

_____

_____

What is the best strategy for selling? _____

_____

_____

What are the key concerns of customers? _____

_____

_____

How important is price in this industry? _____

_____

_____

Are there other important facts I should know about this business and
industry? _____

_____

_____

Customer Interview Guide

Now it's time to gather information from the most important source of all—the customers. Customers buy products and services for many reasons. You need to know those reasons in order to compete effectively in the marketplace.

Your approach to interviewing customers should be similar to the approach you took with competitors. Ask the owner of your prospective business to provide a cross section of customers. Also, ask the owner to identify satisfied customers as well as dissatisfied ones. You need to know both sides of the story.

When you speak to customers, you don't need to emphasize that you are considering buying the business. A better approach is to tell customers that you are doing research on behalf of the company to help it improve. Information directly from customers is part of the strategy to create a plan for that improvement. Because your customer base will be your most important business asset, you don't want to shortchange this part of your analysis.

Your research already will have uncovered the key issues and concerns with which customers can help you. When you talk with customers, your questions will be focused because you will know what you need to find out.

EXERCISE 3.5

Customer Interview Worksheet

Use this worksheet to record information that you collect from customers.

Customer Name: _____

How long have you been a customer of the company? _____

Why do you do business with the company?_____

_____

_____

_____

What was your best experience with the company? _____

_____

_____

_____

What was your worst experience? _____

_____

_____

_____

How does the quality of the product or service compare with the
competition? _____

_____

_____

_____

How well does the product or service meet your requirements?_____

_____

_____

_____

What specific improvements are needed? _____

_____

_____

_____

How much business will you do with the company this year? _____

_____

_____

What would convince you to give the company more business? _____

_____

_____

_____

continued

What must the company do to keep your business? _____

_____

_____

_____

How should the product or service be priced? _____

_____

_____

_____

What is important to you about the product or service? What's not important?

_____

_____

_____

What would cause you to switch suppliers? _____

_____

_____

_____

Is there anything else you would like to tell me about this business? _____

_____

_____

_____

Employee Interview Guide

Before you actually sign on the dotted line and become a business owner, you should meet and talk at length with key employees. After all, if everything goes well, soon they will be your employees.

Approaching employees is often an extremely delicate matter, and most sellers don't want to tip their hand to employees until they're sure the sale is actually going to go through. If the deal falls apart for some reason, the seller is the one who will be required to pick up the pieces and move on. On the other hand, if there are potential employee problems, you must resolve them before you buy. Usually buyers and sellers agree to employee interviews as one of the very last contingencies before closing the deal.

To proceed, determine which employees you want to interview, and give the owner their names. The current owner should then inform the chosen employees at the appropriate time that he or she is seriously considering selling the business to you. As part of the investigative process, you will be talking with them to ask for their views on the business.

Timing is very critical here. Work out a schedule acceptable to the owner that ensures as little lag time as possible between when he or she drops the bombshell and you conduct your interviews. The rumor mill can do a lot of damage.

Make sure that you meet employees one-on-one, without the current owner present. You will have a better chance that they will level with you if the owner isn't in the room. Prepare carefully for these meetings. Think how you would feel if you were in the employee's situation. There's bound to be a great deal of concern about what's going to happen. Employees will have these questions:

> ▷ Will I be fired?

> ▷ Will I have to perform a different job?

> ▷ Will I be able to get along with you?

> ▷ Will I still have input into decisions?

> ▷ What changes will take place, and how will they affect me?

While being completely honest, do everything you can to reassure employees that things will be fine. Brief them on your background and what you bring to the business. Tell employees specifically how you will work with them daily as their employer. Assure them of confidentiality. As long as they understand that you really do want their ideas and that anything they say is for your ears only, you will usually get excellent information.

EXERCISE 3.6

Employee Interview Worksheet

Employee Name: _____

Employee Position: _____

What are your duties and responsibilities?_____

_____

_____

What are the strengths of the business? _____

_____

_____

What are the weaknesses of the business?_____

_____

_____

What do you like about the company? _____

_____

_____

What don't you like about the company? _____

_____

_____

What would you like to see changed? _____

_____

_____

_____

Why would you like to see these changes? _____

_____

_____

_____

How can the company be managed more effectively? _____

_____

_____

_____

_____

What other things are important to know about the company? _____

_____

_____

_____

_____

Be alert to any problems that may change your feelings about the purchase, especially any attitude problems. For example, an employee may agree to stay with the company but will hold you hostage for raises the company can't afford. It's often hard to pinpoint such problems in one meeting, but if you are going to have problems, you had better do everything you can to isolate and deal with them early.

The majority of business buyers have great difficulty making a sound decision regarding whether to buy a particular business. The reason usually boils down to lack of meaningful data. If you have the right information and know how to interpret it, the decision will be much simpler.

Interpreting Financial Statements

Your financial analysis is the single most critical factor in determining a go or no-go decision. The two goals of financial analysis are to decipher the actual history of the company's financial performance and to establish a sales price for the business. Without complete and accurate financials, you can't accomplish either goal. A word of caution: what you will learn about financial analysis and valuation here will not replace your need for an accountant experienced in small business concerns.

The two primary financial records you will need are a balance sheet and an income statement, also called a profit and loss statement. The company's tax returns are an excellent way to verify these financial statements. Do not go ahead with a business purchase unless, as a contingency, the seller agrees to release tax returns to you at some point before the deal is final. In cases where some or all of these documents are not available, proceed with extreme caution. Discuss the situation with your lawyer as well as with your accountant.

The Balance Sheet

The difference between current assets and current liabilities gives you a picture of the company's cash position, or liquidity. *Liquidity* is the working capital that every company needs to manage cash flow effectively. A balance sheet can tell you if the company has enough cash to run the business, what the assets are, and how the assets compare to the liabilities. The balance sheet also tells you how much unused debt capacity is available.

The Income Statement

The income statement compares the company's revenue to its costs. The operating expenses tell you what is happening to the cash generated by the business. These expenses will be reviewed later to determine the true owner benefit. Many small business owners have all kinds of personal expenses or perks embedded in the operating expenses.

Study the sample balance sheet and sample income statement given here. The company is a very small service company—a sole proprietorship with one commissioned sales representative. Ask yourself the following questions:

1. Is the company profitable?
2. Is it carrying too much debt?
3. Does the cost of sales seem high, low, or about right?
4. Are there operating costs that are missing?
5. Do you see any operating expenses that seem out of line?

6. Would you classify this company as a high-profit organization worthy of consideration?

Review the sample Balance Sheet and Income Statement. Determine the answers to the preceding six questions. In some cases, these questions cannot be answered unless you know how the performance of the company compares with others in the same industry. Refer to the section on financial ratios in chapter 2 for information on evaluating performance.

Sample Balance Sheet of a Service Company

Year Ending December 31, 19__

ASSETS

Current Assets	
Cash	$ 3,000
Accounts Receivable	9,500
Total Current Assets	$ 12,500
Fixed Assets	
Equipment	$ 9,000
Vehicle	12,500
Less Accumulated Depreciation	(10,000)
Net Fixed Assets	$ 11,500
Other Assets	
Long-Term Contract	8,000
Total Assets	$ 32,000

LIABILITIES AND STOCKHOLDERS' EQUITY

Current Liabilities	
Note Payable–Vehicle	$ 2,500
Accounts Payable	1,000
Total Current Liabilities	$ 3,500
Long-Term Debt	
(less Current Payments)	$ 0
Total Liabilities	$ 3,500
Stockholders' Equity	
Retained Earnings	$ 7,500
Current Earnings	21,000
Total Stockholders' Equity	$ 28,500
Total Liabilities and Stockholders' Equity	$ 32,000

Sample Income Statement of a Service Company

Year Ending December 31, 19___

SALES	$250,000
Cost of Sales	0
Printing	80,000
Commissions	45,000
Gross Profit	125,000
OPERATING EXPENSES	
Bad Debt	2,500
Advertising	1,000
Depreciation	4,000
Insurance	1,000
Utilities/Maintenance	500
Interest	300
Telephone	1,500
Legal/Accounting Fees	500
Office Supplies	4,000
Vehicle Expense	1,500
Travel/Entertainment	8,000
Miscellaneous	1,000
Total Operating Expenses	25,800
Income Before Taxes	99,200
Provision for Income Tax	3,000
Net Income	$ 96,200

Here are the answers to the questions on the sample service company:

1. Is the company profitable? *Yes.*

2. Is it carrying too much debt? *No.*

3. Does the cost of sales seem high, low, or about right? *High.*

4. Are there operating costs which are missing? *Rent.*

5. Question the owner closely on the Bad Debt figure. Is it a one-time expense? What has the history been over the past five years? Question Travel and Entertainment, also. Is any part of the total really a personal expense?

6. Is this a high-profit company worthy of your consideration? *Yes.*

Whenever you evaluate a company's recent performance record, also be sure to review the prior five years. Knowing their past performance is essential. Last year's track record may not be typical. You need to know the answers to these questions:

▷ Has the company been consistently profitable?

▷ Has the company been growing steadily?

▷ Are operating expenses consistent from year to year?

Owner Benefit Analysis

The true value of a small business is directly related to its capability to generate profit for the owner. To obtain an accurate figure that reflects the actual benefit to the owner, you must readjust the company financial statements. You must extract the direct benefits to the owner that are hidden in the business expenses. This figure is known as *owner benefit*, also sometimes called *seller's discretionary cash*. It's the total of all of the financial benefits accrued by the owner.

The owner benefit figure is the basis for most business valuation formulas. In order to establish that figure, you must reconstruct or adjust the income statement to reflect the true cash flow picture.

Obtaining a true picture of the owner benefit in a small company is sometimes difficult. Business owners try to shelter as much as possible. That's why you will often see company-owned cars, high travel expenses, relatives on the payroll who do little work, unusually high legal and accounting costs, and other questionable expenses on the income statement. When you prepare an adjusted income statement to find the true owner benefit of a company, you will have constructed a before-and-after income statement. The actual, or before, statement was constructed for tax purposes. The adjusted, or after, statement reflects the actual profit to the owner.

Study the following example to understand how to determine true owner benefit. It includes a sample balance sheet and income statement to work from; a worksheet to use to adjust the income statement to reconstruct the owner benefit; and a sample, completed owner benefit worksheet derived from the sample financials, including explanations of all adjustments.

Sample Balance Sheet

Year Ending December 31, 19___

ASSETS

Current Assets	
Cash	$ 2,000
Accounts Receivable	17,500
Inventory	312,000
Due from Officers	200,500
Total Current Assets	532,000
Equipment	
Leasehold Improvements	24,500
Auto	45,000
Equipment	250,000
Less Accumulated Depreciation	(150,000)
Net Property & Equipment	169,500
Other Assets	
Real Estate	375,000
Total Assets	$1,076,500

LIABILITIES AND STOCKHOLDERS' EQUITY

Current Liabilities	
Notes Payable	$ 200,000
Long-Term Debt	
(Current Payments)	50,000
Accounts Payable	300,000
Accrued Taxes	110,000
Total Current Liabilities	660,000
Long-Term Debt	
(Less current payments)	300,000
Total Liabilities	960,000
Stockholders' Equity	

Common Stock, No Par Value,	
250 Shares Authorized,	
Issued and Outstanding	30,000
Retained Earnings	86,500
Total Stockholders' Equity	116,500
Total Liabilities and Stockholders' Equity	$1,076,500

Sample Income Statement

Year Ending December 31, 19__

SALES	$2,000,000
Cost of Sales	1,200,000
Gross Profit	800,000
OPERATING EXPENSES	
Salaries	250,000
Consulting/Contracting	25,000
Payroll Taxes	17,000
Lease Payments	35,000
Utilities	12,000
Telephone	6,000
Advertising	30,000
Repairs	2,000
Insurance	9,000
Travel/Entertainment	41,000
Depreciation	60,000
Auto Expense	20,000
Taxes	7,000
Office Supplies	14,000
Shipping	19,000
Legal/Accounting Fees	3,000
Dues & Subscriptions	1,000
Miscellaneous	3,000
Total Operating Expenses	$ 554,000
Other Expenses	
Interest	150,000
Income Before Taxes	$ 96,000

Worksheet for Adjusted Income Statement

For Year _____ *Ending* _____

SALES   _____

  Cost of Sales   _____
  Other Income   _____
Gross Profit   _____

OPERATING EXPENSES

	Actual	Nonrecurring/ Owner Benefit	Normal Expense
Advertising	_____	_____	_____
Bad Debts	_____	_____	_____
Bank Charges	_____	_____	_____
Car/Transportation	_____	_____	_____
Commissions	_____	_____	_____
Consulting	_____	_____	_____
Contributions	_____	_____	_____
Depreciation	_____	_____	_____
Dues/Publications	_____	_____	_____
Employee Benefits	_____	_____	_____
Insurance	_____	_____	_____
Interest	_____	_____	_____
Legal/Prof. Fees	_____	_____	_____
Office Supplies	_____	_____	_____
Payroll	_____	_____	_____
Payroll Taxes	_____	_____	_____
Rent/Lease	_____	_____	_____
Repairs/Maintenance	_____	_____	_____
Shipping	_____	_____	_____
Taxes	_____	_____	_____
Telephone	_____	_____	_____
Travel/Entertainment	_____	_____	_____
Utilities	_____	_____	_____
_____	_____	_____	_____
_____	_____	_____	_____
Totals	_____	_____	_____
Net Profit	_____	_____	_____
Owner Benefit		_____	

On the worksheet of the adjusted income statement, you will see four entries at the top of the worksheet: *Sales, Cost of Sales, Other Income*, and *Gross Profit*. Record those figures from the actual income statement.

You will see a list under the heading *Operating Expenses*, with three blank columns directly to the right of each item. Go through the operating expenses on the income statement, line item by line item, and record the actual amount listed in the column titled "Actual." Note that the categories are in alphabetical order and that they are more extensive than in the sample income statement. The blank lines at the end of the list are included for you to add categories not covered on the form.

Using the figures from the Actual column, your task is to determine if the expense is a normal cost to run the business that would most likely recur under new ownership. If so, you will record the same number in the third column, "Normal Expense."

The middle column, "Nonrecurring or Owner Benefit," is where you record the cash that was of direct benefit to the owner. As you go through the expenses, isolate what could reasonably be called either owner benefit (those expenses which are not necessary business expenses) or expenses which are unusual, one-time costs that are not likely to recur in the future.

Depreciation is a concept that is often misunderstood. Essentially, depreciation is a dollar amount that is set aside to replace assets that wear out. However, most businesses do not actually set the money aside. It's allowed as a legitimate cost of doing business, even though no cash is paid out. Because it is a cash benefit to the owner, record the depreciation figure as owner benefit.

Now you can see why you need excellent rapport with the current owner. Without it, you will have a difficult time determining what is really owner benefit. Because the owner has a vested interest in showing you how profitable the business has been, you should have little trouble getting cooperation, assuming you have done a good job of creating trust.

Typical areas where you should look for owner benefits are salaries, benefits, payroll taxes, vehicle expense, pension and profit sharing, personal travel and entertainment, and disability and health insurance.

Adjusted Income Statement

*For Sample Year Ending*_____

SALES	$2,000,000
Cost of Sales	1,200,000
Other Income	0
Gross Profit	800,000

OPERATING EXPENSES

	Actual	Nonrecurring/ Owner Benefit	Normal Expense
Advertising	30,000	_____	30,000
Bad Debts			
Bank Charges			
Car/Transportation	20,000	20,000	
Commissions			
Consulting	25,000	25,000	
Contributions			
Depreciation	60,000	60,000	
Dues/Publications	1,000	750	250
Employee Benefits			
Insurance	9,000	5,000	4,000
Interest	150,000		150,000
Legal/Professional Fees	3,000		3,000
Office Supplies	14,000	7,000	7,000
Payroll	250,000	150,000	100,000
Payroll Taxes	17,000	12,000	5,000
Rent/Lease	35,000		35,000
Repairs/Maintenance	2,000	1,0000	1,000
Shipping	19,000		19,000
Taxes	7,000	3,000	4,000
Telephone	6,000		6,000
Travel/Entertainment	41,000	20,000	21,000
Utilities	12,000	7,000	5,000
Misc.	3,000		3,000
Totals	704,000	310,750	393,250
Net Profit	96,000		
Owner Benefit	406,750		

This completed adjusted income statement worksheet shows the true cash benefit to the owner for the sample financials given. Here's an explanation of the owner benefit analysis:

▷ Advertising costs are a normal operating expense, and $30,000 was spent. There was no benefit to the owner personally.

▷ The owner leases his new Jaguar through the company. The automobile is not used for business purposes. It's a perk to the owner and is therefore listed in the owner benefit column.

▷ The $25,000 consulting fee was spent for assistance in developing a five-year marketing plan. As it's a one-time cost that will not recur as an operating expense, it's listed in the nonrecurring column.

▷ Depreciation is one of the benefits of business ownership.

▷ Under dues/publications, only $250 was actual business expense. The other $750 was for books and computer software used by the owner's family.

▷ Of the $9,000 insurance figure, $5,000 was health, life, and disability insurance on the business owner.

▷ Under office supplies, half of the amount was for personal purchases.

▷ The owner and his spouse paid themselves $150,000 out of payroll. The spouse, by the way, spent little time at the business.

▷ Half of the repair/maintenance account was personal.

▷ Note the tax in two categories that are owner benefit.

▷ Of the $41,000 spent on travel and entertainment, $20,000 was personal.

▷ Utility costs were $5,000 for the business; $7,000 were costs associated with operating a second business on the premises. Because that business was running at a substantial loss, the owner allocated the $7,000 figure to his highly profitable business in order to get the deduction. That $7,000 is a nonrecurring expense for any new owner.

The next step is to total each of the three columns. The sum of column one (Actual) will always equal the combined sums of columns two (Nonrecurring/Owner Benefit) and three (Normal). To find the total owner benefit, add the company's net profit and the total of column two (Nonrecurring/Owner Benefit). The net profit is the gross profit less the actual operating expenses (column one).

To summarize, the net profit added to the nonrecurring or owner benefit expenses equals the total owner benefit. This total is the available cash you have to work with, and, it's the figure you need to plug into small business valuation formulas in order to determine a selling price for the business.

Remember this: Don't ever take the financials at face value. A company may be far more profitable than the financial statements indicate. The reverse may also be true.

Valuing a Business

Now that you have a working knowledge of financial statements and the real story they tell, you're ready to establish the market value of your target company in order to arrive at a fair sales price. Valuing a company is not a precise science. Many tangible and intangible factors must be considered to reach a reasonable sales price for a business.

Your purpose here is to establish a ballpark market price from which you and the seller can negotiate a final selling price that both parties can live with. No matter what the final sales price is, there are three fundamental factors to consider:

1. **The company must have the capability of servicing the debt from cash flow.** Typically, buyers will carry debt of between one-half to two-thirds of the purchase price. Any business that you are considering that cannot service the debt is a bad investment, no matter how attractive it may be in other respects. The "Rule of Two-Thirds" states that if the business will not support a debt service of two-thirds of the purchase price, pass or lower the purchase price. This rule of thumb assumes a down payment of one-third. Even if you are putting down more, the business still should generate enough profit to cover two-thirds of the sales price; otherwise, you are paying too much.

2. **The company must give you a reasonable return on your down payment.** After all, if you placed that amount in some other investment vehicle, you would expect a reasonable return.

3. **The company must give you a living wage.** How much you need to live on is, of course, a personal matter. However, a defensible figure for a living wage is approximately equal to what you would have to pay a manager to run the company.

If the cash flow will cover these basic three factors, you have found an attractive company to consider.

The valuation formulas that follow are meant for small, privately held firms. Always value a company several times by using different valuation methods in order to confirm your proposed figure. Remember, no matter what valuation method is used, arriving at an accurate market value always depends on an accurate analysis of the company's cash flow. And be sure to check any valuation with your accountant before presenting an offer to the owner.

Asset Valuation

The first formula is called asset valuation. Use this formula when the company is asset intensive. For an asset valuation, first you must have the value of the company's fixed assets and furniture, fixtures, and equipment that were purchased. The value can be looked at in four ways: replacement value, scrap or liquidation value, depreciated value, and market value.

What you need to know is the market value of the fixed assets and equipment. Market value is the price you would pay if you were to buy each asset or piece of equipment on the open market at a price experts in the industry would agree is reasonable.

To compute an asset valuation, add the market value of fixed assets and equipment to the value of leasehold improvements. Leasehold improvements are additions, modifications, upgrades, renovations, or other changes to the physical property that would be considered part of the property should you not renew a lease or sell the property. You will find the leasehold improvements, if there are any, listed in the financials.

Next, add the wholesale value of inventory, including raw materials, work in progress, and finished goods or products.

To this figure, add in the total owner benefit that you calculated in your adjusted income statement. The final total is the sale price.

The asset valuation is the total of the fair market value of fixed assets and equipment, leasehold improvements, inventory, and one year's owner benefit. This calculation can be stated as the following equation:

$$FMV/FA + LHI + OB + I = MV$$

FMV/FA is the fair market value of the fixed assets.
LFI is the leasehold improvements.
OB is the owner benefit.
I is the inventory.
MV is the market value of the business.

Earlier we analyzed a sample balance sheet and income statement and developed a sample adjusted income statement. Using that same sample, extract the appropriate figures to develop an asset valuation. Here's how it would look:

FMV/FA	=	$169,500
LHI	=	$ 24,500
OB	=	$406,750
I	=	$312,000

Therefore: 169,500 + 24,500 + 406,750 + 312,000 = 912,750. The market value of the business according to asset valuation is $912,750.

Notice that the depreciated value of the furniture, fixtures, and equipment was taken directly from the balance sheet. In reality, the actual market value may be somewhat more or less. Note that the real estate recorded on the balance sheet was not included. In cases where the real estate is part of the sale, its market value would be added. In this case, as in all of these formulas, we are valuing the business alone, not the real estate.

Capitalization of Income Valuation

The second valuation method is called the capitalization of income formula. This method places no value on the equipment and other fixed assets. The assumption is that they have no value other than the ability to produce income for the company. Service companies are often valued using this method.

This valuation method acknowledges the business's intangible value, or goodwill. Because goodwill is subjective, it's difficult to place a number on its value. The first requirement is to reduce the intangible value of a business to a list of factors that affect its value. These are called the capitalization of income rate multiplier factors, and they will help you derive your final formula. The trick is to place an appropriate value on each of these factors.

Rate each of these twelve factors on a scale of 0 to 5, with 5 being the highest, most positive score:

1. **The owner's reason for selling.** The more urgent the reason, the lower the score.

2. **The length of time the company has been in business.** Obviously, the longer, the better.

3. **The length of time the current owner has owned the business.** Again, longevity gets a high score.

4. **Degree of risk.** High-risk businesses, such as restaurants or retail stores, score low marks.

5. **Profitability.** Does the company show acceptable and consistent profit margins for the last five years? (Remember, profit in a small business is owner benefit.)

6. **Business location.** Is the company in the right area of the country and the right part of town? Do employees and customers find the location attractive? Is there an adequate employee pool?

7. **Growth history.** Have gross revenues shown acceptable increases over the last five years?

8. **Competition.** Are there few or many competing companies? Does the company have a competitive advantage?

9. **Entry barriers.** How easy is it for competitors to enter the market?

10. **Future potential for the industry.** Is it growing, stable, or declining?

11. **Customer base.** What is the percentage of repeat business? Referrals? Is the customer list diverse? Growing?

12. **Technology.** Does the company have trained personnel, state-of-the-art equipment, and high quality standards?

You will find it impossible to assign an intelligent value to each of these factors unless you've done your homework and know both the industry and your target company extremely well.

Now, total the figures and divide by twelve. The resulting figure is the multiplier that plugs into the formula.

Next, take the owner benefit figure and multiply it by 75 percent (.75). The result is what is called "buyer's discretionary cash," what you will have after allocating 25 percent of the cash thrown off by the business to service debt.

To arrive at the selling price, the final step is to multiply the buyer's discretionary cash by the multiplier. For example, let's assign a multiplier of 3 to the sample business we've been using. The capitalization of income valuation of the business would be computed as follows:

Cap Rate x BDC = MV

Cap Rate is the multiplier.
BDC is the buyer's discretionary cash.
MV is the market value of the business.

If you use the same financial data as when valuing the business using asset valuation, the number would look like this:

Cap Rate   =   3
OB   = $406,750
BDC   =   75% x 406,750 = 305,062.50

Thus, 3 x 305,062.50 = 915,187.50. The market value of the business according to this formula is $915,187.50.

Owner Benefit Valuation

Here's another formula that focuses on the owner benefit. It's called the owner benefit valuation, and it's used to value businesses whose primary value comes from an ability to generate cash flow and profit.

To use this formula, start with the owner benefit and multiply it by debt service. Remember that the standard figure for debt service is 25 percent. Divide that number by 1.1, which is a standard for return on investment. The formula assumes that if you put that amount of money in a relatively safe investment, you could assume a 10 percent return.

The resulting figure is then divided by 0.3, which gives you the sales price. The 0.3 figure comes from an assumption that most buyers will allow about one-third of the owner benefit for their living wage.

You don't have to go through each step to make this formula work. Simply multiply the owner benefit by a composite factor of 2.2727 and presto—you have the sales price.

The equation is this simple:

OB x 2.2727 = MV

OB is the owner benefit.
2.2727 is the composite multiplier to adjust for return on investment, living wage, and debt service.
MV is the market value of the business.

Plugging in the owner benefit of $406,750 from our example, the market value would be figured as 406,750 x 2.2727 = 924,420.72. The market value of the business according to this formula would be $924,420.72.

Industry Multiplier Valuation

The fourth formula is actually a long list of formulas that apply to specific industries. They are called industry multipliers. Although remarkably accurate in some situations, they tend to take an overly simplistic view of business worth. Nevertheless, these formulas are useful for nailing down a rough selling price in some cases. Here's a list of some common ones:

Advertising Agencies	.75 x Annual Gross Sales
Building Supply Retailers	.25 to .75 x Annual Net Profit + Inventory + Equipment
Collection Agencies	.15 to .2 x Annual Collections + Equipment
Employment Agencies	.75 x Annual Gross Sales
Fast Food (Non-Franchise)	.5 to .7 x Monthly Gross Sales + Inventory
Food Distributors	1 to 1.5 x Annual Net Profit + Inventory + Equipment
Insurance Agencies	1 to 2 x Annual Renewal Commissions
Job Shops	.5 x Annual Gross Sales + Inventory
Manufacturing	1.5 to 2.5 x Annual Net Profit + Inventory or .75 x Annual Net (including work in progress)
Profit + Equipment x Inventory Newspapers	.75 to 1.5 x Annual Gross Sales
Office Supply Distributors	.5 x Monthly Gross Sales + Inventory
Printers	.4 to .5 x Annual Net Profit + Inventory + Equipment
Professional Practices	1 to 5 x Annual Net Profit
Real Estate Agencies	.2 to .3 x Annual Gross Commissions
Rental Agencies	.2 x Annual Net Profit + Inventory
Restaurants	.3 to .5 x Annual Gross Sales or .4 x Monthly Gross Sales + Inventory
Retail Businesses	.75 to 1.5 x Annual Net Profit + Inventory + Equipment
Sales Businesses	1 x Annual Net Profit
Travel Agencies	.05 to .1 x Annual Gross Sales

After you become comfortable with the valuation formulas, try them out on a prospective company. Use all of the different formulas. More often than not, you will arrive at about the same figure using several of the formulas, although sometimes one may give you a result wildly different from the others. If two or more formulas result in roughly the same selling price, you have a good indicator that your valuation is on target.

Before you settle on a price, it's a good idea to do a valuation of your prospective company for each of the last three years. Last year's figures may be an anomaly. In an unstable or developing market, revenue swings may dramatically affect the business.

Making the Deal

The completion of your financial analysis and valuation is an important step in deciding whether to buy a business. But remember that the seller must make an equally important decision—whether to sell. That decision will be heavily influenced by how well you present your case.

Arriving at a point where both sides leave the table feeling that a fair and equitable arrangement has been negotiated is the result of executing a well-planned strategy. No matter how proficient you may be in presenting your case in person, back it up with a written proposal. There are several reasons to do this:

▷ The owner won't remember most of what you said. Later, when the owner is contemplating your offer, the probability is high that your most compelling arguments will be forgotten.

▷ Because most owners will look for advice from both professional and personal sources, a written proposal is a strong visual aid to help convince skeptical advisors that the deal is a good one.

▷ A written proposal presents you as a business professional. Not one person in a hundred will go to the trouble of creating a powerful business proposal such as yours.

The Offer

An "offer to purchase," also called a "letter of intent," is a proposal that outlines your thinking regarding the key issues of the purchase. The most significant issue you must address in your letter of intent is the proposed purchase price.

Before you begin, decide on the top price that you are willing to pay and under what terms you will pay. If the seller's asking price ends up exceeding that figure, resolve to walk away. Your initial position on a selling price should be somewhat less than the top price you would eventually agree to pay. Starting with a proposed sale price of 25 percent below what you are willing to pay will give you room to negotiate.

State the amount of any promissory note and the duration and interest rate for that note. Ask that the length of the note run twice as long as the time you are actually willing to accept. Request an interest rate of 50 percent below what you would pay. Propose a down payment of half of what you would really agree to pay. Outline any other specific financial arrangements you are also proposing, such as balloon payments, a percentage of future revenue or profits, or a performance bonus.

Remember that cash is king. The more up-front cash you can offer, the more power you have to lower the purchase price. Also remember that a dollar is not a dollar. Tax laws have a substantial impact on the real dollars the seller will take home. Use your professional advisors to devise creative ways of putting more actual dollars in the seller's pocket, while minimizing the impact on you.

In addition to the sales price and payment terms, there are a host of other issues that are important to resolve if the deal is going to fly. These additional issues are commonly referred to as "contingencies of the sale."

In your letter of intent, you should indicate that the sale is predicated on the satisfactory resolution of certain contingencies. Then list them. The specifics of resolving these contingencies will be the subject of future negotiations. Each situation will demand different contingencies. Here are some common ones:

▷　The employment arrangement with the seller, if appropriate.

▷　The duration and extent of the noncompete agreement with the seller if he or she is leaving the company.

▷　The assignment of the lease.

▷　The allocation of the purchase price for tax purposes.

▷　A satisfactory review of the company's books and records.

▷　An examination of insurance policies.

▷　Agreements with key employees to stay on.

▷　Evidence that key customers won't defect.

▷　Assurances by the seller that he or she is responsible for liability claims up to the sale date.

▷　The length and terms of any training period.

In your letter of intent, propose a small binder, if the offer is accepted, to ensure that the business is not sold to someone else and to demonstrate that you are a serious buyer.

After you have decided on the details of your initial offer and created a draft of your letter of intent, give copies to your accountant and lawyer for their input. Include their changes when you prepare the final document.

Later, if the deal goes through, your lawyer will prepare a formal purchase and sales agreement, the legal document that transfers ownership. However, the initial offer to purchase should be written by you. Preparing this offer will force you to think through the details, and, therefore, help you to be thoroughly prepared to make your oral presentation.

See the sample letter of intent. Read it carefully and use it as a starting point for your own document.

Sample Letter of Intent

Anne Beck, President
Prescott Systems Inc.
42 Harding Road
Allentown, PA 18101

April 27, 19___

Dear Anne:

I appreciate the time and energy you've expended to supply the information I've requested over the last few weeks. It's been very helpful in making a solid business decision about the possible purchase of your business. I've constructed a purchase proposal which I feel meets both of our needs and at the same time reflects the market value of your business. The purchase price, terms, and conditions are described below.

Purchase Price:
Base price–$100,000; Performance bonus–$50,000.
The performance bonus will become part of the total purchase price when and if Prescott Systems' profit before taxes and before provision for buyer's compensation and fringe benefits equals or exceeds 7 percent of net sales for three years from the date of purchase. Otherwise, the total purchase price shall be $100,000.

Payment Terms:
Payment of $50,000 at closing. The remainder of the base price ($50,000) will be repaid in the form of a note taken back by the seller. The note payments shall be paid quarterly for a term of four years. The first payment shall be due ninety days after closing. The interest rate shall be 10 percent, based on a four-year amortization schedule, with no prepayment penalties. If the performance bonus is payable, a second note shall be written on January 1, 19- for $50,000. Interest and terms of payment shall be the same as for the first note.

Conditions:

The purchase of the business is subject to the following conditions:

1. Buyer shall purchase the assets of the company and form a new corporation bearing the same company name.

2. Buyer shall pledge the assets of the new corporation as collateral for the note or notes.

3. Buyer and seller shall develop a mutually agreeable employment contract between the seller and the new corporation.

4. A covenant not to compete, satisfactory to the buyer, shall be drafted.

5. The existing lease shall be assigned to the new corporation with essentially the same terms and conditions.

6. The existing line of credit with Consolidated Banking Corp. shall be transferred to the new corporation under terms satisfactory to the buyer.

7. A profit-sharing plan satisfactory to buyer and seller will be developed.

8. Upon acceptance of this offer, seller agrees to allow the buyer and his agents to communicate with customers, employees, and vendors.

9. This offer is subject to revision if the buyer or his agents are not satisfied with this offer agreement, the purchase and sales agreement, the company books and records, or any information from any other source which could change the buyer's assessment of the worth or desirability of the business.

10. Life insurance shall be secured by the new corporation on the buyer's life with the seller as the only beneficiary. The amount shall equal or exceed the amount due under the terms of the purchase and sales agreement.

11. Upon acceptance of this offer, the buyer shall pay a $10,000 good faith deposit to a law firm designated by the seller. Said deposit shall be held in escrow and shall be returned to the buyer if this agreement is not executed within ten days.

12. If this offer is accepted, the buyer shall apply the total amount held in escrow as partial payment of the down payment. The date of closing shall be no later than sixty days from the date of this offer.

Sincerely,

J. Welch

Agreement:

Your signature below indicates your agreement to the above.

Signature: _____   Date: _____

Presentation

Negotiating the sale of a business is complex. Think carefully about whether you have the ability to do the actual negotiating yourself. If you have a good relationship with the seller and you are both willing to put a deal together, the two of you will do a better job at striking a deal than any outsider could. On the other hand, if you don't have a working knowledge of law and taxes, it's wise to have your lawyer available. Whatever you do, make it clear that all decisions are subject to the approval of your accountant and lawyer.

If you are to negotiate effectively, you must know where you are going and have a strategy for getting there. These are the steps you must take to prepare for the negotiations:

1. **Prepare a list of every conceivable issue that could be raised by you or by the seller.** Ask your advisors what you've left out.

2. **Write down your position on each issue and your justification for that position.** Base your arguments on logic rather than emotion.

3. **Place yourself in the seller's position and write out every possible objection.** Include emotional arguments as well as logical ones. Write out your response to every argument that the seller might have.

4. **Draw up a list of benefits that the seller will gain when he or she sells the business.** Include in this list not only the monetary pluses but also the less obvious psychological rewards. Remember, the seller's decision will be made with the heart as well as the head.

5. **Create an outline of what you think will happen.** Role-play it with a friend. Practice it again and again. If possible, videotape your performance and evaluate it after you're done.

6. **Establish a proposed agenda and time limit for each negotiating session.** Don't waste time by not knowing exactly what is to be accomplished.

Now it's time for the real thing. Always deliver your offer in person. Schedule a meeting where you won't be interrupted. Sit down and explain your proposal in detail to the seller. Don't ever waste time negotiating with the wrong person. Many would-be buyers never succeed in arranging the sale because they're not negotiating with the person who has the power and the authority to cut a deal. Deal directly with the owner, or with someone who has the express authority to negotiate this sale.

Advance your proposal by documenting with logical arguments why the deal is reasonable and fair. Have the facts available to support your case. If you can document why your position on any issue is rational and reasonable, there's a good chance you can persuade the seller to see it your way.

Don't expect to reach a final agreement at this first meeting. Indicate that you understand that the seller needs time to digest your proposal. Make certain that each issue is understood and then agree on a date for your next meeting. Don't push.

Negotiation Strategies

Meeting number two is the event where the action really begins. The seller will hold center stage for the first part of this meeting. Just listen. And don't be surprised if the seller sees the deal very differently than you. Remember that at this stage of negotiations, differences of opinion are neither good nor bad; there's no right or wrong. Also, keep in mind that for an owner who started the business, there are many personal issues involved in the negotiations. Your goal at this point is to identify the issues that need to be resolved.

After the seller has offered a counterproposal, clarify anything you don't understand. Then go through the proposals together and see where you agree and where you disagree. After you've identified where you both are in agreement and you've isolated the issues that need to be negotiated, point out that perhaps you are closer to an agreement than you originally thought.

Start by resolving the easy issues. Save the hardest ones for last. Starting with the small differences of opinion that can be quickly settled creates an atmosphere of solid progress, and invariably, you will uncover information you can use in later negotiations.

After the easy issues are behind you, define the tough issues that still must be resolved. Direct the focus from attacking each other to attacking the problem. Draw the seller into a partnership in which together you design solutions for mutual problems. Successful negotiation lies in understanding what the other side wants and finding a way to get as close to it as possible. End this session on a positive note by emphasizing your willingness to work with the seller to resolve the tough issues together.

Before your next negotiation session, meet with your advisors and brainstorm options for resolving the key issues. Devise as many solutions as possible. The more opportunities you can give the seller to say "yes," the more likely you will be to reach an agreement.

Remember that the stated issue is not always the real issue, and the first offer is never the final offer. Focus on the interests of the seller rather than on his or her stated position. If you can find a creative way to satisfy these interests, the seller will give way.

In your next negotiating session, start by recapping the issues on which you have already reached agreement. Then begin to attack the major issues. Use solid evidence to support your case, but keep an open mind. If things begin to get hot, back off and tackle another issue.

Never issue ultimatums. If the seller becomes angry, don't defend your ideas. Instead, invite feedback and suggestions. Recast an attack on you as an attack on the problem. Ask for help in shaping a solution. Remember, your relationship to the seller is everything. If it's bad, facts and logic are meaningless. If it's good, together you can move the earth.

If you can't seem to make progress on an issue, sometimes it makes sense to bring in an outsider to help you reach an agreement. The best candidate is a neutral third party. This person could be an accountant or a lawyer who is experienced in negotiating business deals.

Negotiating a good deal is a lot of work, and emotions often run high on both sides. But if you use the strategy outlined here and truly commit yourself to creating a win-win solution, chances are you will come away having purchased your dream business.

Taking Charge

After the deal is concluded, you need to prepare for taking charge of the business. It is important that you prepare for the change in ownership. There are a number of things that you should plan to do:

Set a date for takeover. In many ways, the best time to make the change is on the last workday of the week. There are a number of reasons for this tactic. You can start the new week fresh. Employees can have a less stressful weekend because they won't be wondering what the new boss is going to be like. Also, the end of most work weeks is less busy than the start of a new week.

Meet with the previous owner. Sometimes the previous owner will remain involved with the business. Now is the time to begin your working relationship with that person. Discuss your daily involvement and duties, along with those of the previous owner. When the owner is no longer going to be involved, this meeting should focus on the key information you need to take charge of the business.

Secure access to facilities. Get the keys and any security codes needed to access the company's facilities. Often these will be exchanged when the legal papers finalizing the purchase are signed.

Meet with key employees. It is important to retain the services of key employees. Meet with each one individually. Share your goals and ideas about the business. Assure them of their importance. Ask for their ideas about how to help the change proceed uneventfully.

Meet with key customers. When a business changes ownership, customers can be rightfully concerned. They wonder how the change in ownership will affect their relationship to the company. Meet with them to answer questions and assure them of continued good service and quality.

Communicate with all stakeholders. There are many people who have a stake in your business: employees, customers, other business owners, and government leaders, just to name a few. Prepare a letter or brochure that communicates your vision for the company. Explain what changes you expect to occur. This strategy opens channels of communication that can help you avoid potential problems during the change of ownership.

Take an inventory. Make sure that all office furniture, equipment, supplies, products, records, and other critical items are in place. Most people are honest, but it is important to verify that what you bought is in your possession.

Review all business records. No matter how thoroughly you research a business, there are always surprises you will discover after taking over ownership. The sooner you delve into the details of the business, the better. Ask key employees to help you in this review.

Plan to spend the first few days and weeks at your newly purchased business getting to know more about the company. It is advisable not to make critical changes until you have an opportunity to learn more about the company. Your first few weeks or months at the company should be considered a learning period. Gradually, the business will take on more of your personality. Don't rush the process. Most of all, enjoy the experience of being a new business owner.

Buying a Franchise

According to *Webster's Encyclopedic Unabridged Dictionary,* a franchise is permission granted by a manufacturer to a distributor or a retailer to sell his products and the territory to which such permission extends. The legal definition expands this meaning. A franchise may also extend the right to use a predetermined method for marketing products or services through outlets that use a known name or trademark. The International Franchise Association, the major trade association in franchising, defines the term as "a continuing relationship in which the franchisor provides a licensed privilege to do business, plus assistance in organizing, training, merchandising, and management in return for a consideration from the franchise."

There are four basic types of franchises used by businesses in the United States:

Product franchise. Manufacturers use the product franchise to govern how retailers distribute their product. The manufacturer grants a store owner the authority to distribute goods by the manufacturer and allows the owner to use the name and trademark owned by the manufacturer. The store owner must pay a fee or purchase a minimum inventory of stock in return for these rights. Some tire stores are good examples of this type of franchise.

Manufacturing franchises. These types of franchises provide an organization the right to manufacture a product and sell it to the public, using the franchisor's name and trademark. This type of franchise is found most often in the food and beverage industry. Most bottlers of soft drinks receive a franchise from a company and must use its ingredients to produce, bottle, and distribute the soft drinks.

Business opportunity ventures. These ventures typically require that a business owner purchase and distribute the products for one specific company. The company must provide customers or accounts to the business owner, and, in return, the business owner pays a fee or other consideration as compensation. Examples include vending machine routes and distributorships.

Business format franchises. In this most popular form of franchising, a company provides a business owner with a proven method for operating a business using the name and trademark of the company. The company will usually provide a significant amount of assistance to the business owner in starting and managing the company. The business owner pays a fee or royalty in return. Typically, a company also requires the owner to purchase supplies from the company.

Franchising Terms and Definitions

Several terms are commonly used in association with the concept of franchising. If you are interested in purchasing a franchise, you need to be familiar with these terms. The most important ones are defined here for you:

Franchise. A legal agreement that allows one organization with a product, idea, name, or trademark to grant certain rights and information about operating a business to an independent business owner. In return, the business owner (franchisee) pays a fee and royalties to the franchisor.

Franchisor. A company that owns a product, service, trademark, or business format and provides it to a business owner in exchange for a fee and possibly other considerations. A franchisor often establishes the conditions under which a business owner operates but does not control the business or have financial ownership. McDonald's is an example of a franchisor.

Franchisee. A business owner who purchases a franchise from a franchisor and operates a business using the name, product, business format, and other items provided by the franchisor. For example, McDonald's sells a franchise to a franchisee. This purchase allows the franchisee to open and operate a McDonald's fast-food restaurant. Therefore, if you purchase a franchise, you become a franchisee.

Franchise fee. A one-time fee paid by the franchisee to the franchisor. The fee pays for the business concept, rights to use trademarks, management assistance, and other services from the franchisor. This fee gives the franchisee the right to open and operate a business using the franchisor's business ideas and products.

Royalty. A continuous fee paid by the franchisee to the franchisor. The royalty is usually a percent of the gross revenue earned by the franchisee. You must pay this fee as long as you own the franchise.

Franchise trade rule. A law regulated by the Federal Trade Commission that places several legal requirements on franchisors. It requires that franchisors disclose all pertinent information to potential buyers of a franchise. These disclosures provide you with most information needed to make a wise purchasing decision.

Federal Trade Commission (FTC). A commission authorized by the United States Congress to regulate the franchise business. The Federal Trade Commission oversees the implementation of the Franchise Trade Rule and monitors the activities of franchisors. You can register complaints about a franchisor with this agency. Contact the office of your local U.S. Representative or Senator for information about how to register a complaint with the FTC.

Disclosure statement. Sometimes called an offering circular, it is a document that provides information on twenty items required by the FTC. These items are described later in this chapter. The law requires that a franchisor provide a disclosure statement to you when you inquire about purchasing a franchise.

Trademark. A distinctive name or symbol used to distinguish a particular product or service from others. A trademark must be registered with the U.S. Patent and Trademark Office. It can be used exclusively by the owner, and no one else can use it without the owner's permission. Part of a franchise's value is the right to use a recognized trademark.

The Franchisor's Perspective

What motivates a business to offer a franchise? The answer to this question will help you as a potential franchisee to become a more knowledgeable consumer. Understanding the franchisor's perspective can help you do a better job when selecting a franchise and negotiating its purchase. Here are some common reasons why businesses offer franchises:

More rapid expansion. A primary reason for a business to become a franchisor is the capability to expand more rapidly. A lack of capital and a shortage of skilled employees can slow business expansion. The franchisee provides both when a new outlet is opened. A franchisor may assist you in obtaining financing for a new business, but you bear the liability for repayment of the funds. In addition, the franchisor evaluates you on your business experience and management skills. Thus, a franchise operation is a mutually beneficial proposition for both the franchisor and franchisee.

Higher motivation. When a business franchises its operations, it acquires a motivated group of managers. Each manager is an owner and has a high level of motivation for success. Also, a manager is more accountable for actions because the manager as an owner is totally responsible for business outcomes. You should ask the representative of the franchisor why the company wants you to purchase a franchise. If the only benefit you bring is money, then be cautious and look closely at the franchisor's operations.

Capital. Franchising allows a company to raise money without selling an interest in the business. The franchisor uses franchise fees for business expansion. Issuing stock often results in reduced control and less profit per shareholder. Loans are often given with certain provisions attached and cost a significant amount of money in the form of interest paid.

While franchising is an alternative that has many positive benefits for a franchisor, there are also some disadvantages. It is useful to explore some of these drawbacks so that you understand the motivation behind a franchisor's policies.

Image. The name and image of a company are at risk when it is sold to other individuals. Thus, a franchisor often is quite particular about quality and standards that you are expected to meet. Franchisors usually designate very specific business practices that you must follow. The concern over image also helps explain why many franchisors reserve the right to buy back a franchise operation. You can take comfort in the fact that most franchisors want to see you succeed. A good franchisor provides the support necessary to help you achieve success.

Less profitability. Another disadvantage to a franchisor is the sacrifice of profits. A company-owned outlet is often more profitable than a franchise. In addition, the company owns the outlet's assets. You should consider future motivations of a franchisor when purchasing a franchise. Will the franchisor try to buy back a business after you invest the time and energy to make the operation profitable? Look for a franchisor that views the success of a profitable operation as beneficial to both parties.

Potential competition. Franchising a business also has the liability of training competitors. You may learn how a business operates and then decide to replicate the operation under another name. This situation has happened to some franchisors, so it makes others cautious. A good franchisor will try to establish a positive relationship with franchisees to avoid this problem. The restrictions placed on franchisees are usually balanced by rewards in an attempt to retain their loyalty.

As you review a franchise agreement, keep in mind the franchisor's perspective. Look for an agreement that takes a balanced approach. A good franchisor is one that desires to create a relationship where both parties are winners.

The Franchisee's Perspective

It is important to consider the benefits and costs from the franchisee's perspective before you consider the purchase of a franchise. The following benefits provide a good rationale for starting a business by purchasing a franchise:

Lower risks. Most business experts agree that a franchise operation has a lower risk of failure than an independent business. The statistics on this vary depending on the definition of failure. Whatever statistics are used, they consistently suggest that you are more likely to succeed with a franchise than as an independent business.

Established product or service. A franchisor offers you a product or a service that has sold successfully. An independent business is based on both an untried idea and an operation. Three factors will help you predict the potential success of a franchise. The first is the number of franchises that are in operation. The second predictor is how long the franchisor and its franchisees have been in operation. A third factor is the number of franchises that have failed, including those bought back by the franchisor.

Experienced management team. The experience of the franchisor's management team increases the potential for your success. This experience is often conveyed through formal instruction and on-the-job training.

Group purchasing power. It is often possible to obtain lower-cost goods and supplies through the franchisor. Lower costs result from the group purchasing power of all franchises. To protect this benefit, most franchise agreements restrict you from purchasing goods and supplies through other sources.

Name recognition. Established franchisors can offer national or regional name recognition. Although a new franchisor may lack name recognition, one benefit of starting with a new franchisor is the potential to grow as its business and name recognition grow.

Efficiency in operation. Franchisors discover operating and management efficiencies that benefit new franchisees. Operational standards set in place by the franchisor also control quality and uniformity among its franchisees.

Management assistance. A franchisor provides management assistance to you. This help includes—but is not limited to—accounting procedures, personnel management, and facility management. Even if you have experience in these areas, you may not know how to apply your knowledge and skills in a new business. The franchisor helps you to overcome this lack of experience.

Business plan. Most franchisors help you to develop a business plan. Many elements of the plan are standard operating procedures established by the franchisor. Other parts of the plan are customized to meet your personal needs.

Start-up assistance. The most difficult aspect of a new business is its start-up. Few experienced managers know how to set up a new business because they only do it a few times. However, a franchisor has a great deal of experience accumulated from helping its franchisees with start-up. This experience will help reduce mistakes that are costly in both money and time.

Marketing assistance. A franchisor typically offers several marketing advantages. The franchisor can prepare and pay for the development of professional advertising campaigns. Regional or national marketing done by the franchisor benefits all franchisees. In addition, the franchisor can provide advice about how to develop effective marketing programs for your local area. This benefit usually has a cost because many franchisors require franchisees to contribute a percentage of their gross income to a cooperative marketing fund.

Assistance in financing. It is possible for you to receive assistance in financing a new franchise through the franchisor. A franchisor will often make arrangements with a lending institution to lend you money. Lending institutions find that such arrangements can be quite profitable and relatively safe because of the high success rate of franchise operations. You must still accept personal responsibility for the loan, but the franchisor's involvement usually increases the likelihood that a loan will be approved.

Proven system of operation. An attractive feature of most franchises is their proven system of operation, which has been developed and refined by the franchisor. A franchisor with many franchisees will typically have a highly refined system based on the entire experience of all of their operations.

The benefits to purchasing a franchise explain why more than 600,000 franchise operations exist in the United States. However, there are almost 14 million independent businesses. The drawbacks to a franchise help explain this difference in numbers.

Payment of franchise fee. A major drawback to starting a franchise is the initial franchise fee. This fee can range from a few thousand to several hundred thousand dollars. There are two critical matters that should affect your decision about the cost of a franchise. These are whether you can afford the franchise fee and if you can expect a reasonable return on your investment.

Ongoing royalty payments. Franchisors also typically require you to make continuous royalty payments. The payments are a percentage of the gross income from the business. Usually the royalty payment is less than 10 percent. Some franchisees begin to resent the royalty payments after several years because they have developed experience and built a strong customer base. This success often results in a feeling that the business could continue without the assistance of the franchisor. In addition to the royalty payment, franchisors often require a cooperative marketing payment that amounts to a small percentage of gross income.

Conformity to standard operating procedures. It is important to understand that for most franchisors, there is just one way to do things, and that is *their way*. Success results from proven methods of operation, so the franchisor does not want any variations. You may become frustrated when you believe there is a better way to do things.

Inability to make changes readily. A franchisor may prohibit you from selling products or services other than those approved by the franchisor. These restrictions are difficult to follow when you believe that there is strong customer demand for a new or different product. For example, a frozen yogurt franchise owner may want to offer coffee to customers in the winter, but if this product isn't approved by the franchisor, it can't be sold. Franchisors often have a method for making suggestions, but submitting them through channels can be cumbersome and time-consuming. You are subject to decisions made in the central office of the franchisor. As a franchisee, you must be willing to limit your independence as an entrepreneur.

Underfinanced, inexperienced, weak franchisor. It is important to realize that all franchisors are not equal. You may have more to offer the franchisor than the franchisor has to offer you. It is critical that you carefully check the credentials of the franchisor's management team and board of directors. However, do not ignore a franchisor just because the franchisor is new. New franchisors can be a great bargain. How many people wish they could have bought a McDonald's franchise when Ray Kroc first began selling them?

Duration of relationship. Most franchise agreements last for ten to fifteen years. There is typically no way to extricate yourself from a relationship with a franchisor other than to sell the business. Find out what restrictions exist on selling the franchise to another person. Also, determine what conditions must exist to force the franchisor to buy back the operation. Given the permanency of most franchise relationships, you need to ask yourself whether you want to be involved with the franchisor for the rest of your business career.

Dependent on franchisor's success. The success of a franchise is usually dependent on the franchisor's success. Some well-known franchisors have failed, such as Lums and Arthur Treacher's Fish & Chips. When the franchisor fails, the franchisee usually fails. Carefully examine a franchisor's business plans and financial reports. This research will help identify potential weaknesses. However, many problems occur when a franchisor is purchased by a larger corporation or when a new management team is brought in to run the business. When this occurs, the franchisees are unable to control the situation.

Personal Considerations

People who decide to purchase a franchise are typically happy with their decision. A recent Gallup poll found that almost 95 percent of franchisees considered themselves successful and over 75 percent would buy the franchise again if they had to do it over. The growth rate for franchise operations often outpaces the economy. Thus, franchising can be an excellent choice. But is it the right choice for you?

As you review this section, you can assess both your interest in a franchise and financial ability to purchase one. You may find that there are many advantages for you to purchase a franchise. If so, you will find the next section quite useful, and you will learn how to select a franchise.

Franchising is obviously a good choice for many business owners. However, you need to consider several personal issues when deciding whether franchising is the best option for you. You must live for many years with your decision to purchase a franchise, so it is important that you be compatible with this form of business.

EXERCISE 3.7

Franchise Compatibility Worksheet

The following questions will help you explore how well you might fit into a franchise operation. Check each statement that you agree with.

_____   1. I prefer to limit my risk as much as possible.

_____   2. I am willing to operate the business in exact accordance with the instructions of a franchisor.

_____   3. I am willing to forgo sales on new ideas and products because of franchisor restrictions.

_____   4. I am comfortable with sharing my success, including profits, with a franchisor.

_____   5. I enjoy being part of a well-known organization.

_____   6. I feel that I need the management experience and assistance that a franchisor can provide.

_____   7. I need assistance in developing a business plan.

_____   8. I do not feel comfortable with establishing a business from the ground floor up.

_____   9. My experience in marketing is limited, and a franchisor would help overcome this weakness.

_____   10. The help a franchisor provides in financing might make the difference in my ability to start a business.

continued

_____ 11. I am willing to pay a franchise fee to obtain a proven business operation.

_____ 12. I feel comfortable establishing a long-term relationship with a franchisor.

_____ 13. I am comfortable linking my success with the success of the franchisor.

_____ 14. I enjoy selling products and services created by someone else instead of creating my own.

_____ 15. I am willing to purchase goods and services as directed by the franchisor.

Count the number of items that you have checked. Use the scores below to interpret the results.

0-6: Franchising is probably not a good alternative for you.

6-10: Franchising has some attraction, but you have some doubts that need to be carefully considered.

11-15: Franchising appears to be appealing and would probably fit your personal business needs.

It is also important to determine your financial ability to invest in a franchise. This can be more important than your personal compatibility with franchising. There are three tables that follow. Use the first table to evaluate your personal financial status. The second table will help determine the costs that are involved in starting a specific franchise operation. The third table will assist you in calculating the amount of money that you will need for operating capital during the first three months of operation.

Table 3.1

Personal Financial Statement

Assets		Liabilities	
Cash on Hand	$ _____	Accounts Payable	$ _____
Savings Account	_____	Loans Payable	_____
Stocks or Bonds	_____	Contracts Payable	_____
Loans Receivable	_____	Real Estate Loans	_____
Accounts Receivable	_____	Taxes	_____
Real Estate	_____	Other Liabilities	_____
Life Insurance	_____		
Automobiles	_____		
Other Assets	_____		
Total Assets	$ _____	**Total Liabilities**	$ _____

Net Worth (Assets – Liabilities): $ _____

Table 3.2

Start-Up Costs Estimate

Franchise Fee	$ _____
Building Cost (New or Remodeling)	_____
Fixtures and Equipment	_____
Installation of Fixtures/Equipment	_____
Telephone System/Installation	_____
Utility Deposits	_____
Insurance	_____
Attorney, Accountant, and Other Professional Fees	_____
Licenses, Permits	_____
Supplies	_____
Initial Inventory	
Advertising, Promotions	_____
Signs	_____
Vehicles	_____
Other	_____
Total Start-Up Costs $	_____

Table 3.3

Monthly Expenses

Personal Living Expenses	$ _____
Employee Wages	_____
Employee Fringe Benefits & Payroll Taxes	_____
Building Payment/Rent	_____
Maintenance	_____
Utilities	_____
Insurance	_____
Advertising	_____
Supplies	_____
Postage/Shipping	_____
Transportation	_____
Inventory Replacement	_____
Taxes	_____
Royalty Payments	_____
Other _____	_____
Total	$ _____
Total x 3	$ _____

Multiplying by three provides an estimate of the operating capital that you will need. This amount would be enough money to operate for three months without having any income. Some experts recommend that you also plan on six to twelve months for personal living expenses. The reason for this advice is that it may take that long before you can withdraw any money from the business.

Selecting a Franchise

Franchising has been around since the Middle Ages but reached its economic apex in the 1970s in the United States. It has been enjoying a resurgence that started in the late 1980s. The success of franchising has attracted some inexperienced and occasionally fraudulent franchisors. In 1979 the federal government implemented a law to protect consumers from fraudulent franchisors. However, the Latin saying "caveat emptor," or "let the buyer beware," still applies to the purchase of a franchise.

There is a simple process you can use to evaluate a franchise and protect your investment. The process is not foolproof, and misjudgments can still occur. However, following the process will help you avoid disastrous mistakes made by many other people. The steps that are explained will assist you in finding a franchise that is a suitable match for you and has the potential for financial success.

Process for Selecting a Franchise

There are five steps you can follow to select a franchise that has the most potential. The steps are listed in a logical order; however, you may find that it is possible to carry out more than one step at a time. These steps represent a process based on models frequently proposed in books and articles about franchises.

The first step is to identify potential franchises. There are an estimated 3,000 franchises. In most types of businesses, you will find several franchise opportunities. For example, if you have an interest in a particular type of business, such as a donut shop, you will find at least sixteen franchisors. This number is based on information found in the *Franchise Opportunities Handbook*, published by JIST Works. There are other directories that you can use to expand your search, along with some magazines that periodically publish lists of franchisors. You can also consult several Websites on the Internet that list franchisors. Refer to the resources section at the back of the book for specific sources of information.

You should contact and compare all possible franchise choices. This research gives you an opportunity to review the costs and benefits provided for each franchisor. You will probably want to narrow the possible alternatives to a finalist group of no more than five. This group of finalists should represent those that you want to consider seriously. You need to complete the next four steps with each franchisor.

The second step is to collect specific information about each franchisor. It is important to obtain thorough information from each franchisor about the franchise. In fact, the federal government and several states have laws stipulating the information that a franchisor must provide. The document containing this information is called a *disclosure statement* or may be referred to as a Uniform Franchise Offering Circular (UFOC).

A franchisor may want to conduct a preliminary approval of you before providing this information. The law stipulates that the information must be provided *before* you sign a franchise agreement. Furthermore, you must be given a chance to review this information without interference from the franchisor. The sooner you have this document, the sooner you can begin your screening process. Do not be reluctant to let a franchisor know that you are reviewing this information and comparing it with competitors. Franchisors that are upset with this approach and unwilling to do business in this manner are probably not the kind of organization with which you want to be associated. A strong franchisor is not afraid to compete directly with rivals.

EXERCISE 3.8

Franchisor Information Worksheet

The following questions can be found in the information that must be supplied by a franchisor.

Name of Franchisor: _____

How long has the franchise been in operation?_____

What other businesses are affiliated with the franchisor? _____

_____

continued

What is the business experience of each of the franchisor's officers, directors, and management personnel?_____

_____

_____

_____

Have there been lawsuits in which the franchisor and its officers, directors, and management personnel have been involved? If so, what are they? _____

_____

_____

_____

Has the franchisor, its officers, directors, or management personnel been involved in any previous bankruptcies?_____

_____

_____

What is the initial franchise fee and other initial payments? _____

_____

_____

What are the royalties and other continuing payments franchisees are required to make?

_____

_____

_____

What are the restrictions on the quality of goods and services used in the franchise? _____

_____

_____

_____

What are the limits on where goods and services may be purchased? _____

_____

_____

_____

What assistance is available from the franchisor or its affiliates in financing the purchase of the franchise? _____

_____

_____

_____

What are the restrictions on the goods or services franchisees are permitted to sell? _____

_____

_____

_____

What restrictions are placed on the customers whom franchisees may serve?

_____

_____

_____

What territorial protection is to be granted to the franchisees? _____

_____

_____

_____

What are the conditions under which the franchise may be repurchased or refused renewal by the franchisor? _____

_____

_____

_____

continued

What limits are placed on the transfer to a third party by the franchisee? ____

_____

_____

_____

What are the conditions under which the contract can be terminated or modified by either party? _____

_____

_____

_____

What training programs are provided to franchisees? _____

_____

_____

_____

What assistance is provided in selecting a site for the franchise? _____

_____

_____

_____

What is the current number of the following:

Franchises: _____

Projected Future Franchises: _____

Number of Franchises Terminated: _____

Number of Franchises Not Renewed: _____

Number of Franchises Repurchased: _____

Is the franchisor financially sound based on balance sheets and income statements? _____

_____

Do you have to participate personally in the operation of the franchise? _____

_____

What is the basis for earnings claims made to the franchisee? _____

_____

_____

What percent of existing franchises have actually achieved the financial
results that are claimed? _____

What are the names and addresses of other franchisees?_____

_____

_____

_____

The third step is to analyze and evaluate the disclosure statement.
Information contained in the disclosure statement provides a basis for
thoroughly analyzing the potential for a franchise. However, it is also
necessary to investigate the franchisor to ensure that all information is
truthful and accurate. The information that is collected in the *Franchisor
Information Worksheet* can be analyzed using the following ideas:

▷   The experience of both management and directors can be critical
to the franchisor's competence. These individuals should have
sufficient experience so that they can add significantly to your own
business expertise. They should have special knowledge and
understanding about the type of business operation that they are
selling.

▷   The number of franchisees provides some measure of the stability
and experience of the franchisor. It is possible that a new franchisor
could provide a great ground floor opportunity. However, your risk
is reduced when you select a franchisor that has a large number of
franchisees. Each franchisee provides the franchisor with added
experience in starting new operations. This combined experience
will prove highly beneficial in getting your business started.

▷ You need to find the number of franchisees who have been closed or repurchased by the franchisor or who have gone out of business. This information can be even more important than the number of currently operating franchises. Franchisors will sometimes buy out or close unsuccessful franchisees in order to remove problems. It is important to know how many of these situations have occurred. The more franchisees that have experienced problems, the greater your risk becomes in purchasing a franchise.

▷ The length of experience often indicates stability and a higher potential for franchises to succeed in the future. However, there are some good opportunities with younger franchisors. Do not let this factor alone discourage you from considering an association with a franchisor.

▷ The type and amount of training the franchisor provides can prove critical to your success. The best training programs will include a combination of classroom training and on-the-job training. A few weeks of training should be offered if the franchisor has a highly effective program.

▷ There should be a large amount of assistance provided with the start-up of the business. This period of time is normally the most difficult and requires the greatest amount of assistance. However, there should be continued assistance offered regularly, as well as assistance for unexpected crises.

▷ The certified financial statement provided by the franchisor should indicate a financially healthy organization. Any type of questionable financial problems should make you cautious about developing an association with the franchisor.

▷ Determine the assistance that the franchisor can provide for financing your business. Will the financing include the franchise fee, equipment, building, supplies, and operating capital? A less reliable franchisor may not obtain financing that will be most beneficial to a franchisee. Be sure to examine carefully the interest rate and loan conditions and have them reviewed by a professional attorney or an accountant.

▷ An old expression about retail establishments states that there are three critical elements to business success: location, location, and location. Although this statement is an exaggeration, it illustrates the importance of the site. An experienced franchisor should be able to provide sophisticated techniques for accomplishing the task of identifying a good location. In addition, determine if there is assistance provided in constructing a building. Experts knowledgeable in managing construction can save you a great deal of money. Find out whether there is any additional fee for this assistance.

▷ The franchisor's customers are its franchisees. The best way to determine how you will be treated as a customer and franchisee is to talk with other franchisees. If possible, try to talk with those who are no longer in business. They can offer a unique insight into franchisor treatment and services. More is said about this later in the chapter.

▷ Determine how long a franchisee is expected to operate before revenue will be sufficient to cover expenses. This information will help you to calculate the amount of funds you will need to raise in order to cover this deficit.

▷ A critical element in deciding about a franchise is the amount of annual profits that you can expect. Have a cost analysis done to determine whether the projected profit is enough to ensure a reasonable return on investment. You should ask other franchisees whether the profit they make each year is close to what the franchisor told them to expect. Project the length of time that it will take to recover your initial investment.

▷ The franchise fee and the capital investment requirements are the biggest obstacle for most potential franchisees. Discuss these expenses with a banker to determine an amount of money that you can borrow. (There are other ways to raise capital, but a loan is perhaps the most common way of financing a franchise.) This information can be used to eliminate quickly those franchisors whose equity requirement is more than the amount of money you can finance.

▷ A franchisee needs to be excited and enthusiastic about a franchisor's product or service. There are several reasons why this enthusiasm is important. You will be associated with the franchisor for many years and need enthusiasm for motivation. Another reason for excitement about the franchisor is that your high regard for your product will be sensed by your customers and employees.

Your customers will be more likely to patronize your business when they observe your enthusiasm. Employees will work harder when they are inspired by your excitement. How do you feel about this franchise and the products or services it offers?

▷ The franchise should closely match your business experience and skills. The more you know about the business operation, the higher your potential for success. This does not mean you must have experience with the specific product or service. You should expect the franchisor to provide training and management assistance, but related skills and experience will enhance what they offer.

▷ Many products and services can be successful in one area but may not work well in another. Customs, tastes, traditions, wealth, and other factors affect the success of a product or service in a community. Franchisors will sometimes conduct a market survey to determine the franchise's viability for your community. However, you need to verify the accuracy of such a study. Less honest franchisors may attempt to modify the survey's outcome to use it as a selling point.

▷ The importance of location has already been noted. You need to consider how critical location would be to this particular business. Next, it is necessary to determine whether a location suitable for the business exists within your community. If you have doubts about available sites, you should reconsider your investment in the franchise.

▷ Ask yourself whether the product or service is faddish. To protect your investment, the franchise should have long-term staying power. Try to look past your enthusiasm and be objective. Read what business magazines have to say about the product or service. Ask the advice of experienced business people. Talk with friends who would be typical of your future customers. These combined opinions will help you predict the product's longevity.

▷ Find out the population projections for the community in which you plan to place the franchise. The city government, Chamber of Commerce, Small Business Development Corporation, Economic Development Commission, and other sources can help provide this information. The long-term growth of the population will have a significant effect on the franchise's potential success.

▷ Study the businesses that will compete directly against the franchise. Then study indirect competition. For example, a specialty coffee shop might compete against delis, gourmet shops, and bagel retailers.

▷ The price for the product or service should be consistent with average incomes for people in your area. A high-price product will sell in an area where income is high but would probably be a loser in an area with low-income households.

▷ The amount of advertising the franchisor does locally, regionally, and nationally is important when you consider the value of a franchise. A franchisor with a less expensive franchise fee may lower operating costs by limiting its advertising. This shortage of publicity may hurt your franchise sales and business growth.

▷ The franchisor's marketing expertise is very important to your success. You should expect the franchisor's help in generating sales. A franchisor should offer effective advertising tools that include the creation of newspaper, radio, and television advertisements. These ads should be professionally prepared, along with a marketing strategy that will maximize their use.

▷ Most franchisors require the franchisee to pay cooperative marketing fees. These fees are typically a percentage of revenues. It is important to understand how this money will be used and what impact it should have on your franchise.

The fourth step in the franchise selection process is to investigate the franchisor you consider to be the best potential investment. It is important for you to investigate the franchisor thoroughly. You wouldn't want to become a partner with someone you didn't know or trust. Consider your relationship with the franchisor a partnership and check the franchisor out completely. There are three stages to this investigation. Beware of any franchisor that wants you to make a decision so quickly that you will not have time to go through the following investigative process.

1. **Investigate the credibility and reliability of the franchisor.** This investigation is particularly critical with franchisors that have been in operation for a short time. Information from sources such as the Better Business Bureau and Dun and Bradstreet can tell you a great deal about the franchisor. Try to find a person or company who will

run a credit check on the organization. If the franchisor is a small and little-known company, you may also want to conduct a background and credit check on the management and corporate officers.

2. **The disclosure statement must include information about lawsuits.** If there are lawsuits pending against the franchisor, investigate these by contacting the attorney for the plaintiffs. Ask the attorney to explain anything he or she can about the lawsuit. Question the franchisor about what the attorney tells you. You should feel comfortable that the lawsuit is about an issue that would not affect you.

3. **Talk with franchisees about their experience.** The disclosure statement is required to have a list of franchisees. Pick a group of franchisees at random to contact. Your conversation with franchisees can provide important information. Use the following worksheet to collect information from franchisees.

EXERCISE 3.9

Franchisee Information Worksheet

Use this worksheet to record answers to the following questions as you interview a franchisee.

Did the franchisor follow through on its promises? _____

_____

_____

_____

Does the franchisor provide good management assistance?_____

_____

_____

_____

Does the franchisor provide good marketing and advertising programs? _____

What are the strengths of the franchisor? _____

_____

_____

_____

What are the weaknesses? _____

_____

_____

_____

Do you consider your franchise to be a success? _____

_____

_____

_____

What has contributed the most to this success? _____

_____

_____

_____

Did the franchisor make any mistakes during the start-up? _____

_____

_____

_____

How could the mistakes have been avoided? _____

_____

_____

_____

continued

Have there been management and operational mistakes? _____

_____

_____

_____

How could these have been avoided? _____

_____

_____

_____

How strict is the franchisor about business being conducted exactly as
described in operating manuals? _____

_____

_____

_____

If you could do anything over again, what would it be? _____

_____

_____

_____

Would you recommend that a person buy this franchise? _____

_____

_____

_____

Carefully review the answers that franchisees give you. Are there
consistent problems or concerns raised by the franchisees? A consistency
indicates a pattern that increases the probability that the problem will be
repeated with your franchise. Likewise, positive answers should encourage
you to seriously consider entering into an agreement with the franchisor.

Seek the advice of professionals about the franchisor and franchise agreement. Three professionals with whom you should definitely confer are an attorney, an accountant, and a banker.

An attorney is needed to review the franchise agreement. This is your contract with the franchisor and provides the only written commitment and promises that exist. Anything that has been verbally promised should be in this agreement. The attorney and you should review in the agreement the following items:

▷ What is the contract length? It should be the same length discussed with the franchisor.

▷ Does it provide an exclusive territory? If not, what protection is offered against other franchisees taking business away from you? Proliferation of franchisees can seriously erode your revenue. This possibility is the reason that you need some protection.

▷ Are there restrictions on selling the franchise? The more limitations that exist, the more difficult it will be for you to recover your money. Many franchisors will offer to buy back the franchise, but there are often conditions. You need to have a clear understanding of what you must do in order to initiate the buy-back provision.

▷ What are the criteria you can use to cancel the contract? Likewise, what are the criteria the franchisor can use to cancel the contract? These criteria should be reasonable and provide a clear process for canceling the contract.

▷ Does the franchisor agree to buy back the franchise if it is canceled? This provision is absolutely necessary, or you risk losing all of your initial investment in the company. Furthermore, determine whether the franchisor will compensate you for the goodwill built during your operation of the franchise. Goodwill is a valuable asset and takes a significant investment of time and effort to accumulate.

▷ Are there any franchise requirements that you believe are unwise, illegal, or unethical? Sections of a contract that make you uncomfortable at the start of a business relationship may result in problems at a later date. You will probably feel uncomfortable implementing a provision that you don't believe is right.

▷ Has the attorney identified any problems with the contract? There are a number of legal technicalities connected with most business contracts. An experienced attorney will be able to advise you about these provisions.

An accountant should review two primary items for you. First, the accountant should examine the corporation's financial information that is provided in the disclosure statement. Second, the accountant should review the financial potential of the business. You should ask the accountant the following questions:

▷ Is the initial investment for the franchise fee, equipment, and building reasonable? The accountant may be familiar with fair market value for these things or should be able to obtain this information.

▷ Are the royalties and cooperative advertising rates reasonable? There are ratio tables that illustrate typical expenditures for certain categories of business. The tables can be used to indicate whether these rates being charged by the franchisor are within a normal range.

▷ What will your financial situation be during the first five years of operation? A form that is often used in a business plan is a *financial pro forma*. The financial pro forma is a five-year financial plan. The plan includes projections for income, expenses, cash flow, and profits. Review this plan with your accountant and determine the potential return on investment for the franchise.

Is the investment a reasonable risk? All new businesses are risky. However, you must balance out three key areas to determine the degree of personal risk. These include your personal assets, resources for financing the franchise, and the potential return on investment. You should be able to afford any loss to your personal assets. The financing should provide a monthly repayment schedule that is reasonable and affordable. Your potential return on investment should directly correlate with the risk that is involved.

A banker should be contacted to review the franchise, the financial proforma, and your personal financial statement. The banker can provide insight into the financing issues that will be involved. The banker needs to answer the following questions:

▷ Would the bank consider giving you a loan to finance your business? This question can be directed to your accountant to determine how affordable the purchase is for you. The banker's answers are given from a lender's viewpoint. When a bank turns you down for a loan, the loan officers have noted problems. Ask the loan officer to fully explain the reasons for not making the loan. This information will allow you to evaluate for yourself whether these are serious problems that could impede the franchise's success.

▷ Do the loan officers feel that the franchisor is credible? The bank will take more risk when your personal assets are sufficient to underwrite the loan. This policy doesn't give you any assurance that they have made a positive assessment about the franchisor or the franchise agreement. Make sure that the loan officer provides a complete explanation about the loan review board's evaluation of your potential for success. What strengths and weaknesses do they judge the franchisor to possess?

▷ What are the lending conditions? These conditions, including the interest rate, provide additional information that can be used to assess the viability of the franchise. More liberal conditions indicate a more positive evaluation of the franchise by the loan officers. Also, attractive conditions will increase your profit potential.

You should weigh the review and recommendations of all three professionals before you make your final decision about a franchise. These experts can provide important advice, and you should value their opinions.

The fifth step in the process is to make a final decision. As with all decisions, this action is usually easier said than done. You have reviewed dozens of questions that need to be investigated. Sometimes you will discover positive facts about the franchise, and sometimes negative facts. It is possible that the positive or negative facts will be so one-sided that making a decision will be simple. However, it is more typical to find that the facts must be organized in a manner that facilitates the decision-making process.

A simple but effective decision-making approach is the *T method*. To follow this method, you make a "T" on a page. On the left side of the "T," list all of the positive reasons for purchasing the franchise, and on the right side, list all of the negative reasons. After the two lists are completed, assign each item a number to designate its importance. A simple scale of 1 for unimportant, 2 for somewhat important, and 3 for very important can be used. Total the numbers for both sides. The larger the numerical difference between these totals, the more sure you can be of your decision. Totals that are close will make a decision more difficult. However, an investment of this importance should usually be one that makes you feel confident of success.

After completing the T-method exercise, you should feel certain that your decision is correct. A decision to purchase a franchise should result in enthusiasm for the undertaking. Without dedication and enthusiasm, you may find it difficult to achieve success. If you decide a franchise is for you, get in touch with the franchisor and complete the purchase based on a mutually convenient schedule.

Chapter 4

BECOMING A CONSULTANT OR AN INDEPENDENT CONTRACTOR

Many people today think about becoming consultants or independent contractors. They might be bored working for one company, or they might be worried that their single source of income is at risk in an era of global competition and corporate downsizing. Or they simply might want more flexibility and freedom. If you are one of these people, remember that consulting and independent contracting are businesses. Before you seriously consider either of these options, you need to ask yourself if you are willing also to become a business owner and manager. Chapter 1 can help you to make this decision.

Establishing and building a consulting or an independent contracting business require careful planning and nurturing. Both types of practices require you to sell yourself—your skills, your expertise, and the results that you can produce for clients. To sell yourself successfully, you need a highly marketable skill or expertise that is in demand in the marketplace. In addition, you must possess the desire and motivation to succeed.

Consultant or Independent Contractor?

Distinguishing between consultants and independent contractors can be difficult. The choice of terminology often depends on who is using which term and for what purpose. Sometimes self-employed individuals choose to call themselves consultants because the term seems more prestigious or more of an industry norm. In other situations, the reverse may well be true. Indeed, some feel that the term *consultant* has been overused and mis-applied. Industry or geographical preferences also influence the choice of terminology. Even interim management firms that place individuals with client companies strongly prefer one term to the other.

In general, the more complex the skills are that are needed to execute the required tasks, the more you are likely to be consulting rather than contracting. Moreover, consulting tends to produce more intangible or conceptually driven outcomes than contracting, which is characterized by very specific concrete results.

Consultants are experts who advise and recommend about strategy, policy, or some other significant conceptual matter. A consultant is hired—and paid—by a client to achieve a certain goal. As a consultant, you can only advise or recommend a strategy; it is your client who is in a position to make an actual decision. At the highest level of practice, consultants are usually associated with a specific belief system or body of intellectual work that forms the core of their uniqueness and provides a foundation for their work and relationships.

In contrast, independent contractors are generally not expected to be experts in their fields. They usually fill a specific, day-to-day company need, working in tandem with a client's full-time employees who are doing similar work. They sell time to a company for a specified period—from a few days to a year or more, in some situations. The tasks they perform are often more hands-on than the complex and conceptual projects associated with consultants. Sometimes a contractor may act as an adjunct employee who performs all the tasks required by the company either on or off the premises without actually being on the full-time payroll. However, like the consultant, the contractor generally operates in a specific engagement with no guarantee of future work.

For many people, taking on initial contracting or even subcontractor assignments may be a first step along the road to a new consulting career. Similarly, even full-fledged consultants occasionally will take on a specific contracting assignment or two, as a favor to a client, even though it involves using a narrower range of their skills. Both the consultant and the independent contractor bring skills that are needed by a business. Although there are distinctions between the two roles, most of the entrepreneurial issues discussed in this chapter relate to both consultants and independent contractors.

Considerations for the Consultant

To be successful as a consultant, you need both expertise in your specialty and highly developed interpersonal and communication skills. The heart of the consulting challenge is to convince others to listen to you and follow your advice. Consultants must be adept at bridging the gaps between their own expertise and the client's system of beliefs. Strong interpersonal and communication skills enable the consultant to break through invisible barriers of resistance, ultimately influencing clients to change their current practices, policies, or systems.

Although you may have the skills necessary to succeed as a consultant, you need to consider whether the lifestyle changes appeal to you. Many who have left the ranks of corporate life to become consultants find an attractive freedom and flexibility in this option. Some of the additional advantages frequently cited include the ability to control your own schedule and execute tasks on your terms, the minimum up-front investment required (generally limited to home office equipment), the tax benefits for business expenses, and the potential to accommodate other interests and responsibilities (which, of course, may also diminish earnings).

However, there are some drawbacks. When you become a consultant, your lifestyle may change drastically not only because of the transition involved in switching from employee to entrepreneur but also because beginners often discover that consulting can be an intensive, all-encompassing profession. Consulting generally requires a greater commitment of time, resources, and energy than most people anticipate.

As a consultant, you will have to do much more on your own than ever before—everything from answering the telephone to estimating taxes to negotiating fees. Many people find the transition from being a full-time salaried worker, with a structured schedule and support system of colleagues and coworkers, to being an entrepreneurial independent, with no fixed workday or bustling office environment, highly stressful. In addition, people who dislike clerical details find the lack of ready-made office support services disturbing. Finally, extroverts, who have high affiliative needs, find the personal isolation difficult to manage.

Are you really suited to this role? Consider the following questions:

▷ Do you like using your skills and expertise to solve problems?

▷ Are you confident in your abilities and effective at persuasion?

▷ Do you have the desire and motivation to succeed?

▷ Are you willing to market yourself and your skills assertively?

▷ Can you deal with the lack of structure and deadlines that may conflict with your leisure time?

▷ Can you live with the potential lack of status in an outsider role?

▷ Can you manage erratic income flow and irregular payments for your services?

▷ Will it bother you not to have the power to implement your advice?

Now review these aspects of a successful consultant and weigh them against your own traits and priorities:

Financial. Your strong financial drive is a central motivating factor in your career.

Expertise. You believe that you have unique skills, expertise, and experience to fill market needs.

Need for Control and Autonomy. You have no desire to work for a corporation. You would rather trust your future to yourself.

Self-Confidence. You believe in yourself and your abilities, and you will draw on this foundation to market your services.

Marketing Ability. You can see how your unique skills and expertise should be packaged and presented to your targeted market.

Sales Skills. You are willing to keep in touch with contacts and former associates and market yourself to potential clients.

Resilience. You do not let disappointments get you down for long. In fact, in the face of obstacles, you typically become even more determined to succeed.

Good Interpersonal Skills. You get along well with all kinds of people, without necessarily being close. You are an excellent listener, sensitive to interpersonal issues and obstacles.

Good Communications Skills. You have excellent oral and written communications skills.

Targeting Your Market

Do not assume that your skills or the services you plan to provide will be in great demand. One of the most common reasons consultants fail to make an adequate living is that they didn't take the time to research their market. All prospective consultants, like anyone starting a business, need to know the answers to the following questions:

▷ Who are your customers?

▷ What, specifically, do they need?

▷ How can you satisfy their needs?

▷ Who is the competition?

▷ Is there a way to differentiate your services from those of your competitors?

▷ How are you going to reach clients?

▷ How much do clients customarily pay?

▷ How much are they willing to pay?

The answers to these questions will enable you to determine the opportunities that consulting might provide. The information is also useful in projecting how much revenue you will generate.

Talking with Prospective Clients

Most consultants find that their first few projects come from associates and acquaintances. You can reasonably predict your potential as a consultant by networking. Begin by writing down a list of people you know either personally or professionally who are prospective clients for your consulting business. Identify the five to ten people whose judgment and honesty you trust. Contact these people and arrange a meeting or an extended telephone interview.

When you sit down with people in your network who may later become clients, tell them that you are seriously considering entering consulting as a career and that you would like to draw on their experience and knowledge. Record the information they provide on the following worksheet (you will need to make copies before you start). Be diplomatic when asking the questions about consulting fees, but don't pass up the opportunity to obtain this important information.

EXERCISE 4.1

Prospective Client Worksheet

1. What professional associations do you belong to in your technical field or industry?

   _____

   _____

   _____

2. How are their meetings good ways to meet prospective clients?

   _____

   _____

   _____

3. What professional or technical publications do you find informative?

_____

_____

_____

4. What other ways would you suggest for contacting potential clients?

_____

_____

_____

5. What kinds of problems has a consultant helped you to solve?

_____

_____

_____

6. What role(s) did the consultant play, and how helpful was the consultation?

_____

_____

_____

7. What are the most important things you look for in a consultant?

_____

_____

_____

8. Who else was involved in your decision to use the consultant?

_____

_____

continued

_____

9. Who do you regard as the best consultants in this area?

_____

_____

_____

10. How do you make the decision to use a consultant?

_____

_____

_____

11. What does it take to get you to consider a new consultant?

_____

_____

_____

12. How do you prefer to structure fees?

_____

_____

_____

13. What fee range for consultants are you accustomed to paying?

_____

_____

_____

14. What kind of needs do you have for a new consultant?

_____

_____

_____

15. How could your company use someone with my skills as a consultant?

_____

_____

_____

16. What people do you know who would be interested in my services?

_____

_____

_____

In this kind of networking, be certain to ask open-ended questions (questions that begin with what, how, who, and so on) rather than questions that trigger yes or no answers (Do you . . . , Are you . . . , Can you . . . , and so on). An open-ended question prompts the other individual to provide information, but a yes or no question gives the other person a chance to say no easily and not supply the information you want to collect.

Researching Your Market

As your information about your market sharpens, you may need to solidify your picture of market size. What geographic area do you plan to serve? How many target organizations exist in your targeted geographic area? Additional research may be needed. Your findings will help you determine if any adjustments in your planning are required.

A knowledge of your competition—other consultants delivering services in your same field—will provide you with invaluable information in determining an accurate market size, a clearer market niche, and a more informed market strategy. Whenever possible, suggest a meeting to discuss possible mutual assistance. As you network, keep a file of these individuals and record appropriate comments, such as their areas of specialty, strengths, weaknesses, methods of marketing, size of their firm, location, clients, and fees charged.

You will find this consultant network to be an invaluable source of information, referrals, and general professional satisfaction. Successful consultants nurture all of their contacts and provide business to each other. A consultant network should be an integral part of your marketing strategy. Other ways to meet consultants in your field are to attend seminars, trade shows, and professional meetings.

After you have collected information about consulting, you will need to make a final decision about whether to enter the business. The next step is to establish and manage your consulting business. The remainder of this chapter provides advice about how to do this.

Organizing Your Business

Getting your business off the ground can be a bewildering process, but it will be much less intimidating if you take a systematic, logical approach. The best time to take care of the details is before you get busy serving clients. If you don't make the effort now, you might be faced with legal and tax penalties later.

The first step is deciding how to structure your business. While state law governs business formation and operation, there are two basic ways in which a business can be structured: corporate or noncorporate status. Within these categories, the law classifies any business as a sole proprietorship, partnership, or corporation.

As most consulting businesses grow and evolve, so do their forms. Most begin as sole proprietorships because of ease and low cost. If your market research leads to a short-term consulting job, you can take it immediately because you will be active as a sole proprietor. Later, as you grow, you might want to consider the advantages of another form. Your business will be able to absorb the costs of such a reorganization at that time.

Licensing is sometimes required of consultants. A license is a certification that can establish credentials and expertise in specialized areas. The cost of a business license will vary, depending on your city or town, and can range from $50 to $300. Some professions, such as investment advisors, also have additional licensing requirements, such as filing with the Securities and Exchange Commission.

A DBA (Doing Business As) may be required if you do business under any name other than your own. For example, if your name is Alfred Silliman and you do business in your own name (as in using your personal letterhead in all correspondence), you are a sole proprietor and are not required to file a DBA. If, however, you call your company "Alfred Silliman Associates" or "Technologies Solutions Group," you will have to file a DBA in most states. Also, if you want to establish a commercial bank account using your business name, you will need a DBA certificate or another corporate document.

Filing a DBA is simple. DBAs are usually filed with your local town clerk or with the secretary of state for fees ranging up to $80. Completing the registration form takes just a few minutes. If you are unsure about specific DBA or licensing filing requirements, there are several ways to find the information you need:

> ▷ If you belong to a professional society, talk to an officer about business filings. Many organizations have this information on file or can direct you to the right source.

> ▷ For local requirements, try your town clerk's office. Be sure to review the listing closely so that you don't end up paying too much by overclassifying yourself.

> ▷ At the state level, contact your secretary of state. Phone numbers are usually listed in the blue pages of the telephone directory.

Do not underestimate the importance of selecting a business structure that will meet your specific needs. Talk with an attorney, a professional tax accountant, and other professional advisors.

Selecting a Name

Choosing a name for your business is an important and sometimes overlooked part of the start-up process. It needs to be done before you register your business. The name you select is an important calling card. More than anything else, your name communicates the purpose of your business and the services you provide.

Ideally, your business name will indicate to prospective clients what your business is all about. Although many consultants operate with their own names because of the simplicity of sole proprietorship, you should also consider a name that is creative, as long as it is appropriate to your line of work. Remember, you will be required to do a DBA filing if you haven't incorporated.

If you are developing a unique product or service, you have an additional reason for operating under another business name. In this case, you may want to build brand-name identity—maybe for franchising at a future time. If you follow this route, you should protect your business name with a trademark or registered service mark under federal or state law. Consult a good business attorney for a step-by-step description of the process.

After you have selected a name for your business, investigate if the same name, or one similar to it, is already being used and protected by another organization. You or your attorney can request a name search through the secretary of state's office. The secretary of state can clear a name for statewide use following a simple and inexpensive computer search.

Finally, if you are a licensed professional, contact your licensing agency about its requirements for naming your business entity.

Setting a Fee for Your Services

Because consulting is a customized business, there is no universal standard to guide you about what to charge. Fees can differ by profession, geographic region, or individual assignment. Industry experts offer various opinions on how to price your services. While pricing models can be of some help in projecting fees, no formula, no matter how accurate or appropriate, will be correct for every situation. So how do you set a suitable fee for your services? And how do you determine the bottom line you need to charge in order to produce your required income?

Beginning consultants, in their eagerness to generate new business, commonly underprice themselves. They assume that low pricing, which can work well for industries such as retail sales, will help jump-start their business in a competitive climate. It might, but they also run the risk of working nonstop for starvation fees because clients will perceive them as a bargain. Some may even assume that they are less competent professionals who cannot command true market prices. After they have locked themselves into a low pricing strategy, they may spend years trying to break out.

In the early stages of business development, you may want to quote your standard rate and then give a one-time discount to a new client on the first project in order to establish the business relationship. After you have demonstrated your value to the organization based on the initial project, your fee to that organization is then established at your higher, standard rate.

You should keep three factors in mind when calculating what to charge:

1. How much you need or expect to make

2. What you must charge to achieve this level of income

3. The going rate in your field and geographic area

Calculating Your Fee

The following case study explains the process for calculating your fee. The example given demonstrates how one consultant developed a bottom-up approach to pricing her services that gave her a very clear view of the financial challenges she faced and what it would take to be successful. You'll also see how she applied the concepts to actual client situations. After you read this case study, you'll be in a stronger position to arrive at your own fee range and see how to apply this pricing strategy to actual client situations.

Case Study

Leslie Barnes was a 52-year-old marketing executive at a major computer company. Employed for 24 years, she earned $100,000 at the time of her departure. Always a realist, Leslie knew that she probably would do well to earn $60,000 at another full-time job, given her age, geographical location, and her unwillingness to relocate. She opted instead to become a consultant. She would be self-supporting and make the necessary lifestyle adjustments to get her business going.

Leslie knew that in order to forecast her potential revenue, she needed to estimate her billable days per month or per year. Predicting this number with a reasonable degree of accuracy would be important to her success. She knew that it would not be possible to bill for vacations, holidays, sick days, administrative and marketing activities, and training. Consequently, she began the fee setting process by determining how many hours she could work each year. The following are her calculations:

Estimate Billable Hours

Assumptions	Hours Available
Standard Work Year:	
52 weeks x 5 days/week x 8 hours/day	2,080
Minimum Time Off	
(5 holidays + 5 vacation days +	
5 sick days) x 8 hours/day	(120)
Minimum Self-Training	
5 days x 8 hours/day	(40)
Administrative Tasks	
49 weeks x 5 days/week x 2 hours/day	(490)
Minimum Marketing	
49 weeks x 1 day/week x 8 hours/day	(392)
Total Hours of Work Available	1,038

Of the 2,080 hours, the net 1,038 represents about 50 percent of the time Leslie has available. Note that there is no guarantee that Leslie would actually bill out these available hours.

Estimate Costs of Operating the Business

Next, Leslie estimated the costs associated with operating her business. The costs listed here are associated with running a sole proprietorship with no employees from a home office. She used the *Cost Estimate Worksheet* to do this. The lines have been left blank so that you can return later and add in your own figures.

EXERCISE 4.2

Cost Estimate Worksheet

Expense Item	Estimated Cost
Salary (Estimate amount needed to survive)	_____
Self-Employment Tax (Currently 15.3%)	_____
Retirement (Up to 15% of earnings)	_____
Personal Insurance (Health, Life, Disability)	_____
Overhead	_____
Advertising (*Yellow Pages* and other)	_____
Business Entertainment and Meetings	_____
Business Insurance (Liability)	_____
Car/Transportation	_____
Depreciation on Equipment (Assume 20%)	_____
Dues and Publications	_____
Education and Training	_____
Office Supplies	_____
Postage	_____
Printing (Business Cards, Brochures)	_____
Professional Fees (Lawyers, Accountants)	_____
Telephone	_____
Miscellaneous	_____
TOTAL COSTS	_____

In the next step, Leslie calculated her daily and hourly rate in three different scenarios using three different earnings assumptions. She arrived at her hourly rate by dividing her total costs by her total available billable hours. She rounded her total available billable hours to 1,000. Leslie then calculated her daily rate by multiplying her hourly rate by 8 (hours per day).

Establish a Daily Rate

	Worst Case	Base Case	Best Case
Salary	$30,000	$40,000	$60,000
Expenses	15,000	20,000	30,000
Total Costs	45,000	60,000	90,000
Hourly Rate	45	60	90
Daily Rate	360	480	720

Leslie determined that her lifestyle could be maintained with a salary of $40,000. Her associated operating expenses came to $20,000. Therefore, she set a daily billing rate of $480. This assumed that she would be able to generate enough sales to fill her available hours. If she couldn't fill her 1,000 billable hours, she would not be able to survive on $480 per day. One way to adjust for projected non-billable hours is to estimate the percent of hours you can't bill. In Leslie's case, she estimated this figure to be 40% because she was just getting started. She adjusted her hourly fee upward by 40% to offset this difference and realized that she must charge $85 per hour or $680 per day to generate sufficient income.

Final Market Check

At this point, Leslie switched from her bottom-up approach and tried to find out what the marketplace was paying for someone with her experience and skills. She went to other consultants and learned that subcontracting was commonplace among those starting up. She was told by several contacts that 15 percent of most consultants' fees go to pay other consultants or contractors who assist them in executing their work. Therefore, she gained some idea of the range of pricing in her market. As it turned out, her costs were actually lower than the ceiling for her consulting services.

Now that Leslie had an idea of what the market would pay, she knew who would hire her and how much money she could charge for her services. Here's how this works:

Leslie's Fee Range:

Worst Case	$480
Base Case	$680
Best Case	$760

Here are some examples of how this fee range might be applied to prospective clients and the decisions that a consultant must make when charging a fee to a client.

Client Prospect 1. XYZ Corporation pays $400 per day for "junior tier" consulting. Although the fee is less than her worst case calculation, Leslie would be assured of frequent work. Linking up with this company would also enable her to retain a prestigious initial client. However, the work she would be doing would be at the bottom end of her skill range—work that would be quite mundane. She could aspire to earn eventually $600 per day as a "senior tier" consultant, but she would have to work at least six months to earn the promotion. Leslie's loss would be $80 per day if she accepted work from XYZ. Because XYZ would be a start-up client, she might be willing to subsidize the contract with her own funds and aspire eventually for a "break-even" at $600 per day. Also, the potential of billing most of her hours meant that she could accept a lower fee. XYZ would potentially be a good contract.

Client Prospect 2. Henry Baskin was a competitor marketing consultant. He wanted Leslie to subcontract to him. He offered to pay Leslie $700 per day, and he would bill out her services at a fee of $1,200 per day for a three-month project. Leslie's work would be challenging but low profile. Leslie could afford to accept this engagement. Note, however, that to obtain this offer, she had to be successful at positioning herself in the marketplace at the higher end of her skill range. Could she, in fact, again bill at this high rate in the marketplace in which she is playing? Leslie would need to be realistic about the market value of her credentials, skills, and experience. Note also that this contract would be a shorter term arrangement than the steady revenue she expected from Prospect 1. However, she liked Henry and believed that they would work well together. She would also be generating more than her base case rate for a full three months! This decision was an easy one.

Case Summary

Leslie's approach to pricing her services combined two key elements. One was a bottom-up strategy that established the amount of revenue she needed to survive. Recall that although she had been making $100,000, she now believed she could command only $60,000 in another full-time job. She priced her worst case at an income of only $45,000. She rationalized the $15,000 shortfall as follows:

▷   It was an investment in her business that she made using her savings.

▷   It was a risk deliberately taken to ensure some money coming in the short term.

▷   It was a temporary stop-gap source of income earned while she continued to search for a full-time job.

The second strategy was a top-down one that established what the market would pay for her services at one end of her skill range as a contractor and at the other end of her skill range as a consultant.

As you can see from this example, pricing your services accurately and knowing what you need to earn to survive are essential. The calculation of your fee range gives you a basis for evaluating offers as they come to you. But it is only one half of the ultimate pricing equation. Market research will tell you what value the marketplace puts on your skills, experience, and expertise.

Now that you know what you are going to charge, you also need to decide how to charge. The next few sections present issues to consider as you decide how to charge a client.

Methods for Charging Clients

Hourly Rates. You can determine your hourly rate by dividing your daily rate by eight hours. Hourly rates are sometimes used to start a project, to become acquainted with a client, or to do work in the proposal stages before a client commits to a long-term project.

Hourly rates can also be beneficial for shorter time commitments—less than a day, for instance—or when time commitments regularly exceed traditional eight-hour days. Base the calculation of your hourly rate on your daily rate. However, if travel to a client's workplace is required for only a few billable hours of work, be sure to take this element into consideration when billing.

Another advantage of hourly billing is that it produces a detailed accounting of your time and activities. Clients can track your progress simply by referring to your invoice logs. Many consultants will actually put in more than eight hours a day on an assignment. In this case, you receive compensation for all of your time.

Daily Rates. Daily rates are another standard for pricing in the consultant's environment. Daily rates can be used when you are planning to do work that can be done in day-long blocks of time. It has the advantage of not needing detailed hourly record keeping on your part. Some clients prefer this method when they anticipate your investing more than eight hours a day on average to a project. For the consultant, it is a fair way to bill when an actual day is not spent in direct work on a client's project. Even though the client does not receive eight hours of your time, you are kept from working on another project because of the commitment. This situation often arises when projects require travel.

Project Fees. A project fee, also known as a fixed contract fee, can be useful when you must tailor a proposal to fit a client's budget. Most clients generally do not require you to divulge specifically how you arrived at the total, but be prepared to do so.

In setting a project fee, it is extremely important to establish clear expectations regarding timetables for completing the work. For example, suppose you agree to write a speech for a client by the 15th of the month for a fee of $2,500. In making this agreement, you assume that all reviews and revisions will be completed and returned to you in time to produce the final draft by the 15th. You may want to stipulate that the proposal and estimate must be renegotiated if you do not receive the revisions in time, or if more reviews are suddenly added to the approval process.

Many consultants prefer to bid exclusively on a project basis. They perceive it as more desirable because they have more latitude in how and when the job is done. The client is paying only for the results.

Retainer Fees. Retainer fees guarantee a consultant a certain level of billable hours per month, and they assure the client company of access to the consultant's specific expertise when needed. Retainer fees usually guarantee a consultant work for one or more days per month. Often these fees are paid in advance on the first of each month. If you contract for retainer fees, make sure that the arrangement clearly defines the following:

▷ The exact amount of your fee

▷ The type of work that will be performed

▷ The time commitment

As you consider the billing policies you will use with your clients, keep these points in mind:

▷ Make sure that your financial terms are explicit (for example, net 30 days).

▷ Remember that cash flow is king.

▷ If clients are small and poor, charge for initial consultations. This approach will weed out unprofitable customers.

▷ Aim for a project fee wherever possible. If you finish early, you'll make more money.

▷ When negotiating project fees, don't reduce your fee unless the project scope is also reduced.

▷ Don't nickel and dime your clients. Plan to stay with your fee structure for at least a year.

The Art of Marketing

Solid marketing skills are vital to ensure that your consulting business is successfully launched. Even if you are fortunate enough to start with a solid base of contacts and assignments, energetic and persistent effort is essential. You will soon learn what every good salesperson knows so well— that to generate one actual contract, you will probably need to write several proposals. And to generate those proposals, you will need to solicit an even larger number of prospects.

One of the key issues in marketing your consulting services is the marketing/delivery dilemma: while you are delivering services you have sold, you are obviously too busy to do your marketing; while you are marketing your services, you are not working on assignments for delivery. To deliver services without marketing may mean finishing an assignment and finding yourself with no prospects lined up for your next job.

This dilemma is accentuated by the fact that most marketing efforts have a long incubation period. Often three to twelve months elapse between a successful sales call and the first billable assignment. This sales cycle must be taken into account when you put together your financial plan. If you succeed at your first assignment, you may have more work right away. Or it could take a very long time.

Consider the following questions as you think through the best way to market your services:

▷ In what marketplace do I want to operate? Why?

▷ How specialized or generic is my service?

▷ What client organizations make up my target market, in terms of industry sector, company size, and departments served?

▷ What types of problems do these client organizations have that need consultants for solutions?

▷ How will I convince these client organizations to tell me what they want and need?

▷ Who are the decision makers for consulting services in these client organizations?

▷ Why will they buy my services, and what will be the benefits they receive?

▷ Who will my competitors be?

Your Marketing Strategy

Most successful consultants have found *indirect* marketing to be the most effective approach. This strategy relies heavily on personal contacts and referrals for new business—and it's simply the best way to generate consulting assignments.

In contrast, *direct* marketing often involves advertising, mailings, or promotional campaigns that serve to introduce your services. This approach can be quite expensive—and nonproductive at the same time.

Other consultants opt for a third-party approach, whereby an independent agent actively markets their services, negotiates the terms of work, places them in the client situation, and often even pays for their services. Likewise, many consultants simply subcontract work from other consultants. This third-party approach can be effective when you establish a network of consultants that need your services.

Use the following questions as a personal checklist to assess your selling aptitude:

▷ Do I like to actively go after new leads?

▷ Do I express my pitch effectively?

▷ Do I like to network?

▷ Can I negotiate well and close deals?

▷ Can I write letters and brochures that sell the benefits of my business?

If you answered yes to all of these questions, you are an ideal candidate for an indirect marketing approach. If you answered no in most cases, a third-party approach will better suit you and your business until you have developed better sales and marketing skills.

No matter which approach you choose, it's imperative that you be reachable. Set up an answering machine or message service to handle your calls when you are unavailable. Consider a separate phone line for your business if you work out of your house. Your business line will automatically be listed in the *Yellow Pages* at no additional cost.

Indirect Marketing

Indirect marketing definitely yields the best results for consultants. While this method, based largely on networking and referrals, requires minimal financial investment, it does require substantial time and effort. The major elements of indirect marketing are described separately below.

Networking

For most consultants, networking is the strongest marketing tool. It includes everything from making personal phone calls to key decision makers, to writing letters and talking to contacts at social and business gatherings. Basically, it involves staying in touch with your contacts and potential clients. Start with the *Prospective Clients Worksheet* that you completed earlier to begin your networking.

Because consulting is a word-of-mouth and performance-based business, referrals from former employers, associates, and colleagues who think highly of your work will often be your best initial and ongoing networking resource. Indeed, most successful consultants obtain the bulk of their new business from former satisfied customers or from referrals made by these customers.

Do not overlook anyone as a potential client. Colleagues, friends, neighbors, family members, suppliers, associates from clubs and organizations, editors of trade journals, and professional acquaintances can all be an enormous help to your business. Even competitors are potential clients. They may subcontract your services.

Tell people about your new business. Explain what you will be doing and ask them for the names of one or two additional contacts who might also need your services or want to know of your general availability. Keep expanding this list at every opportunity.

It pays to keep in touch with people regularly, even if they are not now in a position to give you business. The more contacts you make, the more potential you will build for your business. Many of your best leads will come from close personal contacts, so nurture them.

School Ties

College alumni associations are perfect sources to network and uncover business opportunities. Major colleges and universities have very active alumni associations across the country. Many alumni groups maintain job banks for members. If you are not involved with a local alumni chapter, call your school and talk to the alumni relations director. Also, look in the library for the *Directory of College Alumni*, which lists almost every alumni association in the United States.

Professional Societies and Public Meetings

Organizations that specialize in your field or profession make excellent forums for meeting people and networking. And, if you become involved in a leadership or volunteer role, you will find making new contacts easier because of the ongoing nature of the association between you and others over the longer term. You may find this approach more satisfying than trying to chat with strangers during the cocktail party hour. Consider the time and expense associated with such participation as a cost of doing business.

Specialized professional groups are easy to find. The *Encyclopedia of Associations*, published by Gale Research, is an excellent resource available in most public libraries. For general business meetings, contact the American Management Association, which has chapters and meetings in virtually every major American city.

To find a local group, call the national headquarters of an organization that interests you. You can also ask your librarian for a list of local trade associations and contact numbers. When you call, ask for the local program director or someone who can give you information on meeting schedules and locations. Keep in mind that associations commonly take a summer hiatus, so you should expect calendars to be slim from May through August.

Local business associations, such as the Kiwanis and Rotary Clubs; the Chamber of Commerce; and social organizations, from singles groups to theater groups, are also potential networking sources. Some even have recorded telephone messages that provide meeting times. Check your telephone directory for local chapters of these groups. Don't overlook area newspapers and regional magazines that publish calendars of upcoming events. Listings usually appear once a week, in weekend or community sections, so that readers can plan ahead for the following week.

Authoring Articles or Op-Eds

As a consultant, getting published in professional or trade journals or on the opinion/editorial page of your local newspaper is an excellent way to build credibility as an expert in a high-profile public forum. Some publications may even pay for submissions. *The Writer's Market* lists names of editors and addresses for many major publications, as well as their submission guidelines.

Nearly every major newspaper in the country accepts op-ed articles. Op-eds offer views and opinions on issues from readers. If you specialize in a particular field, an opinion piece can help establish your credibility. Most submissions run from 500 to 750 words. They are usually sent to the editorial editor of the local paper. The editor's name and address can often be found in the masthead, under the paper's logo, or at the top of the editorial page. *Bacon's Newspaper Directory* lists newspapers across the country.

Lecturing

One of the most effective ways of meeting people is by appearing on the lecture circuit. Speakers are automatically perceived as experts or authorities on the subjects they are addressing. Why else would they be on the program? Lecturing creates the aura of being a public figure. The best opportunities are before trade, technical, and professional societies; business, civic and community groups; and public organizations, such as the Rotary or Kiwanis Clubs. If you fear public speaking, join your local Toastmaster's Club. There you will learn how to handle a podium and an audience—and you will also find another source of business contacts.

Internet

The World Wide Web provides the newest source of networking. On the Web, you can find sites that allow you to list yourself as a consultant. Some job listing sites provide this service. You can also find sites that allow you to put up a Web page at no cost. Others allow you to post a "business card."

You can also make many contacts through access to list servers. A *list server* provides a means for large numbers of people interested in a similar area to communicate with one another. People often post requests for information on these list server groups. In providing answers to questions and needs, you make other members of the list server group aware of your expertise.

E-mail is also a great way to remain in contact with people in your network. It allows you to communicate instantly without taking up much time for either yourself or your contact.

Direct Marketing

Traditional direct marketing strategies, such as advertising, promotions, telemarketing, and direct mail campaigns, generally are not effective for consultants. However, you may want to use a few direct marketing tools that are important to consultants because they support and enhance networking efforts. Your marketing arsenal should include the following items.

Business Cards

A distinctive, attractive card will build your image and encourage people to call you. Resist the temptation to clutter it with too much information. Give your name, address, phone number, fax number, e-mail or Web address, the name of your organization, and logo, if available. Always carry a supply of your business cards with you. Office supply stores now carry business card stock that you can use to print the cards on your computer and printer.

Resume

A first-class functional resume, which emphasizes problems you have solved and the concrete results you have achieved, will define your services and the benefits that can be derived from them. It will also serve as a guide for developing your brochure.

Brochures

An effective brochure explains your business, its services, and what you can do for your customers. It should be benefit-oriented and focused on your customers' needs. It is better to have a number of targeted brochures than one brochure that tries to say too much. Brochures can be mailed to potential clients, included in proposals, or handed out with business cards.

To be effective, your brochure must be well designed. The most cost-effective brochures use an 8½ x 11 piece of heavy stock paper folded into thirds. Most office supply stores carry attractive paper designed specifically for printing a brochure with a computer and printer.

Although designs vary, here is a good three-fold format to follow:

1. The first fold should simply include your business name, your name and title, a logo, and a telephone number where you can be reached.

2. The second (or inside) fold should identify your specific expertise—what you have to offer to clients, what is unique about your service, and what benefits your clients will obtain by doing business with you.

3. A brief business biography or quotes serving as testimonials from satisfied clients, if available, are appropriate for the third fold. Photographs of yourself are not usually a valuable addition.

Web Page

You can maintain a nicely designed Web page (or site) that costs no more per month than your telephone service. A Web page is particularly a good idea if you are providing technical, graphic arts, or marketing services.

You should have the same information at the site that would be put in a brochure. However, to leverage the marketing capability of the Web, it is a good idea to have free information at your site that attracts Web browsers. Visitors will be attracted to your site because of the free information but also will be introduced to your business. For example, a consultant on learning technology might have a Web site with a short course that provides visitors with an introduction to basic learning technology concepts.

Marketing Letters

These are also called "pitch" letters because they are used by consultants for making follow-up contacts to potential clients to secure business. You should always personalize letters and send them directly to the person who is most likely to use your services. Make sure you spell the person's name correctly and use his or her proper title. Effective letters contain the following components:

1. **Introduction.** A good marketing letter introduces you.

2. **Connector.** A letter can be especially powerful if the introduction mentions that someone known to the addressee has suggested that you make this contact.

3. **Hook.** If you touch on a real need, the decision maker will read on. Make sure you grab his or her attention, or you will lose the reader before the second paragraph begins.

4. **Service.** Describe what you offer and the benefits to the client, including the key elements of your service or business. Tell prospects what you can do for them—and how your service will help them.

5. **Close.** End the letter by keeping the ball in play: "I would welcome an opportunity to discuss how I can help your company. Should you have any immediate questions, please feel free to call me at (phone number). However, I will call you next week to discuss your needs further and arrange an appointment at your convenience."

Attach a business card to the letter and follow up the correspondence with a phone call within a week to ten days.

Cold Calls

Calling people without an introduction is a hard way to make a living, but some consultants do try the telemarketing route. If you have a pleasing voice and excellent telephone skills, you may do better than most. These calls usually consist of a short, rehearsed pitch that amounts to a commercial for your services. Whenever possible, begin by mentioning something you have in common with this individual to establish a bridge. An introductory letter sent prior to this initial phone call that mentions your intention of calling can help pave the way for greater receptivity.

Developing contacts is a job unto itself. Begin with your primary contacts—people you know—and obtain introductions to secondary contacts. Introduce yourself to a secondary contact by using the name of the primary contact, with his or her permission.

After you have exhausted your primary and secondary contacts, then it's time to hit the books. You can find the names and addresses of corporations and leading executives in your local library. The best reference books for this purpose are the Dun & Bradstreet *Million Dollar Directory*, the *Encyclopedia of Associations,* and *Standard & Poor's Register of Corporations.* Your local Chamber of Commerce may also publish directories of local businesses and key executives.

Remember, you need to contact as many people as you can. Numbers count! Any contact may give you a referral that could lead to new business. The bottom line is, the more people you speak with and the more targeted your marketing efforts, the better your results.

Third-Party or Agency Marketing

Not long ago, temporary agencies typically focused on secretarial or clerical employees. As the economy has shifted, interim employment agencies have expanded dramatically and now cover a range of employment roles and responsibility levels—up to and including senior-level executive assignments.

Consultants can benefit from relationships with interim agencies because the agencies do much of the marketing and record keeping work. They meet with employers, match skills with needs, handle the negotiations, and call when an opening arises. Many companies prefer to work through a broker rather than deal directly with an individual. The company will call the broker agency and place its "order." Some companies have even established subsidiaries within their parent organizations, located on company property, which serve as the sole source for all their temporary, contract, or contingency employees.

You can boost your chances of being selected for temporary assignments by registering with more than one agency. Remember that skills, and not previous titles, are what interim firms need to promote you, so a functional resume may prove most helpful. You should also stress that you are flexible and proficient in many areas and, most importantly, that you can step into an assignment and complete it without any training. Plan to stay in touch with three or four selected agencies that have your resume, so that your name is at the top of the list when a job opening occurs.

If you have trouble attracting clients, using a third party to get started can help you validate your resume and give you some experience into how they obtain and manage clients. But remember that as a consultant, you still need to learn how to market yourself.

Selling Yourself

Whichever specific marketing methods you use, the following simple steps will help you sell yourself to prospective clients:

1. **Get out the news.** Announce your availability and what you want to do. Network with decision makers. Talk with former employers, associates, and colleagues. Contact those who regard you and your work highly and support you in your goals, and tell them about your direction. Ask for referrals.

2. **Be visible.** Attend social and business functions. Talk to as many people as possible and speak to everyone in a polite and friendly way. Take the initiative to introduce yourself to those you don't know, when appropriate.

3. **Be alert to new opportunities.** Analyze the needs of an organization to see if it has a need for your skill base.

4. **Be responsive.** Return all phone calls promptly. Thank in an appropriate way everyone who helps you in your business development. Stay in touch and provide progress updates. Examine how you can contribute to the business interests of those in your professional network, and do so.

5. **Develop your personal and professional reputation.** Be on time for appointments. Always dress professionally. Be aware of the potential client company's need for confidentiality, and be discreet with corporate information. Learn about organizations and key players. Do not contribute to the development of negative rumors. Become known for possessing a high standard of personal and professional integrity. Provide excellent value for the fee paid by the contracting organization.

6. **Volunteer.** Volunteer to write business articles or be a guest speaker to demonstrate your areas of expertise. These activities will give your name greater visibility. Be willing to do a small project at a discount in order to establish a business relationship (but remember that too many freebies will diminish your perceived value). Volunteer occasional value-added benefits or services, especially on your first few independent contracting assignments. Show that you are interested in helping your client grow and prosper.

7. **Be flexible, yet focused.** If a business opportunity develops that isn't exactly what you like to do, consider it carefully because it could lead to other possibilities. Develop appropriate guidelines that establish a clear direction for your company or that communicate a specific skill so that potential clients will understand what you have to offer. Trust your instincts. If something doesn't seem right about the deal, politely walk away.

8. **Do excellent work on time.** Establish long-term, repeat business relationships by negotiating what you can and can't do, and by fulfilling the conditions of the contract as promised. If you recognize that any conditions of the contract are unrealistic, renegotiate with the contractor immediately. The best way to establish a repeat business relationship as an independent contractor is to do excellent work on schedule. Most contractor business is follow-up work from satisfied customers or referrals by them.

Building a Foundation

After you have identified a lead, you need to qualify a contact as a potential client by determining the following:

1. Does the contact have a true need for consulting services?

2. Do you have the ability to meet that need?

3. Does the contact have the authority to hire or make the recommendation to hire you?

Relationship building is key to this process. It begins when you meet with a potential client, or someone in the client organization, to discuss consulting opportunities, and it unfolds as the consulting relationship develops.

Relationship building is one of the cornerstones of your business success, and it should be one of your highest priorities. Even if you are working through a contracting or interim agency, where much of the introductory legwork is done for you, it is still your responsibility to maintain good relations with the interim agency contact, as well as with your actual client.

Developing the Relationship

First impressions count. You must create a favorable impression that instills a sense of trust in the client. Even if you have the exact qualifications for an assignment, do not assume that your experience and skills will precede you. Assume instead that the client knows nothing about you. Unless you are told otherwise, tell your contact everything pertinent about yourself.

Present yourself as a qualified professional. Wear business attire for the first office contact, even if the client has a relaxed dress code. Bring marketing materials to leave behind, including your functional resume and business card. Explain why you are qualified for the assignment. Remember to talk not only about what you do but also to discuss how you can help solve the client's problems.

Sometimes more than one person will be involved in the initial contact meeting. If so, try to make everyone as comfortable as possible. You need to win overall acceptance while also identifying and focusing on who will ultimately decide whether to hire you as a consultant. You need to be able to create good rapport under any circumstances.

Qualifying the Client

Your initial meeting has another purpose: to find out if the prospective client really needs your skills and if he or she can actually hire you. But first, in meetings where a number of players are in attendance, you will need to identify the client. This decision maker is not always obvious, especially in companies that work by consensus or in corporations where a buying agent works on behalf of internal clients. For example, large companies often have print brokers on staff to screen and hire printers for printing jobs. Print brokers often act as the go-between by working as the hiring agent. Your client is the person who decides whether to use your services. If you are having problems identifying the client, simply ask, "Who would I be working for?"

After you have determined who the client is, the next step is gauging how ready this individual is to commit the resources necessary to hire you. Several factors come into play here, but money is usually the biggest issue. Time can also be of concern. If the client is on a tight deadline and you happen to walk in the door with the answer to his or her problems, the decision may be immediate. Unfortunately, newcomers often spend too much time talking to organizations where resources are not likely to be committed. If a commitment seems unlikely in the near future, move on and check back with the company periodically to see if the situation has changed.

Use these guidelines to qualify a contact as a client early in the process. Prior to the meeting, ask these questions over the telephone:

▷ Are there any special issues or situations that will be discussed at the meeting?

▷ Do you have an immediate need for a consultant with my skills? Have you used consultants before?

▷ If there is a need, who is the person ultimately responsible for the work?

▷ Who will attend the meeting, and what are their titles and responsibilities?

▷ How long is the meeting expected to last?

Uncovering your customers' needs depends on your ability to probe and question. You should develop a list of high-leverage questions appropriate for your situation. Here are some that have proved effective for selling consulting or independent contracting services during an initial meeting:

▷ Given what is happening in your marketplace, what are the top challenges you face?

▷ What are your most important priorities?

▷ If you are to realize your goals, what key issues must be addressed?

▷ What are the obstacles standing in your way?

▷ If we could solve those problems, what would eliminating them do for you?

There is always an element of uncertainty in initial contacts. Go in well prepared, listen carefully, look for answers that will qualify clients, identify all the players involved, and find out about any pending assignments.

If necessary, schedule a follow-up meeting to continue the process. And always leave on a cordial note. Exchange business cards, and thank the participants for their time and consideration.

Follow-up is critical. Send the key contact person a letter thanking all parties involved in the meeting for their time. Communicate what you understand the outcome of the meeting to be and your intended response. Your response is typically a formal contract proposal detailing the project and services you can provide. Indicate a specific date when they can expect further action from you. Follow the letter with a phone call a few days later. Verify that your letter accurately communicates the client's needs and report on your progress in preparing whatever additional information was requested by the prospective client. Remember to periodically keep in touch with the client even if they don't use your services immediately.

Developing a Contract

If the first meeting went well and the potential client has a need for your services, you move to the next phase—the process of contracting. Contracting entails the development and establishment of the terms of the relationship with the client in a letter of agreement or contract. The contracting process includes several stages, including negotiating and developing an explicit, signed agreement (a contract) that specifies what each party expects from the other. Contracts also contain terms describing how you and your client plan to work together.

The legal aspects of contracting form only a small portion of the process. Much of what leads up to the final agreement is a very personal part of your business. It starts with developing and maintaining the rapport established at the first meeting, and it grows and continues as you develop an understanding of the client's needs.

In the earliest stages of your relationship, you need to be a detective, probing for information about the client's situation and what is expected of you. As the scope of the project becomes clearer, you should discuss your strategies for helping the client. A positive approach, along with a realistic assessment of the project, will build the client's confidence in you.

Writing a Proposal

Unless the assignment is for a specific, repeatable task where the work is completely spelled out, the client may ask you to write a proposal outlining your involvement, time, and fees. There is no formula for writing the perfect proposal—usually the simpler the better. Outside of the federal government, which issues a "Request for Proposal" (RFP) form with detailed requirements, few organizations specify how they want proposals to be prepared.

Writing a solid proposal takes time and effort. Before you begin, make sure that the client agrees that a formal proposal is the next step. Then submit one promptly, which usually means within 10 business days. However, never make assumptions about the client's schedule; ask the client how soon the proposal is needed. If you can't deliver a proposal on time, the decision maker may begin to doubt your ability to complete the project on deadline. If you and the client have already reached an agreement to work together, the proposal can serve as an outline of the project, rather than as a tool for selling your services.

Your proposal should reflect your client's perceptions of the problem, as well as your opinion, even if they differ. This written statement will help convince the client that you can accomplish what you propose within the budget estimate or fixed price you quoted.

Proposals should be prepared in a report format with a cover letter. Organize your proposal as a set of suggestions addressing the problem and a solution based on your understanding of the situation. Prepare the document as a letter or memorandum on your business stationery. Refer to the Contract Proposal Worksheet below for content that should be included in the proposal.

EXERCISE 4.3

Contract Proposal Worksheet

Write a one-sentence heading or title: _____

_____

Write a synopsis of the problem: _____

_____

_____

_____

Provide a short analysis of the problem that reflects the client's observations:

_____

_____

_____

Briefly describe your recommended course of action: _____

_____

_____

_____

Describe the benefits to the client of following your proposal: _____

_____

_____

_____

Outline the required actions: _____

_____

_____

_____

Detail a schedule of service delivery dates: _____

_____

_____

_____

Estimate your time and costs for the first stage of the project or, if the client
requests it, the projected cost of the entire project: _____

_____

_____

_____

Describe your role in the project: _____

_____

_____

_____

continued

Define the proposal's life term, with the expiration date of the agreement.____

_____

_____

_____

Keep the structure of the proposal logical. To prevent complications later, clearly spell out the details and avoid open-ended statements. A written proposal outlines your obligations to the client organization and, in some cases, their obligations to you. If a company agrees to your proposal, you will be expected to honor the terms.

Not every proposal will result in a contract. Clients may not agree to all of the terms, and you may have to revise certain sections to reflect their changes. If you sense the client will never be happy, remove yourself from consideration, especially if you feel the project has less than a 50 percent chance of succeeding. Working with a client who constantly changes the rules before you even start the actual project is a no-win situation.

The Written Contract

A written contract is the final step in the negotiating process. It formalizes the client-consultant relationship and provides a legal foundation for a good working arrangement. As you develop a contract, you continue to build your relationship with your client. Everything you do should reinforce your client's confidence in you.

A contract is an explicit, signed agreement between client and consultant specifying what each expects to receive from the relationship and how they plan to work together. When you begin work with a clear understanding of what is to be done, the project always goes more smoothly. A contract accomplishes the following:

 ▷ Confirms all important terms and arrangements

 ▷ Clarifies all ambiguities

 ▷ Acts as a guide once a project begins

Contracts can be as simple as a letter of agreement or as formal as a document replete with clauses and subclauses. The following overview discusses the major types of contracts, their purposes, and the benefits they provide. Other contract arrangements can be made for special situations.

Letter of Agreement

You will find the letter of agreement—the simplest and least formal of all contracts—sufficient for many consulting jobs. A letter of agreement should include the following:

▷ A clear definition of the terms of the business relationship

▷ An outline of the conditions of the project

▷ Specific deadlines and other important dates

▷ A pay scale and schedule

Letters of agreement can also specify special arrangements, such as any on-site support a consultant may receive, performance expectations, and procedures to handle problems that may arise. Although the tone is less formal than a general contract, a letter of agreement is considered a legally binding contract when it is signed by both parties and when it includes scope, terms, and other special considerations. If you end your proposal with the language "Accepted and Agreed," followed by signature and date blocks, you can save time and effort by converting your proposal into a letter of agreement.

General Contract

General contracts are formal, detailed, and elaborate documents in which every relevant condition of an agreement is specified. These contracts are most appropriate for large or complex projects and are usually drawn up by an attorney. Clients who request a general contract frequently have standard contracts that they use, and they will have an attorney prepare the document.

Commission and Retainer Accounts

Contracts for commission and retainer accounts are variations of general contracts. If your work is directly linked to company performance, you may be paid on commission. To determine the amount of your commission, commission contracts must include specific details of the client's responsibilities and your access to the company's records.

The retainer contract usually indicates the time allotted to the client for the retainer, as well as billing and payment procedures. For most consultants, a retainer agreement makes sense only when they can predict the amount of time the client will need and be able to fit it into their own schedules. The main advantage to the client of a retainer is that the consultant's services can be easily accessed without making extensive arrangements.

Daily Rate Contracts

Consultants might opt for daily rate contracts in situations where the work is repeatable and well-defined by the client. These agreements are also useful in cases where time overruns are the norm. In a daily rate contract, the consultant gives an estimate of time and expenses but is not responsible for overruns. If the work goes beyond a standard eight-hour day, the client must cover the extra time. Contract houses will have you sign their day-rate contract forms if they place you.

Covering All the Bases

Solid contracts include the following basic information:

▷ An opening section identifying the contractor and client parties

▷ The definition and scope of services to be performed

▷ Clearly defined objectives

▷ A breakdown of the consultant's responsibilities

▷ A breakdown of the client's responsibilities

▷ A time frame for delivery of services

▷ Provision for equipment, supplies, and expenses

▷ A fee payment schedule

▷ Terms of ownership of the resulting product

▷ Effective dates of the contract

▷ Conflict of interest/exclusivity/noncompete provisions

▷ Insurance requirements

Please note that not every contract includes each feature listed above. Consult a professional advisor if you have any questions about the terms presented.

Nearly all aspects of a contract are negotiable. If both sides agree to a change in wording, an addition, or a deletion, the change can be written in. If both parties initial the change, the document does not have to be redrafted or retyped. When the agreement is satisfactory to both sides, the contract is signed and dated by both parties at the bottom of the document.

Always keep a final original copy of the agreement for your records. Be familiar with its contents. In the event of a dispute, the party who best knows the contract is likely to win. Realize, however, that the contract will be written to the advantage of the party that paid the lawyer who drafted the document, to the extent allowed by law. Review the contract carefully to be certain that it achieves its purpose and that it is also fair to you. If you do not understand the terms, you should seek legal assistance.

Your Status with the IRS

You should be aware of how the IRS will view your contract with your client company. You may feel that you're working as a consultant, but the IRS may classify you as an employee, depending on the nature and extent of the services you're providing to your client company. How the IRS interprets your relationship can affect your tax status.

In 1987 the IRS issued a ruling that established a 20-point guideline for determining whether someone is an employee or a contractor. Familiarize yourself with these guidelines. The line between consultants, who are considered contractors by the IRS, and employees sometimes becomes blurred. The following factors are used to determine whether there is sufficient control to establish an employer-employee relationship:

1. **Instructions.** An employee must comply with instructions about when, where, and how to work. Even if no instructions are given, the factor is present if the employer has the right to control how the work results are achieved.

2. **Training.** An employee may be trained to perform services in a particular manner. Independent contractors ordinarily use their own methods and receive no training from the purchasers of their services.

3. **Integration.** An employee's services are usually integrated into the business operations because the services are important to the success or continuation of the business. This factor shows that the employee is subject to direction and control.

4. **Services Rendered Personally.** An employee renders services personally. This factor shows that the employer is interested in the methods as well as the results.

5. **Hiring Assistants.** An employee works for an employer who hires, supervises, and pays workers. Independent contractors can hire, supervise, and pay assistants under a contract that requires them to provide materials and labor and to be responsible only for the result.

6. **Continuing Relationship.** An employee generally has a continuing relationship with an employer. A continuing relationship may exist even if work is performed at recurring, although irregular, intervals.

7. **Set Hours of Work.** An employee usually has set hours of work established by an employer. Independent contractors generally can set their own work hours.

8. **Full-Time Required.** An employee may be required to work or be available full time. This requirement indicates control by the employer. Independent contractors can work when and for whom they choose.

9. **Work Done on Premises.** An employee usually works on the premises of an employer, or works on a route or at a location designated by an employer.

10. **Order or Sequence Set.** An employee may be required to perform services in the order or sequence set by an employer. This requirement shows that the employee is subject to direction and control.

11. **Reports.** An employee may be required to submit reports to an employer. This requirement shows that the employer maintains a degree of control.

12. **Payments.** An employee is paid by the hour, week, or month. An independent contractor is usually paid by the job or on a straight commission.

13. **Expenses.** An employee's business and travel expenses are generally paid by an employer, which shows that the employee is subject to regulation and control.

14. **Tools and Materials.** An employee is normally furnished with significant tools, materials, and other equipment by an employer.

15. **Investment.** Independent contractors generally have a significant investment in the facilities used to perform services for someone else.

16. **Profit or Loss.** Independent contractors can make a profit or suffer a loss.

17. **Works for More than One Person or Firm.** Independent contractors are generally free to provide their services to two or more unrelated persons or firms at the same time.

18. **Offers Services to General Public.** Independent contractors make their services available to the general public.

19. **Right to Fire.** Employees can be fired by their employers. Independent contractors cannot be fired so long as they produce a result that meets the specifications of the contract.

20. **Right to Quit.** Employees can quit their jobs at any time without incurring liability. Independent contractors usually agree to complete a specific job and be responsible for its satisfactory completion, or they are legally obligated to make good for failure to complete it.

Since the ruling was developed, many companies have been fined for misclassifying full-time workers as independents in an attempt to evade employer payroll taxes. Some have also been penalized because they were found guilty of replacing employees with contract workers who didn't meet that classification criteria. Take these issues into account when you negotiate your contract.

Record Keeping

Many beginning consultants are so consumed with attracting new business that they forget about protecting themselves from legal and tax problems. Record keeping is one of the most essential elements of your business. Most consulting businesses need records of the following:

> ▷   Client billings
>
> ▷   Expenses
>
> ▷   Accounts receivable
>
> ▷   Payroll

The practical need for records is to meet legal and tax requirements, minimize your liabilities, optimize your collection efforts, and provide data for decision making. If you can afford to hire a part-time bookkeeper to help set up your records, do so. If not, ask your accountant for guidance on what type of record keeping system will be the most efficient for you.

If you are setting up your own books, go to your local stationery store and ask for an easy-to-use business accounting system. There are several good systems on the market. If you have a computer, you will find a wealth of financial record-keeping software programs at your local computer store. Today's programs are relatively easy to learn and use. Record keeping software is a good investment. If your business is successful, you will eventually want to install a computerized record-keeping system. Because the software is related to your business, it's tax deductible.

Accurate record keeping is also essential in tax planning. When it comes to taxes, procrastination can only hurt you. What you neglect to do now may cost you plenty at the end of the fiscal year. You don't have to become as knowledgeable as a certified public accountant or a professional tax advisor, but it helps to have a basic understanding of tax codes and how they apply to you, even if you have an accountant or advisor overseeing your taxes. This tax knowledge will not only enable you to assess intelligently the performance of your accountant or advisor, but also make you more aware of the kind of financial information that you will need to track.

Learning how the IRS operates also can be helpful. Records carry a great deal of weight with the IRS, so the better your record keeping, the better prepared you will be if you are audited. And, unfortunately for you, consultants are among the most frequently audited of all businesses. Use these techniques to help avoid flagging yourself for an audit:

▷   Use your own business letterhead.

▷   Record transactions consistently and immediately.

▷   Keep a diary of business activities, including meetings, meals, and travel, with a description of their business purpose.

▷   Track odometer readings for all business mileage. Save car repair and maintenance records.

▷   Organize your records according to the categories used on the IRS forms relevant to your business.

▷   Select and carefully define your principal business code. Do not mix radically different types of business activities if you are operating as a sole proprietor.

▷   Pay estimated quarterly taxes to the IRS and to your state, if required.

▷   Justify carefully any activities that will send out warning flags. These include home office expenses, more than 85 percent business use of your vehicle, excessive use of contract labor, and significant amounts in any one expense category.

The IRS publishes several booklets that can guide you through the complicated tax laws governing small business.

Tax Planning

The advice of a good accountant can pay for itself. Your accountant can help you develop a tax strategy that best suits your business and your personality. Conservative strategies are designed to avoid anything that might be considered risky and minimize any chance of an audit. Aggressive strategies are designed to take advantage of interpreting any changes in the tax laws to your benefit. You and your accountant should agree on which type of strategy to pursue.

One of the best and safest ways to shelter income from taxes is to save for your retirement. Qualified retirement plans enable you to contribute amounts that are deductible, up to certain limits, from your annual self-employment income. You won't pay taxes on the income until it is withdrawn after you retire. You will probably be in a lower tax bracket, so your overall tax burden may be less. Retirement funds come in many varieties, with options that allow you to pick and choose your investments. Or you can delegate that responsibility to a professional investment firm.

What's best for you? The decision depends on your particular situation. As a general rule, Simplified Employee Pension Individual Retirement Accounts (SEP-IRAs) make the most sense for consultants who are not incorporated. SEP-IRAs are similar to Individual Retirement Accounts (IRAs), but they allow you to shelter much more income than an IRA— up to 15 percent of your annual income, to a maximum of $30,000. Consequently, SEP-IRAs can provide a significant tax benefit.

SEP-IRAs are similar to IRAs in another aspect: you cannot roll them over into a Keogh or a corporate retirement plan, such as a 401(k) plan. So if you should ever work full-time for a corporation again, you would not be able to take the money you've saved in a SEP-IRA and transfer it into the company's plan.

Most SEP-IRAs allow you to invest your money in stocks, bonds, mutual funds, and certificates of deposit. Call your local bank, stockbroker, or insurance agent for more information. SEP-IRAs are also inexpensive to open, usually requiring less than $25.

Keogh plans are very similar to corporate retirement plans, except that they do not allow you to borrow funds from your account without penalty. Keoghs are usually more appropriate for, but not limited to, independents who are incorporated and have a small number of employees.

Many tax advisors recommend considering a prepackaged SEP-IRA or Keogh rather than a customized plan prepared by a lawyer. The cost savings and simplified nature of prepackaged SEP-IRAs or Keoghs provide major advantages for independents.

As your business grows, so will your need to shelter your income from taxes. Be as aggressive about protecting your income as you are about finding new business. Work to amass larger savings by contributing to your retirement fund regularly.

Considerations for Independent Contractors

Like consultants, independent contractors are increasingly finding their services in demand in the business world. Why do many companies find independent contractors appealing? Contractors enable corporations to be flexible in budgeting and managing their human resources, reduce labor costs, and eliminate benefits and other expenses. They enable companies to develop and implement programs quickly, and to grow or shrink at will in response to their business needs. The company has no psychological commitment to long-term employment and also avoids layoff situations.

Contractors also offer the following benefits to the company:

▷ They are highly motivated.

▷ They bring an outside perspective or experience to a situation.

▷ They have skills that companies cannot find in-house.

▷ They provide relief to permanent employees in short-staffed companies.

The Profile of a Contractor

In addition to the traits exhibited by successful consultants, independent contractors also need to cultivate the following:

Humility

Independent contractors are seldom asked to serve in visible, high-profile corporate roles and rarely have the opportunity to make a major impact on management and decision making.

Flexibility

While to some clients your ability to solve problems in unique ways will distinguish you from the crowd and enhance your value, others may actually discourage your creativity. You may be told what to do in very narrow terms.

Learning Skills

You will need to be effective at learning on the fly. As a contractor, you will be faced with many new business decisions and challenges.

Marketing Your Skills as an Independent Contractor

Third-party agencies, interim management firms, recruiting firms, personnel agencies or brokers, and large "contract only" firms target companies that prefer hiring independent contractors. However, if you are operating in a marketplace suffering from an oversupply of contracting talent, you will still need to market yourself! It won't be sufficient to drop off a resume; you will need to visit a number of firms and concentrate on networking your way into a few.

Use the techniques previously discussed in this chapter to establish a personal relationship with some key people and stay in touch regularly. When assignments come in, if you are personally known to these contacts and they think highly of you, your name will be the first one to pop into their minds. This process will not happen if you are just a resume in their files.

What Is Independent Contracting Work Really Like?

Independent contractors enjoy many of the same advantages as consultants, mainly the freedom and flexibility of being their own boss. However, the drawbacks associated with contracting are also the same as with consulting. These disadvantages can be major concerns or minor nuisances, depending on your personal situation. For example, contractors are not entitled to collect unemployment insurance, take paid vacations, or receive sick pay. They must either market themselves or use third-party contract brokers during and between assignments. They can rarely afford fringe benefits, and many of them, especially the beginners, tend to undervalue their services and price themselves too low.

Other frequently cited drawbacks include the following:

▷ Erratic income flow

▷ The constant need to keep skills and knowledge levels current

▷ The danger of acquiring an over-specialized image because of serving repeatedly in the same capacity

▷ Lack of authority

▷ Unpredictable schedule demands

You may also find that you won't be hired in some circumstances unless you have workers' compensation coverage, even if you are a sole proprietor and are not required to carry it by law. You are also not likely to be able to establish new sources of credit, such as home equity or auto loans, until you have been a contractor for two or three years and can show a steady income.

What can you expect to earn as an independent contractor? A useful rule of thumb is that the lower the wage scale, the more likely your contracting work will be technical in nature and process-oriented; the higher the wage scale, the more likely your contracting work will be professional in nature and results-oriented. As in consulting, you must keep accurate records of your earnings and expenses and file taxes as required by local, state, and federal laws.

A Final Word

As you begin your new business, be prepared for extremes. Consulting and independent contracting work are often cyclical. You will experience both slow periods and harried times. Starting your business is challenging, and many consultants and independent contractors consider it the hardest part of the process. Be prepared to experience disappointments and triumphs with no coworkers to support or encourage you.

Give yourself and your new business time. Be realistic as you begin— your business may not stabilize for at least six months. Continue to seek out and seize your opportunities, and you will prosper as a consultant or independent contractor.

WHY BUSINESSES FAIL

By now you no doubt have realized that the research, planning, and effort required to launch your own business represent one of the greatest challenges of your life. But this initial challenge is just the beginning. The hard work isn't over the day you open your business.

Many businesses have enough capital and momentum to survive the first year. It's the second year that will continually test your ability to run a successful business. What is success? For some, business success is growth and profit. For others, it's earning a comfortable living doing something they love. Only you can define what business success means for you and your company.

Business failure, on the other hand, is more easily defined. Either the business survives or it doesn't. Although some companies fail because of circumstances beyond their control, nine out of ten failures are due to incompetent management in one area or another.

Because preventing problems is always preferable to cleaning up after they've occurred, you should be aware of the management problems that most frequently derail entrepreneurs. The following list accounts for the vast majority of business failures:

1. Flawed business idea

2. Inadequate business planning

3. Undercapitalization

4. Excessive operating costs and unnecessary assets

5. Lack of sales experience

6. Failure to seek professional advice

7. Financial ignorance

8. Sloppy credit practices

9. Ineffective promotion and advertising

10. Emotional pricing

11. Growing too fast

12. No commitment to the business

There are many additional mistakes you can make, but these are the ones that can most quickly destroy your business. Examine each one closely and make plans to reduce your risk.

Flawed Business Idea

Your business idea is the heart and soul of your business. Where others see problems, entrepreneurs see opportunities to solve a customer problem or meet a need in a unique way. Building your company around a solid business idea will guarantee an extraordinary business advantage.

However, some entrepreneurs do inadequate market research:

> "I didn't appreciate the importance of demographics and the
> impact this would have on the declining interest in physical
> fitness when I opened my athletic club. I realize now that every
> product or service has a life cycle. I didn't anticipate that so
> many people would virtually give up on fitness as they ap-
> proached their late forties."

Others do solid research, but they are so in love with their idea that
they misread market demand:

> "Although my market research told me that the market had been
> flooded—there were something like 117 temporary agencies in
> a town that could support maybe half that many—I was totally
> committed to my concept. I thought I could prosper in spite of
> the competition. I was wrong."

Don't fall into these traps. Evaluate your business idea objectively
and get feedback from other experienced professionals *before* you make a
commitment.

Inadequate Business Planning

Planning doesn't end when your business plan is complete. To be of
value, a plan must be used. Believe it or not, many business owners spend a
great deal of time planning and then totally disregard the plan! Managing
according to your plan dramatically increases the likelihood of success.

In the often unpredictable business world, your plan must be flexible
enough to adjust to unforeseen circumstances. In recent years, strategic
agility, or the ability to adjust business strategy immediately to react to
change, has become an advantage, particularly for the small company. So if
the marketplace demands it, act boldly and quickly. Don't stick with an
obsolete strategy just because it's in the plan.

Contingency planning also has become a critical success factor in the last ten years. Examine your business plan and identify the critical elements. What can go wrong, and how likely is it to go wrong? Eliminate the most unlikely disasters, such as a flood or a foreign invasion. For each situation where there is a reasonable chance of miscalculation, develop a "plan B." What are some areas to review? Start with the following list:

▷   Lower than expected revenue

▷   New competitors

▷   Unanticipated expenses

▷   Supplier problems

▷   New regulatory requirements

▷   Lawsuits

▷   Manufacturing and product development problems

▷   Technology obsolescence

As your company moves from a theoretical business plan to a living, breathing organization, you'll tend to ignore the plan. Don't make this mistake. Ongoing planning and continual monitoring of your plan are critical management responsibilities. The alternative is to drift along out of control.

At least once a month, you should have a management review. If you have employees, you may want to include them. Many business owners select the first Friday of each month to review the past month's performance and make adjustments to their business plan. These meetings are very important. What you need to discuss is this question: Are we doing exactly what we need to do to ensure that we meet our goals? Here are some additional questions to ask:

▷   Are revenues on target?

▷   Does the variance report indicate that expenses are in control?

▷   Are all of our customers happy?

▷   Are accounts receivable within limits?

▷ Do we have enough potential business in the pipeline?

▷ Are there symptoms of future problems that we should consider?

▷ Are cash flow and cash reserves adequate?

These are fundamental operational issues that you must monitor carefully. If the answers to any of these questions set off yellow lights or red lights in your mind, identify the root cause of the problem and take action immediately.

At least once a year, you and your partners and key employees should schedule a full day to review how you've done and plan for the future. An annual review provides a structured way to learn from experience, to define and put into operation an improvement agenda, and to adjust strategy to reflect new realities. Here are the types of questions you should have on your agenda:

▷ If we had the year to do over again, what would we do differently?

▷ Where were we particularly effective? Why?

▷ Where were we ineffective? Why?

▷ Where did we waste time, money, and effort? Why?

▷ What is happening in our industry that could present an opportunity or pose a threat?

▷ What adjustments should we make to our strategy to strengthen our competitive advantage?

▷ What are the critical factors that will determine our success for the next year?

▷ What new products or services, capabilities, and resources should we add?

▷ What must we increase, decrease, improve, develop, stop, or start?

▷ How will we measure success for the next year?

Effective planning is essential. Make sure that everyone understands this basic concept. The business landscape is littered with the carcasses of those who didn't see the dramatic changes that would transform their businesses.

Undercapitalization

Capitalizing your company should be based on the worst-case scenario that you created when you developed your business plan. Otherwise, your money may dry up, and you'll lack capitalization to meet your ongoing cash flow needs—and that will be the end of your business.

Excessive Operating Costs and Unnecessary Assets

Although a variance report will tell you if your costs are above projections, it won't tell you if costs are excessive. There are two ways to affect your bottom line: raise revenues or lower expenses. If your operating costs are allowing a 5 percent margin and your competitors' are running at a margin of 20 percent, you are at a distinct disadvantage.

You should strive to keep expenses at an absolute minimum, particularly during the initial phase. More mature companies can sometimes get away with higher operating costs (at least in the short term) because they have the revenue to support them. A new business can't. In the beginning, you have little or no revenue, so running as lean as possible should be your goal. The combination of lower revenue requirements and higher margins will go a long way toward ensuring your success.

Many young companies have disappeared because of large investments in assets that were not required to run the business. One entrepreneur who started an insurance business decided that because his market target was successful executives, he should have a very fancy and expensive office. He also bought a $200,000 yacht and outfitted it with the best equipment. The problem was that he had no customers.

Few new companies need a fancy office. In fact, opulence is often viewed negatively by customers. Be brutal. If an asset is not making you money or saving you money, it's an unnecessary luxury. Buy used equipment or lease to conserve cash. Here are some additional suggestions:

▷   Make vehicles do double-duty. Personal transportation and business needs can often be met with one vehicle.

▷ Don't hire employees too soon. Contract labor is cheaper.

▷ Don't leave large amounts of cash in the company checking account.

▷ Make money work in an interest-bearing account.

▷ Outsource manufacturing. If you do, you'll need fewer employees. You'll dramatically reduce your up-front capital costs and interest on debt, and you'll be able to spend your time on more important tasks, such as selling.

▷ Plan business trips as far ahead as possible. Going at the last minute is very expensive. And don't pump up travel costs just because you want to increase your frequent flyer miles.

▷ Stay on top of receivables. Tapping your line of credit because customers are delaying payment is expensive.

▷ Negotiate with vendors. The first price is not always the final price. Negotiate price concessions on volume and buying frequency.

▷ Don't be seduced by electronic gadgets. Do you really need a $3,500 laptop, a fax in your car, or a portable phone?

Lack of Sales Experience

An inability to attract and retain customers kills more businesses than anything else. Your business plan should have a solid revenue development model that will work. If you have no track record of bringing in the business, what makes you think you'll succeed?

Selling is a skill that is acquired with experience. If your business is sales driven and the salesperson—you—has no experience, you're a disaster waiting to happen. Gain some experience before going out on your own, or find a partner with sterling sales credentials.

Failure to Seek Professional Advice

Losing your business and your life savings because you made a serious but avoidable mistake is not something you want to have to live with. Don't use ignorance as an excuse for nonperformance. Rely on the experience and advice of others. Seek out professionals in the business world who will challenge your ideas and disagree with them when necessary. Listen very carefully to what they have to say.

If you have insufficient management expertise to run a business, seek help. Use the free or low-cost help that is yours for the asking from universities and other government and business organizations. In addition, your accountant should be very close to your business until you reach the point where you know how to run it efficiently.

Financial Ignorance

Without financial controls, your business is out of control. Cash is always short. Accounts payable become seriously overdue. Payroll taxes to the IRS are not being deposited on time—or at all. It's impossible to tell whether the company is making money. Suppliers demand cash on delivery. Lines of credit are tapped to pay operating costs. There's not enough money to advertise, promote, and go out to get more business. The bank is asking why the note payment is overdue. There's not enough cash to meet the next payroll.

Sounds grim, doesn't it? Talk with any accountant, and he or she will tell you that this picture is all too common. That accountant will tell you also that this situation might have been avoided—and that it's probably too late now to intervene effectively and save the business.

Sloppy Credit Practices

The best business is a cash business. But the business world doesn't work that way. Credit policies often attract customers. In their enthusiasm to attract business, many young companies extend credit to customers who are not creditworthy, and then they don't act promptly when those customers don't pay. The result is often serious cash flow problems—or worse.

No matter how much sales revenue you have on paper, you can't spend receivables. Unless the cash that customers owe is flowing in, there's nothing to flow out. If cash is consistently short at the end of each month, you need to look carefully at your receivables. Use the following strategies to prevent problems:

▷ Establish a credit policy that benefits your company. If it's not necessary, don't extend credit at all. It's impossible to go under from bad debt if you operate on a strictly cash basis. If you must offer credit, place limits on the amount and time. If possible, arrange financing for your customers with a bank or finance company so that you can conserve your capital and minimize the risk of bad debt.

▷ Write a short, clear credit policy statement and give it to every new customer. Problems often develop because customers don't know what the policy is. Writing a policy statement will be a big help in establishing sensible credit practices.

▷ Stick to your guns. If your terms are thirty days net, that's the time limit for payment. Don't let receivables age. Get on the phone immediately and find out what the problem is. If your customer is having financial problems, remember that the squeaky wheel gets the grease. So squeak!

▷ Make credit checks a routine part of signing on a new customer whenever you anticipate offering credit. Most customers understand that credit checks are a normal part of doing business.

▷ Encourage your customers to pay up front. In many industries—construction, consulting, law, and accounting, for example—retainers and percentage of contract are normal methods of doing business.

▷ Offer discounts for payment within ten days. Charge interest on all overdue accounts.

▷ Pay sales commissions only on revenue received, not on sales written. Not only does this practice preserve your cash, but it puts the pressure on salespeople to get their customers to pay.

▷ Pass on business before extending credit to shaky customers. Many companies have folded because key customers went belly up.

Ineffective Promotion and Advertising

Study the ads in your local newspaper. You will notice that many are simply awful. New business owners waste large sums on ineffective advertising and promotion. If advertising is a critical factor in the success of your business, take the time to learn how to do it correctly. Take courses and attend seminars on advertising, direct mail, and small business promotion. If you don't know what you're doing, hire an expert. It's better to pay for something that brings in business than to create something for free that doesn't.

Emotional Pricing

Many new entrepreneurs devote little thought to pricing decisions. Pricing is usually an emotional decision based on fear. The thinking is, "If I can offer a lower price than the competition, I'll have customers beating a path to my door." But higher prices mean higher revenues. Higher revenues mean you'll reach break-even and start making money sooner. So price as high as possible to punch up your revenues.

If you're pricing without knowing your costs, you're in trouble. Don't think that you can lose money on every sale and make it up in volume—you'll just be losing more. A pricing strategy must be built on knowing your costs, knowing your competition, and knowing your market.

Growing Too Fast

Many companies fail because they didn't control their growth. As sales go up, so do expenses. What most entrepreneurs don't realize is that the cost of doing business often escalates at a far steeper rate than sales. As costs as a percentage of sales skyrocket, cash flow problems become serious.

Here's an example: your young company with three employees suddenly lands a piece of business that will punch up revenue to five times what was projected for the year. You're tickled pink. The only hitch is that it will require nine new employees and a substantial investment in new equipment to do the work. Here are the problems:

▷ The cost and time of employee recruitment and training needs to be factored into the equation.

▷ Green employees operate at 50 percent of the productivity of the experienced three.

▷ Debt has to be incurred for the new equipment.

▷ You borrowed cash at a high interest rate to pay those new employees.

▷ Because of the workload, you have no time to prospect for new business.

These problems are just the beginning. But consider what happens when the work is completed: you've created an infrastructure that requires five times the revenue you had been generating. Where is it going to come from?

If you've created your company to make a good income and a reasonable profit, don't equate growth with profitability. A 500 percent increase in revenue does not translate into a 500 percent increase in profitability. Think carefully about growth. Small and profitable is better than big and broke.

No Commitment to the Business

Someone once defined an entrepreneur as someone who works twelve hours a day for herself so that she doesn't have to work eight hours a day for someone else. Running a small business is a serious commitment. Be prepared for a dramatic loss of personal and family time. Unless you are truly committed, you will ultimately run out of enthusiasm, and your business will pay the price.

Many entrepreneurs simply do not give enough consideration to whether they are suited to this lifestyle. And many don't give enough thought to the type of business that's going to get them up in the morning and keep them excited all day long.

Before you take the plunge, take time to find out what running a small business is really like. Resolve not to go into a business you don't love—no matter how attractive the deal may seem. Would you change jobs to take a demanding position you hated just because you might make more money?

Inadequate family support may also be an issue, and it could serve to undermine your own commitment. Your spouse or children may initially volunteer to help out, but don't expect them to make the same commitment you do. They may begin to complain about how the business is draining time you used to spend with them—and how you are always tired and in a bad mood. Establish an understanding before this new commitment becomes a problem.

Remember to take care of yourself. Your business should be a part of your life; it's not life itself. You are the boss, so resolve to maintain a balance. Burnout is as common in the entrepreneurial world as it is in the corporate rat race. Take vacations, exercise regularly, and pursue leisure activities.

Before you start on your new venture, consider what reasons might cause you to have problems. If your business fails, you'll know why. But ensure that it doesn't fail by applying what you've learned in this book. If you have completed the work as suggested, you have prepared more than most people do when starting a business. And you've substantially increased the odds of making your new business a successful one.

RESOURCES

T his section offers a wide variety of resources to assist you in planning and starting your new business. Included are reference books, business books, career books, periodicals, professional associations, and Internet sites. Where necessary, titles are followed by a brief description of their contents. Many of these resources are available free of charge at your public library. Consider the time you spend there a low-cost investment in your business. Remember, the quality and depth of your research will help ensure the success of your new venture.

References

Career Guide to America's Top Industries: Presenting Job Opportunities and Trends in All Major Industries. 2nd Edition. Provides trends and other information on more than forty major industries and summary data on many others. Includes details on employment projections, advancement opportunities, major trends, and a complete narrative description of each industry. (JIST).

Corporate & Industry Research Reports. Quarterly updates. This microfiche collection contains industry analyses from investment research firms. Index and abstracts are also available on CD-ROM. (Silver Platter).

Dictionary of Occupational Titles. 4th Edition. U.S. Department of Labor. Provides descriptions for more than 12,000 jobs, covering virtually all jobs in our economy. This book can be used to identify jobs. It contains information on skill requirements and common duties and responsibilities. (JIST).

Directory of Business Development Publications. Offers publications to help you build and manage your business. (Small Business Administration).

Encyclopedia of Associations. The most comprehensive source of detailed information on over 21,500 trade and professional associations, as well as nonprofit organizations. (Gale Research).

Encyclopedia of Business Information Sources. Arranged by over 1,100 subject headings, this source provides a quick, concise overview of the major information sources related to a topic. These may include abstracting and indexing sources, directories, financial ratios, statistics sources, and trade associations and professional societies. (Gale Research).

Franchise Opportunities Handbook: A Complete Guide for People Who Want to Start Their Own Franchise, by the U.S. Department of Commerce and LaVerne Ludden. Lists 1,500 franchise opportunities and information on selecting and financing a start-up. (JIST).

Government Giveaways for Entrepreneurs. Lists 300 government programs and 9,000 sources of free help for persons wanting to start or expand a business. (Information USA).

Luddens' Adult Guide to Colleges and Universities by LaVerne Ludden and Marsha Ludden. Up-to-date information on more than 500 adult-friendly college and university programs in the U.S. A great resource to find educational programs that can be used to keep your skills and those of employees current. (JIST).

Million Dollar Directory. An industry standard that lists over 160,000 private and public companies. (Dun & Bradstreet).

National Business Telephone Directory. An alphabetical listing of companies across the United States, including addresses and phone numbers. This book includes many smaller firms. A good resource to use for marketing your business. (Gale Research).

Occupational Outlook Handbook. Published every two years by the U.S. Department of Labor's Bureau of Labor Statistics, this book provides thorough descriptions of the 250 jobs that cover about 85 percent of the workforce, including information on skills required, working conditions, duties, qualifications, pay, and advancement potential. Very helpful for preparing job descriptions and setting salaries. (JIST).

Oxbridge Directory of Newsletters. Editors of newsletters related to a company's target industry can supply important information not found elsewhere. Some of these editors are very forthcoming in providing insights about a company within their sphere of interest. Updated regularly. (Oxbridge Communications).

Seminars Directory. Covers 8,000 seminars given by 2,000 organizations. (Gale Research).

Small Business Sourcebook. Profiles more than 282 specific types of small businesses. Each profile contains lists of start-up information, associations, educational programs, reference works, sources of supplies, statistical sources, trade periodicals, video, trade shows and conventions, consultants, franchises, databases, business systems and software, information services, libraries, and research centers. Also lists sources of general small business information and assistance, including federal and state agencies, professional associations, small business development centers, educational programs, consultants, venture capitalists, incubators, and related publications. (Gale Research).

Standard & Poor's Register of Corporations, Directors, and Executives. S & P first appeared in 1928 to provide a national directory of directors. It now includes 55,000 leading public and private U.S. corporations. (Standard & Poor's).

States and Small Business: A Directory of State Small Business Offices and Activities. Covers over 750 state government small business offices, legislation committees, and small business conferences. (Small Business Administration).

Study of Media & Markets. Statistics on the characteristics of consumers of specific products. An index is available in the Technical Guide notebook. (Simmons Market Research Bureau).

Thomas Register. Lists more than 100,000 companies across the country, including name, type of product made, and brand name of products. Catalogs provided by many of the companies are included. (Thomas).

Ulrich's International Periodical Directory. Provides information on all of the periodicals published in the world. By looking up a subject area or industry of interest, the user can identify all of the periodicals published that report on that topic. (R. R. Bowker).

Ward's Business Directory of U.S. Private and Public Companies. Comprehensive guide to more than 133,000 companies. Ward's offers an alphabetical list, rankings by sales within SIC code, and an index by state. (Gale Research).

Indexes

Business Index. This indexing service for business information covers over 800 sources, including the *New York Times* and the *Wall Street Journal.* It's a treasure trove of company and industry information. Available on microfilm. (Information Access).

Business Periodicals Index. BPI indexes approximately 300 trade, popular, and research periodicals from all of the major fields of business. Excellent source for identifying competitors. (H. W. Wilson).

The New York Times Index. The *New York Times* publishes a separate index for its newspaper. References are available for every article appearing in the *New York Times.* Published semimonthly with annual cumulations. (New York Times Co.).

Predicasts F & S Index United States. F & S coverage extends to over 750 business periodicals, with a heavy emphasis on trade journals. The indexing is divided into two sections: one by industry (colored pages) and the other by company name (white pages). The white pages are the easiest to use in searching for product or company information. Excellent source for identifying high-growth industries. (Predicasts, Inc.).

The Wall Street Journal Index. The *Wall Street Journal* publishes an independent index for coverage of its articles. (Dow Jones & Co.).

Books

AMA Complete Guide to Small Business Marketing by Kenneth Cook. Four-step guide to marketing for entrepreneurs and small business owners. Includes questionnaires and worksheets to construct a sales and marketing plan. (NTC Business Books).

The Brass-Tacks Entrepreneur by Jim Schell. Provides information for small businesses on all phases of growth, from start-up to selling. (Henry Holt & Co.).

Breakaway Careers: The Self-Employment Resource for Freelancers, Consultants, and Corporate Refugees by Bill Radin. (Career Press).

The Business Planning Guide: Creating a Plan for Success in Your Own Business by David H. Bangs. (Upstart Publishing).

The Consultant's Manual: A Complete Guide to Building a Successful Consulting Practice by Thomas L. Greenbaum. (Wiley).

The Contract and Fee-Setting Guide for Consultants and Professionals by Howard L. Shenson. (Wiley).

The Customer Is Usually Wrong! by Fred Jandt. A practical guide to providing exceptional customer service. (JIST).

Creating Customers: An Action Plan for Maximizing Sales, Promotion, and Publicity for the Small Business by David H. Bangs. Covers inexpensive marketing research, pricing goods and services, writing a marketing plan, and public relations. (Upstart Publishing).

Dare to Change Your Job and Your Life by Carole Kanchier. Practical and motivating guidance on achieving career and personal growth and satisfaction. (JIST).

Do-It-Yourself Direct Marketing: Secrets for Small Business by Mark S. Bacon. Covers mail order, telemarketing, radio and television, newsletters, print advertising, and other media. (Wiley).

The Entrepreneur's Guide to Building a Better Business Plan: A Step-by-Step Approach by Harold J. McLaughlin. Includes sample business plans. Explains how to go about acquiring initial or other capital. (Wiley).

Franchises: Dollars & Sense by Warren Lewis. Aids prospective franchisees in evaluating franchise earnings information based on sales and profit data from 145 franchise systems in 70 business categories. (International Franchsise Association).

Gallery of Best Resumes: A Collection of Quality Resumes by Professional Resume Writers by David F. Noble. Advice and more than 200 examples from professional resume writers. With lots of variety in content and design, this is an excellent resource. Consider it the best resume "library" available. (JIST).

Getting Business to Come to You: Everything You Need to Know About Advertising, Public Relations, Direct Mail, and Sales Promotion to Attract All the Business You Can Handle by Paul and Sarah Edwards. (J. P. Tarcher).

Getting New Clients, 2nd Edition, by Richard A. Connor and Jeff Davidson. (Wiley).

Guerrilla Marketing Excellence: The 50 Golden Rules for Small Business Success by Jay Conrad Levinson. (Houghton Mifflin Co.).

The Home-Based Entrepreneur: The Complete Guide to Working at Home, 2nd Edition, by Linda Pinson and Jerry Jinnett. (Upstart Publishing, 1993).

Home but Not Alone by Katherine Murray. Starting a home-based enterprise opens the door to a rewarding and challenging new lifestyle for you—and your family. From building a business plan to preparing your kids for the adjustment, you will find practical advice in this book. (JIST).

How to Become a Successful Consultant in Your Own Field, 3rd Edition, by Hubert Bermont. (Prima Publishing).

How to Make It Big as a Consultant, 2nd Edition, by William Cohen. (AMACOM).

How to Organize Your Work and Your Life, Revised, by Robert Moskowitz. (Doubleday).

How to Start, Run, and Stay in Business, 2nd Edition, by Gregory F. Kishel and Patricia G. Kishel. Step-by-step guide to starting a business. Covers choosing a business, site selection, financing, sales, promotion, and insurance. Includes checklists and examples. (Wiley).

How to Succeed as an Independent Consultant, 3rd Edition, by Herman Holtz. (Wiley).

Jumping the Job Track: Security, Satisfaction, and Success as an Independent Consultant by Peter C. Brown. (Crown Trade).

Making the Most of the Temporary Employment Market by Karen Mendenhall. (Betterway Books).

Marketing Your Services: A Step-by-Step Guide for Small Businesses and Professionals by Anthony O. Putman. Explains how to market a service, concentrating on packaging, presenting, pricing, networking, and other topics. (Wiley).

Million Dollar Consulting: The Professional's Guide to Growing a Practice by Alan Weiss. (McGraw-Hill).

Mind Your Own Business! Getting Started as an Entrepreneur by LaVerne Ludden and Bonnie Maitlen. A good book for those considering self-employment, with lots of good advice, practical questionnaires, assessment forms, useful worksheets, and exercises. (JIST).

Money Sources for Small Business—How You Can Find Private, State, Federal, and Corporate Financing by William M. Alarid. Sources of financing for small business. (Puma Publishing).

New Venture Creation: Entrepreneurship for the 21st Century by Jeffrey A. Timmons. A complete guide to starting and running a small business. (Irwin).

Nobody Gets Rich Working for Somebody Else: An Entrepreneur's Guide, 2nd Edition, by Roger Fritz. Includes case studies, worksheets, checklists, and examples. (Crisp Publications).

On Your Own: A Woman's Guide to Building A Business, 2nd Edition, by Laurie B. Zuckerman. (Upstart Publishing).

The Quick Resume & Cover Letter Book: Write and Use an Effective Resume in Only One Day by J. Michael Farr. Starting with an "instant" resume worksheet and basic formats that you can complete in an hour, this book takes you on a tour of everything you ever wanted to know about resumes. (JIST).

Self-Employment: From Dream to Reality! by Linda Gilkerson and Theresia Paauwe. The authors show that most people can start a very small business without previous business experience—even with little money to invest. A step-by-step process for getting a business started. (JIST).

Selling the Dream: How to Promote Your Product, Company, or Ideas—and Make a Difference—Using Everyday Evangelism by Guy Kawasaki. (Harper Collins).

Target Marketing for the Small Business: Researching, Reaching, and Retaining Your Target Market, 2nd Edition, by Linda Pinson and Jerry Jinnett. (Upstart Publishing).

Telemarketing That Works: How to Create a Winning Program for Your Company by Ray Harlan. (Probus Publishing Co.).

The Temp Track: Make One of the Hottest Job Trends of the 90s Work for You by Peggy O'Connell Justice. (Peterson's).

We've Got to Start Meeting Like This! by Roger K. Mosvick and Robert B. Nelson. Organizations must change how they get things done. This book shows how task-oriented teams holding fewer, shorter, more focused meetings can get more done in less time, making your organization more competitive in a rapidly changing global environment. (JIST).

Working from Home: Everything You Need to Know About Living and Working Under the Same Roof, 4th Edition, by Paul and Sarah Edwards. (Putnam).

Working Solo Sourcebook: Essential Resources for Independent Entrepreneurs by Terri Lonier. (Portico Press).

Career Books

Career Satisfaction and Success: A Guide to Job and Personal Freedom by Bernard Haldane. This is a complete revision of a classic by one of the founders of the modern career planning movement. Not so much a job search book as a job *success* book. Contains solid information. (JIST).

The Complete Job Search Handbook: All the Skills You Need to Get Any Job, and Have a Good Time Doing It by Howard Figler. A very good book. (Henry Holt).

Getting the Job You Really Want: A Step-by-Step Guide, 3rd Edition, by J. Michael Farr. Career planning and job search materials are provided in a workbook format with lots of worksheets. More than 150,000 copies have been sold. (JIST).

Job Savvy: How to Be a Success at Work 2nd Editionby LaVerne L. Ludden. This book is a down-to-earth approach to the development of basic job skills. A great resource for training entry-level employees. (JIST).

Job Strategies for Professionals: A Survival Guide for Experienced White-Collar Workers by the U.S. Employment Service. Job Search advice for professionals and managers who have lost their jobs. (JIST).

The PIE Method for Career Success: A Unique Way to Find Your Ideal Job by Daniel Porot. Written by one of Europe's premier career consultants, this book presents powerful career planning and job seeking concepts in a visual and memorable way. (JIST).

The Quick Interview & Salary Negotiation Book: Dramatically Improve Your Interviewing Skills in Just a Few Hours! by J. Michael Farr. This substantial book offers lots of information, but it's arranged so you can read the first section and do better in interviews the same day. (JIST).

Sweaty Palms Revised: The Neglected Art of Being Interviewed by Anthony Medley. (Ten Speed Press).

Using the Internet and the World Wide Web in Your Job Search by Fred E. Jandt and Mary B. Nemnich. For new or experienced users of online computer services, this book gives lots of good information on finding job opportunities—which often include consulting opportunities—on the Web. (JIST).

The Very Quick Job Search: Get a Better Job in Half the Time! 2nd Edition, by J. Michael Farr. This is a thorough job search book, and it includes lots of information on career planning and, of course, job seeking. (JIST).

What Color Is Your Parachute? by Richard N. Bolles. This is the best-selling career planning book of all time, and the author continues to improve it. (Ten Speed Press).

Who's Hiring Who? by Richard Lanthrop. Another good book. (Ten Speed Press).

Periodicals

Entrepreneur. Advice for small business owners and prospective owners. Includes franchise advertisements. Monthly.

Home Office Computing. Provides technical advice for operating a business from your home, plus general articles on starting and running a small business. Monthly.

Inc. Bills itself as the magazine for growing companies. Monthly.

Success. Covers small business issues and concerns. Monthly.

CD-ROMS

ABI/Inform (UMI). *ABI/Inform* is designed to meet the information needs of executives and covers all phases of business management and administration. *ABI/Inform* stresses information that is applicable to many types of businesses and industries. Specific product and industry information is included but is not the primary emphasis. Approximately 800 primary publications in business and related fields are currently scanned for inclusion in the database. Monthly updates.

Business NewsBank (NewsBank, Inc.). *Business NewsBank* is an excellent source of information on companies reported on in smaller regional newspapers. Frequently this coverage provides a more intimate point of view on local companies than national newspapers. Monthly updates.

Infotrac (Information Access). Although its coverage is aimed at the general public's interests, *Infotrac* provides excellent business information. Monthly updates.

JIST's Enhanced Electronic Dictionary of Occupational Titles (JIST). This disk contains almost 13,000 occupational descriptions. It is useful for writing job descriptions, setting salaries, and assessing competition in each occupational area.

Moody's Company Data. This disk contains descriptive and financial information on more than 10,000 U.S. public companies. Updated monthly.

Moody's International Company Data. Moody's presents descriptive and financial information on more than 7,500 public corporations in 90 countries outside the United States. It includes news on mergers and new products. Updated monthly.

Standard & Poor's Corporations (Standard & Poor's). This disk comprises several databases on U.S. companies. It contains business and financial information on over 12,000 public companies and gives basic information on nearly 45,000 private companies. Biographical profiles of 70,000 key executives are also provided. Updated bimonthly.

Wilson Business Database (H. W. Wilson). In addition to providing this CD-ROM equivalent to its print directory (*Business Periodicals Index*), many libraries have the system connected to Wilson's online database. After searching your subject on the CD-ROM, the computer automatically accesses Wilson's online business database and searches for new citations available since the CD-ROM was last updated.

Associations and Organizations

American Consultants' League, 1290 Palm Avenue, Sarasota, FL 34236 (813/952-9290).

American Management Association, 135 W. 50th Street, New York, NY 10020-1201 (212/586-8100).

American Marketing Association, 250 S. Wacker Drive, Suite 200, Chicago, IL 60606 (312/648-0536).

Association of Small Business Development Centers, 1313 Farnam, Suite 132, Omaha, NE 68182 (402/595-2387). Members are local small business development centers providing advice for those planning to establish a small business. Facilitates the exchange of information among members and represents their interests before the federal government.

Center for Entrepreneurial Management, 180 Varick Street, Penthouse Suite, New York, NY 10014 (212/633-0060). Serves as an information resource for small business owners and managers.

Direct Marketing Association, 11 W 42nd Street, New York, NY 10036-8096 (212/768-7277).

Entrepreneurship Institute, 3592 Corporate Drive, Suite 101, Columbus, OH 43231 (614/895-1153). Provides encouragement and assistance to entrepreneurs who are creating and developing new companies. Offers consulting on accounting, marketing, banking, and legal issues.

International Council for Small Business, St. Louis University, 3674 Lindell Blvd., St. Louis, MO 63108 (314/658-3896).

International Franchise Association (IFA), 1350 New York Avenue NW, Suite 900, Washington, D.C. 20005 (202/628-8000). Purpose is to build and maintain a favorable economic and regulatory climate for franchising. It enhances and safeguards the business environment for franchisors and franchisees nationwide with lobbying efforts, legal and consultation services, seminars, and publications.

National Association for the Cottage Industry, P.O. Box 14850, Chicago, IL 60614 (312/472-8116).

National Association for Female Executives, 30 Iring Pl., 5th Floor, New York, NY 10011 (212/645-0770). This support organization for women in the business community offers financial assistance, legal programs, insurance savings, and other benefits to women.

National Association of Home-Based Business, P.O. Box 30220, Baltimore, MD 21270 (410/363-3698).

National Association for the Self-Employed, P.O. Box 612067, Dallas, TX 75261-2067 (800/551-4446).

National Association of Small Business Investment Companies, 1199 N. Fairfax Street, Suite 200, Alexandria, VA 22314 (703/683-1601).

National Association of Women Business Owners, 1010 Wayne Ave., Suite 900, Silver Spring, MD 20910 (301/608-2596).

National Federation of Independent Business, 53 Century Blvd., Suite 300, Nashville, TN 37214 (615/872-5800).

Small Business Administration (SBA), 409 3rd Street SW, Washington, D.C. 20416 (800/8-ASK-SBA or 202/205-6600). Created to help people get into business and stay in business. Offers business development programs, financial services and loans, government contracting opportunities, information on legislation and regulations, small business facts, an online service and newsletter, and small business minority programs. Call to locate a regional office near you.

Internet Resources

Federal Government Sources

Commerce Business Daily   http://cbdnet.access.gpo.gov

CBDNet is the official, free online listing of government contracting opportunities that are published in the *Commerce Business Daily*. This is an excellent source for entrepreneurs who want to work with government clients. The paper edition of this periodical is expensive, so it is a great service to have access to the information free of charge.

Library of Congress:

Explore the Internet   http://lcweb.loc.gov/global/explore.html

There is a wealth of information contained at this site. It provides access to the catalogs of the Library of Congress. It also lets you access THOMAS, a database of information on Congress, including legislation.

U.S. Business Advisor   http://www.business.gov

This site is a one-stop electronic link to government for business. The U.S. Business Advisor exists to provide business with one-stop access to federal government information, services, and transactions. Its goal is to make the relationship between business and government more productive.

U.S. Small Business Administration   http://www.sba.gov

The SBA is an important resource for entrepreneurs, and this site provides valuable resources. This is one of the first sites you should visit. It contains information about the services that the SBA provides to small businesses, including assistance and loans. The site provides information on how to start a business and directories, shareware programs, and links to almost 2,000 other sites.

Small Business Sources

Be The Boss   http://www.beyourownboss.com

Interested in a franchise business? This is a good place to get started. This site offers everything from a tutorial on franchising to online applications for some franchises. You'll find a directory of about 1,500 franchisors that you can search alphabetically or by type of business.

Dun & Bradstreet Internet Access   http://www.dnb.com

If you are thinking about buying a business, this is a useful site. You can purchase a business background report for a small fee. This report provides financial, historical, and operational information for approximately 17 million businesses. It can be a useful tool for initial investigation of businesses that you are interested in buying.

EntrepreNet   http://www.enterprise.org

This site features information and links for entrepreneurs and small business owners. EntrepreNet provides extensive connections to other Internet sites of interest to entrepreneurs and maintains an extensive online reference library containing information on a variety of topics. The site is operated by the Enterprise Corporation of Pittsburgh, which provides assistance to start-up companies in the southeastern area of Pennsylvania.

***Inc.* Online**   http://www.inc.com

This site is brought to you by *Inc.* magazine. It provides tools, advice, and shared experiences to help visitors learn how to use the Internet for their businesses. It is a good place to start learning about the Web and its application to your business.

JIST   http://www.jist.com

This site contains more detailed information on JIST books cited in this section and ordering information. It has an online job search workshop, a free job search book, and links to nearly 100 useful Websites.

Management Consulting
Online   http://www.cob.ohiostate.edu/~fin/jobs/mco/mco.html

This is an excellent site to visit if you are interested in starting a consulting business. This site is run by Tim Opler, an assistant professor of finance at Ohio State University. It contains a career guide, directory of management consulting firms, and links to related sites. While it is designed with college students in mind, it has useful information for anyone contemplating a consulting career.

Smalloffice.com   **http://www.smalloffice.com**

This site is operated by the editors of *Home Business Computing* and *Small Office Computing*. There are many articles, shareware, and links for the budding entrepreneur.

Yahoo: Small Business Information

http://www.yahoo.com/Business_and_Economy/
Small_Business_Information/

Yahoo is the grandfather of clearinghouses and search sites on the Web. There are thousands of sites listed in their small business information directories.

INDEX

F

G

T

America's Top Resumes
for America's Top Jobs™
381 Resumes for More Than 200 Jobs
By J. Michael Farr

The ONLY book with sample resumes for all major occupations covering 85 percent of the workforce!

Sample resumes for more than 200 major jobs! Nearly 400 of the best resumes submitted by members of the Professional Association of Resume Writers, grouped according to occupation and annotated by the author to highlight their best features—plus career planning and job search advice from Mike Farr.

1-56370-288-6
$19.95

Beat Stress with Strength
A Survival Guide for Work and Life
By Stefanie Spera, Ph. D., and Sandra Lanto, Ph.D.

Includes a Personal Stress Test that pinpoints sources and effects of stress

Modern life is more hectic and complicated than ever before. Sources of stress are all around us—in our homes, on the job, in our personal relationships. Here's expert advice on how to fight stress and win. Compiled from more than fifteen years of intensive study, formal research, and hundreds of interactive workshops with thousands of participants!

1-57112-078-5
$12.95

Tricks of the Trade
An Insider's Guide to Using a Stockbroker
By Mark Dempsey

An ex-Wall Street broker shares a first-ever, behind-the-scenes look at the brokerage industry.

Today, millions of Americans invest their money with the help of full-service brokerage firms. But are they getting what they pay for? What exactly *are* they paying for? And how can they avoid costly mistakes? At last, here's a book by a Wall Street insider with all the answers presented in a lively, entertaining, informative style!

1-57112-084-X
$14.95

We've Got to Start Meeting Like This!
Revised Edition
A Guide to Successful Meeting Management
By Roger K. Mosvick & Robert B. Nelson

"Valuable insight and techniques for handling the grow-ing problem of excessive and ineffective meetings in business."

-Ken Blanchard, coauthor of *The One-Minute Manager*

Almost every business person would like to have more productive meetings—and fewer of them! Here's advice based on a four-year research project by two communication professionals that shows business people how to get the most out of their meetings. The first edition sold more than 50,000 copies!

1-57112-069-6
$14.95

Home but Not Alone
The Parents' Work-at-Home Handbook
By Katherine Murray

A comprehensive survival guide for today's work-at-home parents

The rise of the home office in the 1990s has led to the rise of the number one home office headache: dealing with the kids. Katherine Murray, an experienced work-at-home mom, provides invaluable insights and advice that can help people who work at home balance their careers and their families.

1-57112-080-7
$14.95

Healthy, Wealthy & Wise
A Guide to Retirement Planning
From the editors of JIST Works, Inc.

Preparing the largest generation in American history to meet the challenges of retirement

Millions of American baby boomers in the 40s and 50s will soon create a tremendous retirement boom. Here's the book that all baby boomers need right now: a strategic planning guide to help them understand and prepare for the emotional and financial realities of retirement.

1-57112-081-5
$12.95